Critical Essays on Evelyn Waugh

Critical Essays on Evelyn Waugh

James F. Carens

G. K. Hall & Co. • Boston, Massachusetts

Library of Congress Cataloging in Publication Data

Critical essays on Evelyn Waugh.

(Critical essays on British literature)
Bibliography: p.
Includes index.
1. Waugh, Evelyn, 1903–1966. 2. Novelists, English — 20th
century — Biography. I. Carens, James F. (James Francis), 1927–
II. Series: Critical Essays on modern British literature.
PR6045.A97Z629   1987   823'.912   [B]   87-17669
ISBN 0-8161-8762-2 (alk. paper)

This publication is printed on permanent/durable acid-free paper
MANUFACTURED IN THE UNITED STATES OF AMERICA

CRITICAL ESSAYS ON BRITISH LITERATURE

The Critical Essays on British Literature series provides a variety of approaches to both the classical writers of Britain and Ireland and the best contemporary authors. The formats of the volumes in the series vary with the thematic designs of individual editors and with the amount and nature of existing reviews, criticism, and scholarship. In general, the series represents the best in published criticism, augmented, where appropriate, by original essays by recognized authorities. It is hoped that each volume will be unique in developing a new overall perspective on its particular subject.

In his long insightful introductory essay James Carens goes carefully through Waugh's novels, summarizing and illuminating the writer's intellectual and biographical development. The last segment of the introduction surveys critical opinions of Waugh over the years.

Carens divides the essays into three groups: the first includes responses to an entire group of novels or several books within the whole body of Waugh's work; the second group treats individual works and essays that offer responses at variance with prevailing critical views; and the third deals with characteristic aspects of Waugh's life or qualities of his writing in representative works.

Only those essays which make some significant contribution to our understanding of Waugh have been included. Within each group, essays are arranged chronologically, indicating developing critical attitudes toward the writer and providing an idea of the range of critical response to his work.

Zack Bowen, GENERAL EDITOR

University of Miami

CONTENTS

INTRODUCTION

I

"All fates," wrote Evelyn Waugh about three years before he died, "are 'worse than death'" (*Diaries* 787). For over thirty years he had been expertly pushing words about on the page, and it had not been his habit to employ the cliché. His bleak apothegm, however, projects the commonplace phrase — "a fate worse than death" — into so startlingly new a context of irony that we comprehend and accept the depth of Waugh's melancholia at the same time that we admire the verbal play of a wit that pains us. The apothegm is and could only have been the utterance of a defeated man, of a writer dying and welcoming death before his time. Even closer to the time of that death in 1966, Waugh finished reading a new book on Jonathan Swift and observed that he had "found many affinities with the temperament (not of course the talent) of the master" (*Letters* 634). During the final years of his life, in fact, Waugh often seemed to have affinities with the narrator of *Gulliver's Travels* who has come to disdain all men as Yahoos. Yet the melancholia and disillusionment of Waugh's final years — when even the rock of Roman Catholicism seemed to him to be crumbling under the onslaught of modernism — were but an acute phase of emotions that had been with him from the start of his career. The misanthropy often ascribed to Jonathan Swift, Waugh ascribed to himself, as early as 1936, when he warned the woman who became his second wife that he was "restless & moody & misanthropic" (*Letters* 104). We laugh outright at Waugh's early novels and then we wince as we realize that the horrid, the horrible, and the absurd are implicit in the events that have just made us laugh. It was Waugh's essential genius that he could invent characters and situations that propel us beyond our delight in their looniness to a recognition of the appalling nature of man and the abysmal nature of reality. It was the triumph of his art that he scarcely ever abandoned himself in his writing to the melancholia that beset him throughout his life, finding in satiric laughter and brilliant fictive patterns of ironic detail a more distinguished response to the follies he discerned.

There seems, indeed, little evidence of misanthropy in Waugh's first novel, *Decline and Fall* (1928). This satire, which drew upon his own experience at Oxford and on his subsequent brief career as a schoolmaster, was originally to be called *Picaresque or The Making of an Englishman*; the book fairly bursts with the high spirits we expect of the picaresque form and with an extraordinary cast of colorful characters. The adventures of a dim young man named Paul Pennyfeather, who is expelled from Oxford for indecent behavior (of which he is innocent), becomes a schoolmaster at a bogus public school, is taken up by a notorious and amoral society woman, is arrested for white slavery on the morning of his wedding to her, and is imprisoned but then liberated when a sham death is arranged for him, *Decline and Fall* is charged with satiric energy and comic inventiveness. Its cast of grotesques includes a phony headmaster, hairy and clawed, but always elegantly attired; a one-legged (and, if one reads between the lines, sodomitic) master who is always "in the soup" and always escaping from it; a school butler who assumes one false identity after another and invents one lie more improbable than another; and a clergyman who has taken to schoolmastering after losing his faith and resigning his living, and who then becomes, as a "Modern Churchman," an incompetent prison chaplain. These grotesques are all defined by an art of brilliant and rapid caricature. And yet, even in this spirited first novel, there were darker shadings and oblique traces of metaphysical concern. Grimes, the debauched schoolmaster, twice "dies" only to be reborn as his depraved self; Paul, the naive antihero, also "dies," only to be "reborn" exactly as he was at the start of the novel. This recurrent pattern of "death" and "rebirth" is projected against chapter headings and textual details that evoke Easter, the agony in the garden, and resurrection — and therefore an archetypal pattern that mocks the imperfect cycles of death and rebirth in the novel. An image that is introduced (albeit by an absurd character) to explain the illogic of society and the fates of different types within it, "the big wheel at Luna Park," is no circle of perfection but an emblematic wheel of chance. Elaborating on the image, Otto Silenus persuades Paul Pennyfeather that he is meant to stay off the wheel and observe those who recklessly sit as far out on it as they can. The image of the wheel implies that the brilliantly reckless and dynamic may triumph in a world of chance; but the best hope of someone as static as Paul is to remain in the stands, watching. At this point in his career, no hater of his kind and even an admirer of certain amoralists, Waugh nevertheless suggests in the image of the wheel of fortune and in the irrational events of the novel the determinism of sheer accident and the necessity of a safe retreat from it.

The absurd and irrational preside also over Waugh's second novel, *Vile Bodies* (1930), in which luck, chance, and accident play a far crueler role than in *Decline and Fall* and in which the circle again functions as an image of futility. If none of the comic grotesques of this novel is developed as fully as those of the first novel, there is, nevertheless, a large cast of memorable monsters, among them a Jesuit of popular fantasy, with a Jewish name; an American Evangelist of dubious morality; two equally ineffectual prime ministers; an eccentric and vulgar hotelkeeper; and numerous Bright Young People, all trailing clouds of depravity as they pursue their tedious and trivial pleasures. The surface of this novel, which is "laid in the near future," is bright, naughty, and apparently indulgent of all the eccentricities and excesses depicted. But Adam Fenwick's futile pursuit of a fortune, which he won accidentally and which is valueless when he finally does receive it, concludes on "a wasted expanse" of battlefield as the sounds of the battle return "like a circling typhoon." In dream delirium, following an absurd racing accident, the Hon. Agatha Runcible, one of the Bright Young People, imagines that she and her friends "were all driving round and round in a motor race and none of us could stop." Her drunken race to nowhere and nothing symbolizes the futile and hectic life of her generation.

In time, Waugh came to criticize harshly *Vile Bodies* and the influence on the book of Ronald Firbank (Heath 80). But Firbank's brief novels, at once decadent and satiric, exercised the most significant technical influence on Waugh, an influence perhaps more happily assimilated in other Waugh novels. Firbank's influence was, indeed, far more substantial than the influence of P.G. Wodehouse, to whose comedies Waugh later directed attention in a series of reviews. Firbank was the master of economical and detached techniques that made it possible for him to suggest, below the silly surface of his fictions, depths of feeling and moral significance; and, whatever Waugh may later have said in disparagement of the Firbank precedent, a book like *Vile Bodies* also owes its success to that same capacity. In an "Author's Note" which precedes the novel, Waugh draws attention to the relations of his novel's climactic events to the Advent season and Christmas; but even without this mordant afterthought on Waugh's part, his readers cannot help but recognize that a dying Edwardian society, which had been ordered but empty, is succumbing to an emerging society which is chaotic and futile. While it is the nearly concealed narrator of *Vile Bodies* to whom we are indebted for the observation that "black misanthropy . . . waits alike on gossip writers and novelists," it is less the creature man than his condition in the world of becoming that Waugh reprehends: "all that succession and repetition of massed humanity. . . . Those vile bodies."

Vile Bodies, which was a much greater popular success than *Decline and Fall*, brought Waugh celebrity. Already linked by ties of friendship and interest to a circle of colorful and aristocratic friends, he now began to move in an even more fashionable world, one remote, indeed, from the sedate milieu of his middle-class father, a publisher and minor "man of letters." After a hesitant period following his departure from Oxford, when he moved uncertainly toward his métier as a novelist, Waugh had seemed to be coming into his own; but his brief and ill-considered marriage to Evelyn Gardner, daughter of the widowed Lady Burghclere, was a catastrophe, which came to its inevitable and painful conclusion while he was at work on *Vile Bodies*. Christopher Sykes has stated, in his biography of Waugh (unfortunately more a memoir than a definitive "life") that Waugh's conversion to Roman Catholicism in 1930 was not the consequence of the failure of his marriage (Sykes 105). Nor does it seem to be the case that Waugh was (as was many an Aesthete or Dandy from the nineties on) merely drawn by the liturgy and ceremony of the Church. The first volume of Waugh's unfinished autobiography, *A Little Learning* (1964), a work markedly reticent on the details of his psychosexual development at Oxford, stops short of the time of the first novels, the unsuccessful marriage, and the conversion; it thus contributes little to our understanding of the immediate grounds for that conversion. But, looking back on the event in 1949, Waugh stated that he had found life "unintelligible and unendurable without God." He suggested, too, that he believed Catholicism to be more historically legitimate and coherent than Protestantism, and civilization itself powerless to survive without the authority of Catholic Christianity (Carens 92–96). Many would find these notions of his reasonable, understandable, and acceptable; others would dismiss them as romantic and reactionary. In any case, there can be no doubt of their sincerity. In terms of our understanding of his development as a writer, we must recognize that Waugh's commitment to a coherent faith did not clash with the vision we find in his first novels of a world subject to irrational accident. For centuries before Waugh, Christians had been able to reconcile the Roman notion of the fickle goddess Fortuna who reigns over the things of this world with their belief in a providential God, superior to the inconstancies of fortune. The intelligibility Waugh found in Catholicism was apparently the very certitude he needed to endure the irrational incoherence he discerned in the modern world.

It was, however, certainly not to the operation of divine Providence that Waugh turned in his next several novels. Restless following the collapse of his marriage and already attracted to travel, for almost a decade he sought out not the charms that beckon more indulgent tourists, but remote places that satisfied his fascination with the bizarre, the violent, and the barbaric — Ethiopia, East Africa, Aden, Kenya, British Guiana, Brazil, Mexico. *Black Mischief* (1932) and *A Handful of Dust* (1934) were the brilliant products of these years.

Black Mischief, inspired in large part by what Waugh had observed, as a correspondent to the *Graphic*, at the coronation of Ras Tafari as Haile Selassie, Emperor of Ethiopia, revealed that Waugh was not content to repeat his earlier successes, that he was extending the breadth of his interests, and that he was successfully stretching his range as novelist and satirist. The protagonist of this novel is Basil Seal, polar opposite to the victim protagonists of the first two novels. An utter cad who steals his mother's emeralds as shamelessly as he pilfers the effects of a cabin companion, Basil manages to be both sleazy and glamorous. Abandoning his candidacy for Parliament, following on a drunken "racket," and bored with England, Basil heads for Azania — an imaginary island off the coast of Africa — to exploit his brief Oxford acquaintance with Seth, who is about to accede to the throne.

Azanian society permits Waugh to introduce a number of grotesques, most memorably Mr. Youkoumian, the Armenian trader who knows that everything and anyone can be bought. But Waugh has not relinquished his role as a satirist of English society, for much of the satiric force of *Black Mischief* derives from his cinematic shifting back and forth between England and Azania. Once again Waugh contrasts England's expiring Edwardian generation and the disorderly heirs it has created. But the truth is, the decorous life Lady Seal wants to imagine Basil living and the disorderly existence he and his friends actually share are equally futile and escapist. Moreover, as Waugh depicts Azania, we see that European culture transposed to Africa becomes absurd; and western notions of reform, absurd in themselves, become yet more aberrant in translation, for they are simply irrelevant to the uncontrollable forces of a primitive culture.

Attacked by a fellow Catholic in the *Tablet* for having written so immoral a book, Waugh defended himself in an open reply in which he maintained that the motif of cannibalism was one of the implicitly moral details of his work (Heath 102). Indeed, it has not been sufficiently noted that *Black Mischief* has much in common with Joseph Conrad's *Heart of Darkness* (1902). Basil Seal's career parallels that of Conrad's Kurtz, an Emissary of Light, who comes to the Congo to introduce European civilization, but who depraves the natives he commands and is himself drawn into their savagery. Both *Heart of Darkness* and *Black Mischief* share the awful recognition that savagery is at the heart of the creature man and that civilization maintains but the most fragile control over savage impulses. Whereas Conrad expressed his vision of the horror of human evil through an irony approaching the tragic, Waugh expressed his comparable and equally legitimate vision through an irony of mocking laughter. Earlier in the century, when the myth of Haile Selassie as a proponent of enlightenment and as a noble opponent of Italian fascism imposed itself on us, Waugh's satiric treatment of Ethiopia seemed to many liberals both supercilious and racist. More than fifty years later in the light of Selassie's later career and its aftermath, and in the light of recent decades of political terror and starvation, Waugh's account of arbitrary power, irrational belief, cruelty, and misery seems no overstatement of the deathly congruence of civilization and barbarism.

Although Waugh turned in his next novel, *A Handful of Dust*, to the subject of upper-class adultery and to a group of aristocratic and fashionable characters, this notion of the congruence between savagery and civilization continued to hold sway over his imagination. More than a decade after he had written the novel, he described how he had first written "a short story about a man trapped in the jungle" and then concluded that he had to explain how his character got there by adapting the story as the conclusion to a novel about "other sorts of savages at home and the civilized man's helpless plight among them" ("Fan-Fare" 33). Curiously enough, for all the skill and economy with which Waugh could handle episodes within his novels, his short stories are thin and undistinguished. Even "The Man Who Loved Dickens," stronger than the other stories, lacks the devastating irony it came to have when transformed as the conclusion of A Handful of Dust. But as Waugh contrived the events leading to the conclusion, he also arranged and titled the chapters so as to emphasize the painful ironies of the book. "Chapter I" is mockingly called (after Proust) "Du Côté de Chez Beaver"; and the penultimate "Chapter VI" is "Du Côté de Chez Todd." Thus the bogus house of the decorator Mrs. Beaver and of her falsely civilized son, the lover of Brenda Last when she grows bored with her marriage to Tony, corresponds to the wretched hut of the illiterate half-caste bastard of a Barbadian missionary, Mr. Todd, who holds Tony prisoner — probably for life — so that Tony can read to him from a disintegrating edition of the works of Charles Dickens.

Accident plays a role in Tony's absurd destiny, as it plays a role throughout the novel — most conspicuously in the accidental death of the Last's son at a fox hunt, a piece of folly from which all are absolved of blame, though all involved are responsible. A messenger, who has led Tony into the jungle, is killed accidentally; Tony himself stumbles accidentally upon the hut of Mr. Todd. A Handful of Dust is another novel in which the chaotic forces of chance reign. At the time of John Andrew's death, a character who is briefly introduced for ironic purposes sits in the library at Hetton brooding over her game of patience. It has been suggested by Jeffrey Heath, who is very interesting on the subject of fortune (112–13), that this brazen blonde symbolizes Fortuna herself. But Waugh was no writer of allegory. Indeed, Mrs. Rattery's card game, like a number of the silly games in the novel, is a futile effort to bring "order . . . out of chaos," "sequence and precedence into being"; it is an effort to find symbols that are "coherent, interrelated." Waugh's irony is that in a world ruled by accident, empty people attempt to discover an order in a game of chance itself, "a heartbreaking game," as Mrs. Rattery exclaims. To add to the excruciating ironies of the novel, in the chaos of fortune into which Tony plunges, it is only his captor, Mr. Todd, who has achieved some kind of order — and that, a vile one. Todd triumphs over accident, for, when a search team arrives to rescue Tony, Todd is forewarned and drugs his captive so as to retain him as a reader of Dickens.

In 1930, after he had seen a performance by the American actress-monologuist Ruth Draper, Waugh complained in his diary that she was "too humane and philanthropic." He made a further note that helps to illuminate the unique quality of Black Mischief and A Handful of Dust.

Of Ruth Draper he wrote, "a brilliant artist if she was satirical but always sentimental and sympathetic" (*Diaries* 314). There are reasons for thinking that Waugh was sympathetic to Tony Last, whom he described as a "civilized man" ("Fan-Fare" 33). And though Tony is dull, in the context of the novel's amoralists, he is also appealing and decent. Brenda, too, is made attractive and appealing in numerous ways. The reasons for her boredom with Tony and Hetton are apparent. Even after her betrayal of Tony; even after the awful moment — one of the most painful in modern literature — when she expresses relief that her son, not her lover, has died; and even after the appalling divorce demands she makes — in effect, that Tony buy Beaver for her — she is pathetic when her fortunes sink low. At the time he wrote *Black Mischief* and *A Handful of Dust*, if, like Swift, he was no lover of "that animal called man," Waugh was also, like the master, able to love "John, Peter, Thomas and so forth." If he could not create what E. M. Forster meant by "round" characters, he could create multidimensional ones — a Tony who is decent but dull and spiritually blind, a Brenda who is charming but empty, bitchy but pathetic. At the time he produced these two novels he also was master of an art of distance, detachment, and significant ironic motif. No longer need he, as in the earlier novels, devise ways for minor characters to interpret events. He was master of a deadly satiric tone, and of a subtle, complex, and mordant irony that eschewed sentimental indulgence at the same time that it evoked in the reader emotions inextricable from judgments of value.

In 1939 Evelyn Waugh abandoned work on a novel which was both technically and thematically a departure from his earlier books. *Work Suspended*, published as a fragment in 1942, is a love story narrated retrospectively by its main character, John Plant, a successful writer of murder mysteries. At one point Plant observes of his novels that he feels "in danger of becoming mechanical, turning out year after year the kind of book I know I can write well." Thinking that he has "got as good as I ever can be at this particular sort of writing," Plant needs "new worlds to conquer." Plant's words may be taken as a reflection on Waugh's own situation and on his desire to develop in new ways as a novelist.

Of *Scoop* (1938), which was completed before the experiment of *Work Suspended*, one should observe to start with that it is a very funny book. Still, in its comic account of the blundering and circular quest of a young man and in its African setting, it exploited again certain of the things Waugh had already done in *Decline and Fall* and *Black Mischief*. Its antihero, William Boot, is another innocent, a naïf, a creature of chance. By accident Boot, who writes a biweekly half-column of nature commentary for Lord Cooper's *Beast*, is confused with the novelist John Courtney Boot, who is being puffed by the fashionable Mrs. Algernon Stitch. As a result of Mrs. Stitch's efforts to promote her friend, Lord Cooper's foreign editor mistakenly employs the entirely inexperienced William as a special correspondent to cover the confused political situation in Ishmaelia, an imaginary African republic loosely based on Liberia and Ethiopia. Though Boot is incompetent as a correspondent, he accidentally picks up information about the imprisonment of President Jackson during a communist coup. Thus Boot scoops his fellow journalists. Then, disdaining the honors and the career Lord Cooper offers him but accepting a fat contract from the befuddled foreign editor, Boot seeks refuge from the excesses of modern journalism and modern politics by returning to his family's country house, Boot Magna Hall. He is almost as untouched by his experiences as was Paul Pennyfeather in *Decline and Fall*.

There is amusing satire in *Scoop* — of the press lord who orders up battles and victories to entertain his readers, of newspapers and their perversions of truth, and of journalists who fabricate events as easily as a column. There is pertinent satire of both communism and fascism as they manifest themselves in Africa. But the satire in *Scoop*, even the satire of the totalitarians, seems less intense than the satire in the earlier novels; *Scoop* is the most genial of the books Waugh produced during the 1930s. At the close of the novel Boot returns to the atrocious prose of his newspaper column ("maternal rodents pilot their furry brood through the stubble"), but the very last words of the novel, the narrator's own ("Outside, the owls hunted maternal rodents and their furry brood.") suggest that Boot's prose evades the real facts of nature. So there is an ironic implication that Boot's return to Boot Magna is an escape from reality that may not be as secure as he takes it to be. Still, the dominant implication of the novel is that Boot has done well to reject the public life of action in favor of the private pursuit, and that he has done well to repudiate the unrealities of journalism and of political involvement.

Scoop was written at a time of personal fulfillment in Evelyn Waugh's life, for he had married Laura Herbert, a fellow convert, in April 1937; secured a country house, Piers Court, Gloucestershire, well before the wedding; and then become the father of a first child (of six) shortly before the publication of the book. Seldom has biography better provided grist for the mill of those who argue that intense satire and irony are produced not by the happy but by the disgruntled! Still there are intrinsic literary as well as biographical determinants to be noted. Christopher Sykes and others have pointed to the influence on *Scoop* of the comic novels of P. G. Wodehouse, which Waugh was reading during the gestation of *Scoop*; and the genial quality of the book has something to do with the free play given to such farcical elements as are found in the work of Wodehouse. In *Scoop*, as farce becomes dominant, satire is diminished. There is also a far more obvious element of wish-fulfillment fantasy in *Scoop* than in other Waugh novels, for just after President Jackson has been "locked in the woodshed" and the Soviet Union of Ishmaelia has been proclaimed, a fairy godfather appears in response to William Boot's prayer for "a god from the machine," in the person of the novel's major comic grotesque. Partly a bizarre contrast to the stodgy prime minister, Stanley Baldwin, partly a parody of a Wildean aesthete of the Nineties, partly a comic embodiment of capitalist individualism, Waugh's Mr. Baldwin sports purple hair, emerald and ruby jewelry, and pointed snakeskin shoes. Moving behind the scenes throughout the novel, he emerges at the climax to take control of the counterrevolutionary forces and to restore President Jackson, from whom he has gained a concession to the mineral rights of Ishmaelia. In its farcical wish-fulfillment conclusion, *Scoop* is revealed as a Waughian *marchen* for our times. Had it not been preceded by the devastating ironies of *A Handful of Dust* and *Black Mischief*, this novel, on the manuscript revisions of which Waugh expended considerable time and energy (Davis 89–91), might seem far more impressive than it does. Even improving on the comedy of Wodehouse, Waugh had not moved far from the kind of book he had already learned to write very well.

By the time Waugh produced his next novel, *Put Out More Flags* (1942), World War II had broken out and he was an officer in the Royal Marines. Waugh's "Dedicatory Letter" to Randolph Churchill, which prefaces the novel, apologizes for this "race of ghosts, the survivors of the world we both knew ten years ago." Thus Waugh seems to align the book with the earlier novels and to define it as another of the kind of book he knew how to write well. Waugh apologizes, too, that the book deals with characters "no longer contemporary in sympathy" and therefore not "acceptable" to Churchill's "ardent and sanguine nature." Basil Seal, the ultimate cad as hero, appears here once again, as do the Edwardian simpletons Lady Seal and Sir Joseph Mainwaring, and the once Bright Young People Alastair and Sonia Trumpington and Peter Pastmaster. Waugh's handling of these recurring characters and of many new ones is dazzling, as is his tracing of several careers "in that strangely cosy interlude between peace and war, when there was leave every week-end and plenty to eat and drink and plenty to smoke, when France stood firm on the Maginot Line and the Finns stood firm in Finland. . . ." Basil Seal, more sadistic than ever, takes over from his sister as billeting officer and extorts large sums from various respectable householders upon whom he imposes three hideous slum children, "one leering, one lowering, one drooling." Then, having tricked his way into a post in Internal Security, Basil offers up as sacrificial goat to the director, his old friend, the Jewish, homosexual aesthete Ambrose Silk, whom he contrives to represent as a Nazi agent. Aesthetes do not fare well in *Put Out More Flags*: Ambrose, tipped off by Basil that he is about to be arrested, does escape to Ireland, but merges with the mythic Wandering Jew by the novel's close; the poets Parsnip and Pimpernell (W. H. Auden and Christopher Isherwood), who have emigrated to America, are taunted throughout; and Cedric Lyne, who has made a career of grottoes and gardens, dies needlessly in an early campaign in Finland.

In fact, despite Waugh's dedicatory remarks, the mood of the novel is ebullient and hopeful, expressive of the Churchillian renaissance. In what is surely the novelist's own psychic enactment, Ambrose is exiled and Lyne disposed of not just to make it possible for Basil to marry Angela, his mistress of many years, but to emphasize the novel's commitment to public action. Peter Pastmaster is commissioned in a regiment and, beginning to "suffer from pangs of dynastic conscience," marries to beget an heir; Alastair Trumpington enlists in the ranks, refusing a commission, to atone for past irresponsibility; even Basil Seal eventually joins a special corps d'élite, in which he will serve with both Peter and Alastair. As the novel closes, Sir Joseph Mainwaring, who has, to this point, been wrong about every aspect of the war, finally gets something "bang right": "there is a new spirit aboard."

It is not this spirit of optimism, suffusing the later sections of the novel and allying it to its genial predecessor, however, that is, in terms of Waugh's development as a novelist, the most interesting aspect of the book. *Put Out More Flags* is the first of Waugh's novels in which there is substantial evidence that, to use John Plant's words, he will conquer new worlds. Among the novel's characters one finds the usual contrasting types of Waugh's early fiction — the comic grotesques and those who are developed by means of understated ironies. In this novel, however, there is also a new and sympathetic capacity on Waugh's part to get inside his understated characters. Among the victims of the novel — a dark strand in the novel's bright design — are Angela Lyne, always "poor Angela" to her friends because of her long, painful, and humiliating liaison with Basil; Cedric Lyne, hero to his son, utter failure as a husband, and yet one of the few decent and sympathetic parents in all of Waugh's books; and Ambrose Silk, part charlatan, part idealist and individualist. Observed from outside, Angela wears "the livery of the highest fashion"; her face "might have been carved in jade, it was so smooth and cool and conventionally removed from the human." Late in the novel, we see Angela, blind drunk, sitting on the sidewalk. We are not surprised because, tracing her gradual surrender to alcoholic depression, Waugh has been able to reveal the pain she endures beneath the mask of perfection. From the point of view of his superiors, Cedric Lyne is utterly incompetent as a soldier, but, overhearing his final words as he goes to death in battle, we realize that the futility of his life and his notion of warfare are something other than what outsiders discern: "I suppose, thought Cedric, I'm rather brave. How very peculiar. I'm not the least brave, really; it's simply that the whole thing is so damned silly." We enter the stream of Ambrose Silk's thoughts, too, and we see him as he sees himself and as he knows himself to be seen by others: "Born after his time, in an age which made a type of him, a figure of farce; like mothers-in-law and kippers, the century's contribution to the national store of comic objects; akin with the chorus boys who tittered under the lamps of Shaftesbury Avenue. . . ." Whatever else may be said of it, *Put Out More Flags* was the novel in which Waugh, relinquishing none of his capacity to draw a caricature, began to develop characters with psyches as well.

II

It was with *Brideshead Revisited* (1945) that Waugh made his real breakthrough into a new world of fiction. One way of understanding the difference between this work and the books preceding it is to make use of Northrop Frye's distinction between the romance — symbolic, expressive, fabulous — and the novel — realistic, concerned with character, and conflicts of value within a particular social setting. From this point of view, though there were novelistic elements in Waugh's early satiric and ironic romances and romance elements in the later novels, *Brideshead Revisited* is dominantly a novel, a fiction developing three-dimensional portraits of characters caught in religious and emotional conflicts over a period of more than twenty years, from the 1920s until World War II. At last satisfying the impulse he had revealed in *Work Suspended* to experiment with a first-person narrator, Waugh uses as narrator Charles Ryder, who becomes involved with a family of English Roman Catholics of title, owners of Marchmain House in London and of the more important country seat, Brideshead, which is at the center of the novel. Framed by a prologue and an epilogue in which, during the war, Ryder finds himself encamped on the grounds of Brideshead House, the novel has a formal beauty of design, though in 1960 Waugh divided the two books into three, as he had originally wished to do. In the setting of the great house with its exquisite grounds — though Ryder is pained to find the extent to which earlier encampments have scarred the place — Ryder finds that the "winged host" of memory soars about him, evoking the retrospective account he gives of his love first for Sebastian Flyte and then for his sister Julia. These profane loves, we eventually understand, are but earthly manifestations of Ryder's longing for God.

Brideshead Revisited was an enormous popular success for Waugh, both in England and in the United States — though Waugh himself was certain not "six Americans will understand it" (*Letters* 177). The novel, moreover, has retained its popular interest as witnessed by a BBC television serial production of particular excellence nearly four decades later. But the novel gave Waugh a notoriety he did not enjoy and also damaged his reputation among the critics, losing him, as he put it, "such esteem as I once enjoyed among my contemporaries" (Sykes 258). The strengths of the novel are considerable. There is the beauty of the book's architecture. There is the beauty of much — though not all — of the book's rich and subtle prose. There is a brilliant series of central character portraits, shining among them that of the charming Sebastian Flyte, a holy sinner, declining from epicene beauty at Oxford to alcoholism in

North African exile, until destitute at a Tunisian monastery he finds the
God he had sought to escape. There are his saintly and deadly mother,
Lady Marchmain, and his father, Lord Marchmain, a saturnine exile who
has himself fled the saintliness of his Lady. There are Bridey, elder son of
the Flytes, as stodgy as Sebastian is abandoned, and Cordelia, youngest of
the Flytes, engaging child, homely spinster, virtuous servant of the
suffering. There are numerous lesser figures, rich and varied in treatment,
all rendered with brilliant economy: Rex Mottram, the Canadian climber,
who marries Julia; Celia Mulcaster, efficient, hygienic, and faithless wife
to Ryder; Nanny Hawkins, all gentle banality, nursemaid to the Flytes and
therefore sheltered under the dome of Brideshead; Kurt, Sebastian's
disreputable German companion, a lisper and an eventual suicide in a
concentration camp; Mr. Samgrass, Oxford don, failed mentor, ingratiat-
ing and dishonest. There is also the figure of Anthony Blanche, a grotesque
in the style of the earlier books but given depth by his ironic role as
destroyer of illusion, surely the most brilliant portrait in modern English
literature of the homosexual dandy.

But then there are problems with the novel that have provoked,
among professional and academic critics, intense debates, vehement
attacks, and defenses of ingenious subtlety. There are extended passages of
overindulgent and overripe prose. (Waugh revealed his own consciousness
of these when he pruned back some of the excesses in a revised later
edition.) There is the problem of the first-person narrator, untouched
himself, except for Anthony Blanche's mockery of his paintings, by any
irony searching enough to call into question his values and judgments; and
there is the awkward contrivance by which he withholds an admission of
his own conversion until the novel's close. There is the problem of Ryder's
snobbery, more obvious now than ever, not just a sense of superiority or an
affection for certain aristocrats (either of which one might endure) but a
detestation of all those Ryder considers beneath him. There is the artistic
discrepancy between the idyllic early sections dealing with Sebastian and
Oxford, a paean to an Arcadian homosexual love so tactfully (some would
say evasively) handled that many readers may not even recognize it as
such, and the later melodramatic, overblown, and unconvincing account
of Ryder's love affair with Julia, who is the least realized of all of the
novel's characters.

According to Waugh, the best of his early novels was *A Handful of
Dust*: "It was humanist and contained all I had to say about humanism"
("Fan-Fare" 34). *Brideshead* he regarded as a distinct departure from his
earlier work and not only because of its technical achievements. "Vastly
more ambitious, perhaps less successful" than *A Handful of Dust*, *Brideshead* was, he declared on the dust jacket of the English edition, "an
attempt to trace the workings of the divine purpose in a pagan world."
Thus the ultimate returns to the Church of Lord Marchmain, Sebastian,
and Julia — who sacrifices the possibility of marriage to Ryder in order to

return—and the conversion of Ryder himself, all reveal God's providence and his sanctifying grace. If the "glaring defects" he eventually saw in the book (Sykes 258) were a consequence of the circumstances of its composition—his escape from the restrictions of military service and from the exhaustions of the war—Waugh still saw no reason to retreat from his desire henceforth to treat man in relation to God. A writer who had in a succession of satiric novels explored the derangements of chance and the horrors of modern chaos from which ironic laughter alone might save man's sanity now seemed determined to embody in his fiction the very answer to chaos, Roman Catholicism, which he had long ago found in his own life.

But in the years that followed *Brideshead*, Waugh's high theological resolve was not always or obviously apparent in the works he produced. In less than a decade, Waugh published two novels, *Helena* and *Men at Arms*, and three short novels, *Scott-King's Modern Europe*, *The Loved One*, and *Love among the Ruins*. Since *Men at Arms* was the first part of a trilogy that Waugh always considered a single work and later even published in a one-volume redaction, it seems appropriate to consider it later, apart from the three short novels and *Helena*. To *Helena*, a work that seems essentially devotional, the short novels stand in glaring contrast, for in none of these does Waugh's religious commitment find overt expression as it does in *Brideshead* and *Helena*. All three of these short novels were occasioned either by Waugh's travels in the postwar period or by his resentment of postwar conditions. Though they differ in quality, the short novels all demonstrate that the form of the *nouvelle* was better suited than the short story to Waugh's talent.

The least of the three is *Scott-King's Modern Europe* (1947), which narrates a "dim" classical master's journey to Neutralia for the tercentenary of the imaginary Latin poet, Bellorious, in 1946. Alas, totalitarian Neutralia—which suggests Yugoslavia, though drawing also on Franco's Spain—bears little resemblance to the "virtuous, chaste, and reasonable" utopian community described in the master work of Bellorious. Understated and farcical, *Scott-King's Modern Europe* has some amusing satiric and comic moments, but, though written in the detached manner of the earlier books and recording largely fortuitous events, it lacks their bite and sting. Its account of the shoddy ceremonies of the celebration, of propaganda manipulations, and of the difficulties of Scott-King's return to England through an underground for displaced persons, is almost as dim as the classicist himself. Faced at the short novel's conclusion with the news that there are fifteen fewer classical students to start the year, Scott-King still refuses to take on another subject. His insistence that it would be "very wicked to do anything to fit a boy for the modern world" seems more a crotchet than a principle.

In *The Loved One* (1948), however, Waugh found a subject well suited to his talent for the macabre. Waugh told his agent, who advised him against publication, that "the tale should not be read as a satire on morticians but as a study of the Anglo-American cultural impasse with the mortuary as a jolly setting" (*Letters* 259). To another correspondent, he cited these two themes, adding that *The Loved One* would also show that all Americans are exiles; that Europeans visit America as raiders bent on taking spoils; and that the reality of death must be recognized rather than evaded (*Letters* 265–66). *The Loved One* does indeed touch on all these themes. It also ridicules America's polyglot names, Hollywood's artificially created starlets, the "Momism" of American males, English expatriates in Hollywood, studio politics, pet cemeteries, advertising jargon, the synthetic religions of California, newspaper columnists who dispense advice to the lovelorn, health foods, and even the quality of American peaches. Almost all of these were appropriate targets for ridicule, and Waugh mostly hit the bull's-eye when he aimed at them. But if not a satire on morticians, *The Loved One* is certainly predominantly a satire on American mortuary customs and on Hollywood's vulgar Forest Lawn Cemetery, and it is most successful when ridiculing these. The book's greatest weakness is its utterly amoral but bland antihero, Dennis Barlow, who lacks the panache of a cad like Basil Seal and never really convinces us that he is to be taken seriously as a lover or as a poet. When Dennis disposes of the suicide Aimée Thanatogenos (his own victim) for his rival Mr. Joyboy, by incineration at the pet cemetery where he has been employed, he prepares the way for a macabre joke: Yearly Mr. Joyboy will receive a postcard reminding him that "your little Aimée is wagging her tail in heaven tonight, thinking of you."

Very, very funny, to be sure, but this is satire on a far different level from that which describes the murderous pyromania of the anti-hero of *Love among the Ruins*, who incinerates countless numbers of people by various acts of arson. Though it has never been given the kind of attention *The Loved One* has received, and though Waugh himself described it as "hastily finished and injudiciously published" (*Letters* 404), *Love among the Ruins* (1953) is a better focused and sustained satire. Placed some twenty years into the future from its time of composition and appropriately inviting comparison with the dystopias of Aldous Huxley and George Orwell, this short novel ridicules the shabby welfare state Waugh saw emerging in England and its system of justice and social psychology, which Waugh felt rewarded the criminal at the expense of his victim. The amoral Miles Plastic who is both victim and victimizer is a product of a state orphanage and corrective treatment. His pyromania, however, is his anarchic act of rebellion against a sterile, impoverished, and empty society in which love is "a word seldom used except by politicians and the Department of Euthanasia flourishes." In this deathly atmosphere, Miles finds that life takes on meaning when he meets Clara, a ballet dancer whose career has been ruined by a faulty sterilization procedure that has given her "a long silken, corn-gold beard." When a second operation provides her instead with a salmon pink synthetic facial mask, Miles, deprived of the one exceptional thing in his experience, again commits arson. As the novel closes, denied real expression of choice or freedom, Miles is to be used as a government exhibit of the success of the correctional system and he is to be married to a "gruesome" young woman.

In the concluding passage of the novel, Waugh introduces a sinister, black comic conceit. The detachment and obliquity of his early style are triumphantly preserved, for, as Miles plays with his cigarette lighter, "there burst out a tiny flame—gemlike, hymeneal, auspicious." Interpreted variously as an act of creative rebellion and as a suicidal impulse, Miles's final gesture surely implies that when values die and men are shaped like plastic objects anarchic and destructive impulses will provide an outlet for the human spirit. *Love among the Ruins* was Waugh's way of dealing with the tendencies of the present by projecting a narrative into the future. It came closer than either *The Loved One* or *Scott-King's Modern Europe* to dealing with Waugh's religious concerns, but only obliquely in that it included a description of Santa-Claus-Tide, a holiday on which an "obscure folk play" involving "an ox and an ass, an old man with a lantern, and a young mother" is performed. The obscure play is of interest to the public inasmuch as it deals with "maternity services before the days of welfare."

In *Helena* (1950), however, Waugh turned back to the third and fourth centuries for a subject that would permit him to comment on the modern world and also fulfill his promise to treat man in relation to God. According to Christopher Sykes, Waugh expended considerable energy on this, his sole historical romance (which is also his sole piece of doctrinal or apologetic fiction), devoting several years to research and composition; and Sykes also tells us that until the end of his life Waugh considered *Helena* his best book (Sykes 187–317). Not many have agreed with this estimate.

Waugh had little solid historical information to go on in developing his portrait of St. Helena, mother of Constantine the Great, to whom is ascribed the "invention" (or discovery) of the cross and the tomb of Christ. Imagining Helena as a young woman of the English upper class of his own time, working highly selectively with the body of legend and myth, depending upon his own power of invention, Waugh devised an account of a British princess, daughter of Coël (the old King Cole of nursery rhyme), of how she is wooed by Constantius, who, after several years of marriage, puts her aside for another wife when he is adopted as Caesar for the Western Empire by the Emperor Maximian. Years later, Helena's son becomes Emperor, and she is brought to Rome as Empress Dowager. In her old age, performing holy works as she goes, Helena sets out for the Holy Land, where she makes her discoveries.

Like every book Waugh wrote, this one is distinguished by its craftsmanly prose; and there are superb portraits—satiric grotesques imagined as boldly as those of the Italian film satirist Federico Fellini—of the megalomaniac Constantine and the "fat common little woman," his depraved Empress, Fausta. The decadent atmosphere of Rome with its murderous power struggles and its mingling of Christian beliefs with pagan, esoteric, and magical practices is splendidly realized. Waugh is able to suggest too the theological conflicts—Arius versus Athanasius—raging within the Church, as these became involved in Roman politics. And he does not shirk from depicting impurities of motive within those who accept Christianity.

But artistic and thematic conflicts and difficulties mar the book. Scarcely any political act in *Helena* is untouched by the corruption of centralized power, and Constantine is associated with both Napoleon and Hitler. And yet in one of the numerous allusions to modern conditions, Helena, sounding more like an apologist for totalitarianism than for Christianity, laments that a time may come when people "may forget their loyalty to their kings and emperors and take power for themselves." (Reading that, one cannot help but thank a writer like E. M. Forster, for having offered instead two cheers for democracy.) Moreover, as a literary form, the saint's legend is really a naive form in which myth, folk tale, and religious belief mingle fantastically. Waugh had wanted to write a highly sophisticated legend in which myth and folk tale would be replaced by Christian symbol and thematic meaning directed by right reason. Still, it is not at all clear why major events in the life of the pragmatic Helena, who dismisses legend and myth as "rot" and "bosh," who regards theological debate as obscurantist, and who wants to find a "solid chunk of wood" to persuade others that Christianity is historical fact, are on a different level from the events of other myths and cults of Helena's time—except that Waugh believed they must be. At the climax of the novel, Helena has a dream in which the mythic Wandering Jew (whose unfortunate and awful accent is strictly from London's West End) lead hers to the place where the true cross may be found. He leaves the print of a goat's hoof in the dust. We are to understand then that God's will and providence operate even through accidental and diabolical forces. This climactic episode, both unpleasant and unconvincing in itself, demonstrates the novel's greatest weaknesses: that its religious ideology is too insistent and too obvious, and that a myth of Waugh's *own* invention, shaped by *his* theological convictions, is offered as superior to, more solid than, all other myths.

By 1946 Waugh was so distressed by the conditions of life in postwar England that he seriously considered moving to Ireland, even undertaking a house-hunting expedition there. In his diary he listed among the attractions of a move to Ireland "the luxury of being a foreigner, of completely retiring from further experience and sitting in an upstairs library to garner the forty-three-year harvest." The passage is interesting not only because it reveals the conflict present throughout Waugh's novels between the secluded life and the life of action, but because it points to Waugh's sense that he had a vast store of material yet to be transformed into works of fiction. Waugh did not abandon Piers Court; indeed it remained his retreat until 1956, when he moved to Combe Florey House in Somerset, where he was to end his days. In his later years, Waugh traveled abroad frequently and made regular excursions to London, but the sequested life was necessary to him, as was the need to return to a rich store of experience. "In youth," Waugh wrote, "I gadded about and in those years and in the preposterous years of the Second World War I collected enough experience to last several lifetimes of novel writing" ("Fan-Fare" 30–31).

It was to those preposterous years of World War II that Waugh turned in the major work of his final years. The three Guy Crouchback novels appeared at intervals over the course of a decade, and at a time when Waugh's health was badly deteriorating. As early as his forty-fourth birthday, Waugh could complain to his diary that he was "a very much older man than this time last year, physically infirm and lethargic" (*Diaries* 690). From Oxford on he had, like many in his social set, drunk to what may, with understatement, be called an excess. Moreover, as early as the mid-1940s, he is complaining to his diary that he does not sleep and that he has had to "take drugs every night this week" (*Diaries* 560). An insomniac for the rest of his life, Waugh dosed himself liberally with various sedatives and sleeping draughts. Both alcohol and these dangerous medications surely contributed to the steady physical decline of the last decade of his life and to a bout of hallucinations he suffered in 1954. When he published the second of the Crouchback novels Waugh indicated, on the dust jacket, that it completed the first, even though he had at first "thought that the story would run into three volumes." However, Waugh added, "I find that two will do the trick. If I keep my faculties I hope to follow the fortunes of the characters through the whole of the war. . . ." When, after several years, he published the third of the Crouchback novels Waugh declared, again on the dust jacket, that in his earlier statement he had not been "quite candid." He admitted now that he had known that "a third volume was needed," but that he "did not then feel confident that I was able to provide it." Behind his uncertainty lay, we now know, the mental collapse he experienced in 1954.

Like his war experiences, however, the hallucinations turned out to offer Waugh more material for fiction. Partly as therapy but partly because he wished to harvest this rich new material quickly, Waugh interrupted his work on the Crouchback trilogy to write a fictionalized account of his own mental collapse, *The Ordeal of Gilbert Pinfold* (1957). The extent to which the book is a prose record of what actually happened to Waugh during a journey to Ceylon is open to question, for in his memoir Christopher Sykes explains that Waugh offered widely varying accounts of his experience to his friends and, in other demonstrable respects, selected what he chose to emphasize (360). Nevertheless, that Waugh wanted us to recognize Gilbert Pinfold as a self-portrait seems inescapable. The opening chapter of the book gives a portrait of the artist in which the ironic tone is beautifully understated and controlled. Thereafter, Waugh gives an account of paranoid delusions in which Pinfold cannot escape the voices of tormentors who condemn, threaten, and ridicule him. Pinfold is accused of being Jewish, homosexual, and masochistic. He is denounced as a "common little communist pansy" and as a "priest-ridden puppet." He is accused of impotence, religious hypocrisy, drunkenness, drug addiction, fascism, and snobbery — indeed, of many of the things for which Waugh himself has been denounced by his detractors and perhaps by himself. He is sexually tempted by a young woman who bears the name of a daughter upon whom Evelyn Waugh's letters reveal that he quite doted. *The Ordeal of Gilbert Pinfold*, just a little beyond the limits of the short novel or *nouvelle*, was a startling performance, for Waugh dredged up from the depths of the unconscious mind almost every guilt or shame the psyche might seek to conceal. At the novel's close, Pinfold, suddenly restored to sanity by his wife's appeal to reason and by the ministrations of priest and doctor, sits down at his desk, puts aside an unfinished novel, and begins to write *The Ordeal of Gilbert Pinfold*. Thus from his own physical disorder and mental collapse Waugh distilled a witty fable about the artist and his processes.

No more than *Pinfold* can the Guy Crouchback novels be regarded as the unrefined raw material of Waugh's lived experience, though Guy Crouchback's military career closely parallels that of Evelyn Waugh, and Waugh's experiences in the war were the harvest he expected to garner in the trilogy. Sykes has set forth a detailed account of Waugh's military service "in three different units and in three extraregimental appointments," and Sykes's conclusion about Waugh's military career is remarkably frank. There was gallantry certainly in Waugh's volunteering, given his age, as there was in his conduct under fire on Crete. But Waugh remained a junior officer throughout his service, because, as Sykes sees it, he proved to be "critical and disruptive." According to Sykes's account of Waugh's service, "The prestige he had justly accumulated as a writer of shining talent made him welcome, but the discovery that the energy of his wit was the expression of a deep-rooted and searching and destructive skepticism applied indiscriminately to small things as well as great, made commanders from company to divisional level doubt if the retention of this officer was profitable in the circumstances of war" (199). From the viewpoint of a sympathetic observer, then, Waugh's military career was pretty much of a burden to others. To Waugh himself the experience of military service was thoroughly disillusioning. It might be argued that Guy Crouchback was Waugh's idealized notion of himself and Guy's military career a self-gratifying fantasy version of his own service. But if one adopts this view, one must also grant that what Waugh made out of disillusionment and rationalization went far beyond either of these. Guy Crouchback and his story have the substance of virtual reality about them.

Men at Arms (1952) introduces Guy at the moment of the Russian-German Alliance, which he hails, since it presents him with an enemy he wants to defeat: "the modern age in arms." Descended from an English Catholic family so distinguished that it includes martyrs in its genealogy, Guy has lived in self-imposed exile in Italy "for eight years of shame and loneliness," following on the collapse of his marriage. A cuckold with a "deep wound," he is not quite a whole person. For years his soul has languished in a "waste land." In his memoir-biography of Waugh, Christopher Sykes admits that, though Men at Arms was dedicated to him, he "never greatly cared for the book" (354) and, indeed, Sykes finds the entire trilogy to be gravely blemished by its protagonist, whom he recognizes as in antiheroic descent from Paul Pennyfeather. To be sure, Sykes recognizes that in the Crouchback novels Waugh was making amends for the defects of Brideshead, against which he had quite turned, but Sykes fails to see that, from Pennyfeather to Charles Ryder to Crouchback, the Waugh male protagonist developed from a flat into a round character, that Crouchback has an "inside," a psyche, and that he grows over the course of the novels to the point at which a hero emerges from the antihero. In undertaking the Crouchback novels as a repudiation of Brideshead Waugh made, moreover, a vitally important technical and aesthetic decision. Guy Crouchback does not, like Charles Ryder in Brideshead, narrate his own story. Consequently, there is a distance between the detached narrative voice of the Crouchback novels and the consciousness of Guy as protagonist; and, of course, Guy is constantly being shown as others see him and in dramatic and ironic relation to the complex motifs and themes of the three books.

Like Men at Arms, the two succeeding novels, Officers and Gentlemen (1955) and Unconditional Surrender (1961), the last published in the United States as The End of the Battle, were artfully formed. (Varied arrangements of books, prologues, epilogues, and one interlude constitute the structural divisions of the three novels.) Throughout the trilogy, for dramatic and thematic purposes, Waugh employed the rhythm of heightened expectation and deflation. Then, to suggest the confusion and disorder of wartime as well as the nature of one man's military service, Waugh employed another rhythm, that of alternating chaos and order, a strategy that succeeded well in conveying the tedium as well as the excitements of wartime. Finally, in each of the three novels, exploring discrepancies between reality and illusion, Waugh created a vivid series of characters who either represent Guy's ideal of action or else mock, parody, or ironically betray that ideal.

In Men at Arms, three books of which bear mock-heroic titles ("Apthorpe Gloriosus," "Apthorpe Furibundus," "Apthorpe Immolatus") the eponymous Apthorpe is Guy's foil. As the two older men are trained by their regiment, the Halberdiers, they are addressed by the younger officers as "uncle" and both sustain leg injuries during the course of their training, though neither in martial exploit. Throughout training the apparently knowledgeable Apthorpe succeeds wherever Guy fails and eclipses him in regimental award and rank by the end of the training. Yet Apthorpe is the *miles gloriosus* of Roman comedy, a braggart soldier who lacks any real authority and whose apparent sophistication masks an undistinguished background and a failed career in the tropics. He dies at the novel's close succumbing to what he calls "Bechuanaland tummy" — a combination of alcoholism and various jungle fevers — though Guy is regarded as culpable for bringing him whiskey when he is in the hospital. While Apthorpe waxes as a comic pretender and wanes as a warrior, Ben Ritchie-Hook supplants him and emerges as a more compelling and ideal figure. Bemonocled, mustachioed, maimed in one hand, Ritchie-Hook "was the great Halberdier *enfant terrible* of the first World War." A notorious prankster, he engages in a battle of wits with Apthorpe over the latter's "thunderbox," a chemical toilet, driving Apthorpe ever deeper into paranoia, until he finally booby-traps the prized piece of equipment right under the unfortunate Apthorpe. For Ritchie-Hook warfare is "biffing" the enemy: engaging in intense surprise assault. When Guy himself does finally see action, it is on coastal Africa, after a withdrawal order, when he accompanies Ritchie-Hook on an unauthorized raid. Ritchie-Hook bags one black soldier's head and takes a bullet in the leg. Guy's service earns him a "black mark."

Throughout *Officers and Gentlemen*, Ritchie-Hook's fate is associated with that of Guy Crouchback, for, when Ritchie-Hook is saved from the consequences of his folly by the direct intervention of the prime minister, Guy too is apparently redeemed. As the "personal property" of the colonel he now "loves," Guy is attached for training purposes to a commando force; but Ritchie-Hook disappears when his plane crashes in the jungle, not to appear again until the final Crouchback novel, though he continues to be felt as an influence even when his fate is not known. As in *Men at Arms*, the rhythm of the earlier part of the novel is dominated by a series of false starts, confusions, and futile training procedures, until Guy finds himself in Cairo, still attached to "Hookforce," though in the absence of Ritchie-Hook, a deputy commander is in charge. But in Cairo Guy comes to admire the elegant Ivor Claire. Guy idealizes this dandiacal figure as the fine flower of English chivalry. In the second part of the novel Guy finally sees action on Crete, as the English are routed by the Germans and withdraw in utter chaos and confusion. During this withdrawal, the admired Ivor, though ordered to remain with his men and surrender, instead abandons his troops and his honor and conveniently seizes an opportunity to escape. Even before the Cretan debacle, Guy had begun to dissociate himself from the army in matters of real concern, and now with

Ivor's defection from the ideal of duty, he has to admit that "the man who had been his friend had proved to be an illusion."

From the earliest of his novels on, Waugh was intrigued by characters with multiple identities—like Grimes and Philbrick of *Decline and Fall*—by jack-in-the-boxes who startlingly spring forth into a new life. Among the comic grotesques of *Officers and Gentlemen* is Corporal Major Ludovic, whose accent changes suddenly from "plummy" to "plebeian" and who communicates his exquisite reflections to a journal that comments ironically on the characters and incidents of the novel. In *Unconditional Surrender* Ludovic reappears, broadly comic but also rather sinister, and something of a polymorph, too. Guy's rescuer from the Cretan defeat, possibly the murderer of a cowardly officer, the certain murderer of a deranged sapper on the escape craft, Ludovic, we now learn, was once the lover of the homosexual diplomat, Sir Ralph Brompton. Ludovic turns up, too, as the commanding officer of the base where Guy takes his parachute training. Madly fearful now that Guy will expose him, Ludovic attempts to send Guy to his death. Eventually, he emerges as a literary man, author of a volume of aphorisms and then of a highly romantic and awful popular novel, *The Death Wish*, which is described as if to ridicule *Brideshead Revisited*. At the novel's close, already a bizarre parody of Ivor Claire, Ludovic has purchased the Crouchback Castello and thus parodies Guy's prewar exile. In effect, Ludovic's apotheosis as aesthetic recluse is the novel's satiric repudiation of escape from the world.

Yet in public action Guy Crouchback finds no satisfactory alternative to the aesthete's withdrawal from life. In the early pages of *Men at Arms* Waugh established Guy's belief that the Russian-German Alliance presented England with its proper enemy, "the modern age in arms"; and, by the conclusion of *Officers and Gentlemen*, Guy is depicted as regarding England's alliance with invaded Russia as a dishonorable blunder. Moreover, Guy learns in Yugoslavia that there can be no honor in war. In the context of a policy designed to reinforce the partisans, Ritchie-Hook, now clearly no more than the superannuated hero of an earlier war and consumed with a desire for death, plays his final game. He throws away his life in an assault staged to make the partisans look good to an American observer. Guy's good intentions as a member of the British mission come to naught or worse. His efforts to help Jewish refugees are defeated by the malice of the partisans; a gesture he makes out of kindness to the refugee's spokesperson, Mme Kanyi, leads to her imprisonment or execution by a People's Court. Aesthetic sequestration having been made ludicrous and sterile by Waugh's satiric treatment of Ludovic, public action having been revealed as at best futile and more likely as catastrophic, did Waugh reach an emotional and artistic impasse at the close of the Crouchback trilogy—*Sword of Honour*—as it was called in his one volume redaction?

By 1965, he was so distressed at the changes in the Catholic Church, in particular at the banality of the democratized vernacular Mass, that in his journal he prayed God he would not apostatize (789); and both his public and private utterances over the years during which he worked on the trilogy and the redaction substantiate his despair. But the trilogy was, in fact, a triumph over despair, and a triumph, too, over the defects Waugh had come to recognize in *Brideshead*. While the Crouchback novels are an account of a man's disillusionment with warfare and public causes, they are also an account of the dispelling of illusions, of a man's discovery of the reality of his own nature and of his circumstances. Thus they record not just the defeat of Guy Crouchback but his triumph over the various falsehoods of the modern world. Much of *Unconditional Surrender* is devoted to the conditions of civilian life, to episodes involving Guy's father, his Uncle Peregrine, and Guy's former wife, Virginia. When Guy learns that Virginia (who has now managed to cuckold her third husband) is penniless and also pregnant by the bogus lower-class war hero Trimmer, her former hairdresser whom she now loathes, he performs what he terms the one "single, positively unselfish action of his life." He remarries Virginia and accepts Trimmer's child as his heir. In the closing pages of the novel, following the death of Virginia and Uncle Peregrine, who are victims of a flying bomb, we learn that Guy has married Domenica Plessington, that, his family estate being much reduced, he and Domenica live in the agent's house with Virginia's son and "two boys of their own." In a later decision, Waugh denied Guy and Domenica children of their own—as can be seen in *Sword of Honour*—thus reenforcing the thematic significance of Trimmer's bastard as heir to the Crouchback line. That Guy and Domenica farm and that they live not in the manor but in the small agent's house is a development of greater import than the painful contrast in *Brideshead* between the former glories of the great house and its degraded present condition. Of course, Waugh is recording a substantial economic change diminishing a particular class in English society, but he is also symbolizing the persistence of private humane values in a disordered world.

The significance of the conclusion of *Unconditional Surrender* may be illuminated by considering it in relation to the endings of E. M. Forster's *Howards End* (1910) and D. H. Lawrence's *Lady Chatterley's Lover* (1928). Odd though it may seem to associate these diverse works, each of them is concerned with class values, bastardy, and the rural retreat. It was E. M. Forster's effort in resolving the conflicts of *Howards End* to shape a possible future for England that would heal class conflicts, unite culture and power, liberate men from the encroachments of the machine, and elevate the impoverished imagination of the proletariat. Forster's was a noble aim, and yet many of his readers have felt the marriage of the cultivated and intellectual Margaret Schlegel to the materialistic business-man Henry Wilcox to be more imposed by Forster than suggested by experience. Moreover, many readers have sensed an aesthetic strain in the resolution of *Howards End*, when the illegitimate son of Leonard Bast, a clerk one generation from the land, is depicted as heir to the suburban farm of the spiritually sensitive Mrs. Wilcox. In *Lady Chatterley*, Lawrence's concerns were essentially the same as Forster's, for beyond the sexual theme of the novel is a concern with class barriers, the dehumanizing machine, the destruction of the countryside, and the debased quality of popular culture. Regarded as a prophetic novelist by Forster, in the final *Lady Chatterley*, Lawrence found a resolution more personal than the symbolic and national one of Forster's *Howards End*. At the conclusion of Lawrence's novel, Constance Chatterley, having cuckolded the impotent and mechanistic Clifford Chatterley, plans to leave her class behind. Mellors, the gamekeeper, whose child she carries, has already abandoned his class — really that of the miners — now lifeless from mechanization and the vulgar distractions of popular culture. These two déclassé people will depart, it is implied, for a small farm, perhaps in British Columbia. The vast political and religious expectations of *The Plumed Serpent* abandoned, Lawrence's solution to the social problems he sets forth is, in short, a modest individualist one.

Like both Forster and Lawrence, Waugh found it impossible to imagine a good independent life without also imagining a working farm. Decades after Forster and Lawrence, he depicted in a number of his novels many of the social problems with which they had sought to deal. Unlike Forster he could not imagine a national solution to the problems of modern society; indeed, for him, national solutions were one of the problems. The conclusion of Waugh's trilogy, however, goes beyond the individualist conclusion of *Lady Chatterley*. In making Trimmer's bastard Guy's heir, moreover, a writer often accused of social snobbery and often guilty of it implies that the seed of the awful Trimmer may not only inherit the shrinking wealth of the Crouchbacks' but also their culture and undiminished moral values. The private act of *caritas*, a limited but redemptive deed, is Guy's alternative to the dichotomy of public action or aesthetic retreat. "One day," Guy has reflected long before the conception of Trimmer's son, "he would get the chance to do some small service which only he could perform, for which he had been created. Even he must have his function in the divine plan." The three Crouchback novels are filled with accidents and with chance, for Waugh never lost his sense of the power of fortuity. But accident in the trilogy is less the irrational and absurdist chance of the early novels than the consequence of human error and frailty. Guy's reflection indicates that Waugh was still adhering to the promise he made at the time of *Brideshead* "to trace the workings of the divine purpose in a pagan world." Still, in the design of the trilogy, Waugh has not confused the divine plan with the social status of the Catholic aristocracy. Avoiding the defects of *Brideshead* and *Helena*, in the major work of his later career Waugh allows his readers to listen to Guy, form their own conclusions about the relation between chance and providence, but not to ignore the human importance of decency. His Crouchback trilogy ridicules and lashes with satire the follies of his age. But transcending the misanthropy of which Waugh accused himself and triumphing over the despair of his declining years, it affirms a simple goodness as within the reach of man.

III

As is the case with other important writers of the earlier part of our century, there is now a substantial body of criticism and scholarship devoted to Evelyn Waugh. It was, however, not until the 1940s that much criticism worthy of note was produced, and not until the 1960s was Waugh's work given the kind of extensive and sustained scrutiny that it deserved. Right from the start of his career, however, Waugh had the attention of reviewers, in part because he had a circle of well-placed friends who were reviewing in various English papers and journals. One memorable response to the early Waugh was that of a novelist of an earlier generation, Arnold Bennett, who admitted that *Decline and Fall* provoked him to frequent laughter but then had so many reservations about the kaleidoscopic naughtiness of *Vile Bodies* that he concluded that Evelyn's pot-boiling brother Alec Waugh "was weightier than his cadet." By the middle of the 1930s Waugh had attracted enough attention in the United States to have gained the enthusiastic support of Alexander Woolcott. Not very important as a critic and not taken at all seriously in academic circles, Woolcott yet had the sense to reprint *A Handful of Dust* in his widely circulated *Woolcott Reader* (1935), to see that Evelyn Waugh was more important than his brother, and to declare him "the nearest thing to a genius among the young writers who have arisen in post-war England." From this point in the mid-1930s on, Waugh was certainly regarded on both sides of the Atlantic as a writer to be reckoned with — even by those hostile to his books.

The essays reprinted in this collection were not, however, selected to provide a historical record of Waugh's reception by the critics or of fluctuations in his critical reputation. To be sure, within each of the major groupings of essays, the selections are arranged chronologically and thus incidentally provide a sense of developing critical attitudes toward Waugh and his work; but each essay has been selected primarily because it makes some significant contribution to our understanding of this writer, and also indicates the range of critical response to his work. The first group of essays is composed of criticism that responds to the entire group of Waugh's novels or to a number of books within the oeuvre. In the second group of selections are essays that treat individual works or offer responses to the works in question that are at variance with prevailing critical views. Finally, there is a group of essays that deal with characteristic aspects of the life of the writer, or with certain groups of books, or with significant conclusions about pervasive qualities within many of the works. With the exception of Richard Voorhees's essay on the travel books and two reviews of *A Little Learning,* concentration throughout the entire selection is on the novels. Waugh's biographical works—his books on Rosetti, Edmund Campion, and Ronald Knox—are treated only incidentally, as are the various collections of his short stories.

Malcolm Cowley's early review of the first three Waugh novels and of one of the travel books has first place in this collection. An influential and respected interpreter of major American writers of the period, Cowley signals in this review the start of that concern with Waugh's political views that was to shape many a critical response to the novels. Prepared to recognize that the first novels were "brilliant," Cowley nevertheless reflects the political mood of the 1930s when he is so outraged by the opinions expressed in *They Were Still Dancing* that he can only see Waugh as a latter-day Kipling and utterly fails to recognize the strengths of *Black Mischief.* A decade later, Nigel Dennis (who himself achieved some fame as satiric novelist) was more moderate in his political response to Waugh and more searching in his critical analysis of the works through *Put Out More Flags.* Seeing Waugh as in conflict with the generation of W. H. Auden and more sympathetic to the radical mood of the 1930s than to Waugh's conservatism, Dennis was, nevertheless, one of the first to recognize the discipline and skill of Waugh's novels. The single essay one would most want to have on the subject of Waugh was that which George Orwell would have written had he lived, in which Orwell would have raised the issue of Waugh's Catholicism. Written more than a decade after Malcolm Cowley's review and following on the publication of *Brideshead Revisited,* Orwell's notes, brief as they are, are fascinating. In their personal correspondence, Waugh and Orwell are decorous, formal, perhaps a little wary of one another; still one can recognize that there is respect on both sides, and Orwell's notes on Waugh center upon a sharp distinction between Waugh's opinions and his talents.

Written a little earlier than Orwell's notes, Edmund Wilson's "Never Apologize, Never Explain" probably did more to advance Waugh's reputation than anything hitherto written about him. Wilson's essay, appearing first in the *New Yorker* and then in a collection of Wilson's criticism and reviews, placed an influential and widely respected critic solidly behind Waugh; going a little further than Alexander Wolcott, Wilson described Waugh as "the only first-rate comic genius that has appeared in English since Bernard Shaw." When Wilson returned to the subject of Waugh again (1946), however, it was on the publication of *Brideshead Revisited.* While Wilson discerned, as one would expect him to, the strengths of *Brideshead,* he had to admit that the new novel was "a bitter blow" to him. He assailed *Brideshead* as "a Catholic tract" and developed a case that would frequently be heard thereafter against the element of snobbery in Waugh. Reading Wilson on the subject of *Brideshead*, one cannot help but recognize that his are the strictures of an American secular liberal whose heritage was Protestant.

During the 1950s, two Irish writers, with perspectives on Catholicism very different from that of either Waugh or Edmund Wilson, produced books on the modern novel. Writing then as Donat O'Donnell, Conor Cruise O'Brien produced an indictment of Waugh's Catholicism and a lively exploration of Waugh's romanticism. O'Brien is, moreover, particularly interesting on the sources of Waugh's satire in cruelty and adolescent fantasy. That master of the short story, Sean O'Faolain wrote of Waugh in *The Vanishing Hero* with greater sympathy, though O'Faolain's comments on the Catholic element in *Brideshead* were also severe. While recognizing the element of snobbery in Waugh, O'Faolian placed that element in another perspective than O'Brien's by the attention he gave to Waugh as a detached moral satirist. Preferring the earlier works, O'Faolain insisted of them "that they would live as long as literature lasts." Stephen Spender, a poet of the Auden set frequently ridiculed by Waugh, joined O'Brien and O'Faolain in criticizing *Brideshead*. But Spender's grounds for complaint were aesthetic rather than religious. Like many another, he preferred the pre-*Brideshead* books. However, Stephen Spender was the first critic to recognize the element of the absurd in Waugh; and he also took a new line in praising Waugh as more of an observer of manners than a satirist.

Nigel Dennis and others had pointed out the symbolic significance of the great house as a symbol of order in the novels of Evelyn Waugh, but in "The Wall and the Jungle" Alvin Kernan went further than his predecessors in defining the wall as a principle of order and the jungle as a symbol of anarchy; he described these as central patterns in the carpet of Waugh's novels. In Kernan, too, one begins to find a spirited defense of Waugh against those who attacked him on political and social grounds; pointing out that Waugh's satire is directed against all social classes, Kernan argues that Waugh was a defender of tradition but not of the status quo, of social order but not of the social establishment. Treating the entire body of Waugh's work, Herbert Howarth, another vigorous defender, develops a subtle and eloquent defense of the way in which Waugh remained his own man throughout his entire career; Howarth praises Waugh's "truculent and wilful resistance to the norms of his day," and he finds that the conflict between the demands of Catholicism and the anarchic impulses of Waugh's own nature is a source of Waugh's creative energy.

These two important essays of the 1960s contrast with an essay of the 1970s which returns to a critical method of the 1930s. The element of a "social" literary criticism in Malcolm Cowley's early review was a slight trace of the Marxist strain in modern literary criticism which pretty well dissipated itself in the 1950s; in the past two decades, however, a recrudescent Marxist criticism has emerged. Terry Eagleton is the proponent of both a theoretical and a practical Marxist criticism. His examination of Waugh as an exponent of the upper-class novel is rigorous and challenging. Indeed, the approach of a critic like Eagleton is one that needs to be reckoned with, even though one may feel that to achieve his ends Eagleton must wear mechanist blinkers and exercise his very considerable ingenuity to prove what he must.

Among the essays in the second grouping of this collection, the first is Edmund Wilson's shocked response to *Brideshead*, already commented upon, and the last is a passage from Ian Littlewood's recent book on Waugh. The thesis of Littlewood's book is somewhat paradoxical, for he argues that the various techniques of Waugh's novels were strategies by which Waugh sought escape from the pressures of reality. In the passage on *Brideshead* included here, however, Littlewood sets forth the notion that the nostalgia for childhood frequently ascribed to Waugh is constantly subverted by the language of the novel. Some of the other essays in this group also advance highly individual theses that run counter to the prevailing critical view of the work. The satiric novelist Aubrey Menen (also a Catholic) offers an ingenious defense of *Helena* as a piece of baroque art and terms the novel a "masterpiece"; and L. E. Sissman celebrates the formal qualities of *Put Out More Flags*, which he considers to be "the greatest of Evelyn Waugh's great novels."

Certainly the most provocative of all pieces in this collection is J. B. Priestley's essay on *The Ordeal of Gilbert Pinfold*, which provoked a response from Waugh himself, so characteristic of the satirist's talents that it has been included in the collection. Priestley adopts the disarming tactic of insisting that his subject is Pinfold not Waugh; he proceeds to a layman's psychoanalysis of Pinfold and then gives a warning to Waugh — no, no, to Pinfold, of course. Reading Waugh's uproarious and trenchant rejoinder, one wonders if Priestley can have anticipated it. In any case, most readers will wish to thank him for having given a master an appropriate occasion for sport of a deadly kind.

Two of the remaining essays in this group are an essay on *A Handful of Dust* by Richard Wasson and, from my book on Waugh, a chapter dealing with the Guy Crouchback novels. The Wasson essay argues the thesis that *A Handful of Dust*, far from romanticizing the past, constitutes a profound criticism of the ethical values of the Victorian period and, in its Arthurian motif, develops an ironic account of the heroic quest as imagined by the Victorians, and particularly by Tennyson. My chapter on the trilogy was an attempt to demonstrate the essential unity of the work and to describe it as the triumph of Waugh's later manner and religious vision. Excepts from books by Robert Davis and Jeffrey Heath, helpful as accounts of the stages by which the Crouchback novels and the one-volume redaction came into being, also reveal the extent to which the redaction differed from the original books. To a degree, these two writers reinforce one another, yet they also offer certain distinctly opposed responses to the redaction as it modified the trilogy.

In the final group of selections are two reviews of *A Little Learning*, the first volume of Waugh's never-completed biography, and an essay on Waugh's travel books. The reviews of the biography by the prolific novelist Anthony Burgess and by John Gross, both of which deal with the language of the book, with the relation of Waugh to his father, and with the significance of Waugh's entire career, offer intriguingly different emphases and conclusions. Richard Voorhees's essay on the travel books is one of the few critical examinations we have of these works as an element in Waugh's whole creative endeavor; the essay is particularly interesting on the incidental subject of Waugh's complex attitudes toward class and color.

Finally, there are selections here from some of the important full-scale studies of Waugh. Frederick Stopp's early *Evelyn Waugh: A Portrait of an Artist* was not really a critical life but a piece of biographical criticism with an understated Jungian emphasis. Stopp's chapter on fantasy and myth suggests the extent to which he regards Waugh's novels as not only accounts of, but the product of unconscious psychic processes. Robert Davis's book on Waugh, a detailed study of the available manuscripts and other materials, explores the revisions, whether of local details or of major structural elements, to arrive at an understanding of Waugh's artistic processes. The final chapter of the book succinctly summarizes Davis's conclusions. As utterly committed to Waugh as Davis, Jeffrey Heath has also drawn upon manuscripts and biographical materials, his intent being to fuse biographical and aesthetic criticism. If one were to find fault with Heath's thesis, it would be at his insistence upon the fixed moral and spiritual consistency of Waugh's entire oeuvre; but his chapter on Waugh's religious and aesthetic impulses surely makes a persuasive case for essential concerns that shaped the writer's career.

Readers will find a brief and highly selective list of suggested readings at the back of this book, but it seems more than appropriate in closing to recommend the *Evelyn Waugh Newsletter* to any reader who has chosen to examine this collection. Edited and produced by Paul Doyle since 1967, this scholarly labor of love is a publication in which those interested in Waugh may expect to find varied and useful news, notes, reviews, and criticism.

JAMES F. CARENS
Bucknell University

Works Cited

Carens, James F. *The Satiric Art of Evelyn Waugh.* Seattle and London: University of Washington Press, 1966.

Davis, Robert Murray. *Evelyn Waugh, Writer.* Norman, Okla.: Pilgrim Books, 1981.

Heath, Jeffrey. *The Picturesque Prison: Evelyn Waugh and His Writing.* Kingston and Montreal: McGill–Queen's University Press, 1982.

Sykes, Christopher. *Evelyn Waugh: A Biography*. London, Glasgow: Collins, 1975.

Waugh, Evelyn. "Come Inside." In *A Little Order*. Edited by Donat Gallagher. Boston, Toronto: Little, Brown and Company, 1981.

————. *The Diaries of Evelyn Waugh*. Edited by Michael Davie. Boston, Toronto: Little, Brown and Company, 1976.

————. "Fan-Fare." In *A Little Order*. Edited by Donat Gallagher. Boston, Toronto: Little Brown and Company, 1981.

————. *The Letters of Evelyn Waugh*. Edited by Mark Amory. New Haven and New York: Ticknor & Fields, 1980.

General Essays and Reviews

Decline and Fall

Malcolm Cowley*

Evelyn Waugh is a young writer whose first two novels were praised by good critics and neglected by the public at large. He is often confused with his older brother Alec, the industrious author of fifteen books in which it is hard to find either salt or substance; Evelyn has both. His favorite theme is the Bright Young People of 1927–28, children of King Edward's Best People, inheritors of wartime frenzy without the sobering hardships of war: they rush from parties at Lady Metroland's to parties at the Prime Minister's, to parties in a furnished room over a chemist's — everywhere parties, absinthe, caviar, checks drawn against nonexistent bank accounts, love affairs with Maharajahs and Negro singers — everywhere music and international glitter, a life enjoyed because "it's all too too utterly bogus." Evelyn Waugh describes this side of English society in a fashion that makes Aldous Huxley seem evangelical and the Sitwells pedantic.

Decline and Fall, his first novel, is the story of a divinity student expelled from Oxford as the result of an unfortunate meeting with Sir Alastair Digby-Vane-Trumpington. Suddenly the timid and amiable young student discovers himself among the Bright Young People, engaged to Mrs. Beste-Chetwynde, about to be arrested as a white slaver: it is first-rate comedy; the author enjoys himself and his characters. In Vile Bodies, a much better novel, many of the same people are plunged into wilder adventures, but this time a hard-boiled pathos is mingled with the wit, and there is a new mood of ennui and revulsion. The story ends abruptly with the declaration of another world war, biggest and best in history; it is as if the author had suddenly grown tired of these bright puppets, had determined to sweep them aside and abolish his own past. As an ending, it is arbitrary and disappointing, but it left one eager to read what Evelyn Waugh would write and see where he would go. . . . He wrote Bachelor Abroad, an unimportant travelogue. Then he went to Africa and wrote They Were Still Dancing, another book of travels.

Scratch an Englishman and, if the scratch goes deep enough, you find

*Reprinted from the New Republic, 16 November 1932, 22–23.

an Englishman. Take the brightest, hardest, most cosmopolitan of England's Bright Young People, ship him out to an English colony, expose him to any hardship, fleas, garlic, customs officers—and suddenly he goes native, goes Trollope-and-Kipling, talks of the Anglo-Saxon heritage, looks down his nose at Hindus, Somalis, French and other niggers. That is what happened, briefly, to Evelyn Waugh. In his long journey from Abyssinia to Zanzibar, thence through the East African plateaus and the Congo south to the tip of the continent, he saw perhaps as little as any traveler has ever seen, being afflicted with a congenital blindness toward landscapes and foreign customs. But he had two encounters that revealed two sides of his nature and contributed to the triumph of one over the other: he met an Armenian trader and he visited Kenya.

The Armenian represented the cosmopolitan side of him, the side expressed in his first two novels. M. Bergebedgian kept a sort of hotel at Harar, in southern Abyssinia, where he impartially cheated Europeans and natives. "I do not think I have ever met a more tolerant man; he had no prejudices or scruples of race, creed, or morals of any kind whatever; there were in his mind none of those opaque patches of inconsidered principles, it was a single translucent pool of placid doubt." M. Bergebedgian was a proper guide and companion for the Bright Young People; and the Armenians as a race, Mr. Waugh reflected, were the only genuine men of the world; in his own life or books he could not hope to equal them. "Sometimes when I envy among my friends this one's adaptability to diverse company, this one's cosmopolitan experience, this one's impenetrable armor against sentimentality and humbug, that one's freedom from conventional prejudice . . . and realize that whatever happens to me and however I deplore it, I shall never in actual fact become a 'hard-boiled man of the world' . . . then I comfort myself by thinking that if I were an Armenian I should find things easier." It was as if, in comforting himself, he had decided to put away the cosmopolitan, the sophisticated, the Armenian side of him and revert to another nature.

That nature was objectified in Kenya Colony. There, in the African highlands on the sharp edge of the equator, he found two thousand English families reliving "The Chronicles of Barset" (with just a touch of Michael Arlen)—riding to hounds, inspecting their vast estates, keeping open house for their English neighbors, amiably cuffing their servants, then motoring into Nairobi for a grand binge at the Muthaiga Club—in a word, perpetuating "the traditional life of the English squirarchy . . . to which, now that it has become a rare and exotic survival . . . we can as a race look back with unaffected esteem and regret." But Barset-on-the-Equator survives as a system of exploitation. Below the two thousand county families are nearly three million natives, who furnish them with low-priced agricultural labor and servants to be treated with "half-humorous sympathy." In an intermediate position there are forty thousand Hindus eager to exploit the natives in their own dingier fashion. The domination of the English settlers is continually threatened, like that of the slave-owning families in the South before the Civil War. Evelyn Waugh became their partisan, "going a little mad," as he said, on the color problem. He began seriously to consider "the possibility that there may be something valuable behind the indefensible and inexplicable assumption of superiority by the Anglo-Saxon race."

On his return to England, Mr. Waugh completed his book of travels and — since he is almost as industrious as his brother Alec — determined to utilize part of his adventures in a novel. The scene of *Black Mischief* is laid in a Negro empire, an imaginary island which combines Abyssinia with Zanzibar while retaining the worst features of each. The natives are described with a half-humorous contempt which suggests the author's adventures in Kenya. As for the story, it deals with Basil Seal, one of the Bright Young People. Hearing that a Negro he knew at Oxford is about to ascend the throne of Azania as Emperor Seth I, Basil takes the next boat for the island and becomes its Minister of Modernization; with a very unscrupulous and polite Armenian he runs the country. There is a lot of superior comedy; Seth is deposed and murdered; Basil's mistress, the daughter of an English diplomat, is captured by the natives. This young lady represents qualities by which the author is attracted, others by which he is obviously repelled; and her fate is more interesting psychologically than artistically. Basil makes a last hazardous journey into the interior and discovers that he has helped to eat his mistress in a cannibal stew.

Back in London, the decade of the Bright Young People is ending. Lady Metroland has gone to America; Sir Alastair Digby-Vane-Trumpington is married without glamor and living next door to a pretty shady sort of chemist. "D'you know," says his wife after a dull evening with the former Azanian Minister, "deep down in my heart I've got a tiny fear that Basil is going to turn serious on us too." Evelyn Waugh himself has turned just a little serious; next year it wouldn't be surprising to learn that he had entered the diplomatic service or become a Member of Parliament speaking in favor of a strong imperial policy (and no misguided mercy to the Hindus). He has abandoned an attitude which produced two brilliant novels; he has resumed old loyalties which, in their day, gave themes to Kipling and Trollope; I don't know what they'll do for Evelyn Waugh. His latest novel is no fair test of their value, since it belongs to a period of transition. It is fairly amusing to read, if you don't read too carefully, but it's the sort of book a gifted author shouldn't have written, or at least should have published under a pseudonym.

Evelyn Waugh: The Pillar of Anchorage House

Nigel Dennis*

When Evelyn Waugh's last novel, *Put Out More Flags*, appeared in the summer of 1942, the *Retail Bookseller* summed it up for the American trade: "The Waugh type of cleverness is for a definite market, faithful but limited."

It was a precise tribute to England's foremost contemporary comic novelist. Here, far more than in England, Waugh has tended to be a special taste established in the first years of Depression and savored devotedly by a handful of people through ten years of proletarian novels, monsters of historical romance, and dubious charts for liberal futures. Uneasily reviewed in the line of duty, this author of two incomparable period pieces (*Decline and Fall, Vile Bodies*) has received no serious recognition. Woollcott called Waugh the nearest thing to a genius the English 30s had produced, and chose *A Handful of Dust* as the best English novel in 100 years. But Woollcott called so many thing so many things.

One of the problems has been what the *Retail Bookseller* blandly calls "the Waugh type of cleverness." The same descriptive terms have been used for Waugh by intellectuals who should know better. Waugh has been shrugged off on grounds that are his most serious claim to distinction. The nature of his best fiction; its fantastic gravity in the face of the ridiculous, its levity over accepted forms of seriousness, its high narrative flash-point accompanied by one sleight of hand after another—these admirable gifts of the satirical novelist have frightened even his admirers into the hole-and-corner approval that family men whisper behind their hands about prostitutes, but never admit to their wives. So rubbed away in Waugh's finished work are the pain and labor of the writing, that the artist is condemned as frivolous. He is frowned on for his dexterity when, five characters in each hand, he can develop, in smoothly interlocking conversations and exits and entries, the reader's understanding of his people, their immediate situations, and the theme of the novel. He is mistrusted because he can pull anything from performing seals and oranges to acute major materials out of an air of nonsense at a second's notice, fit them perfectly into narrative-place, and flick them out again with none of the second-rate writer's passion for clutching his material. Time and place are fixed with admirably brief descriptive passages, only to be ignored and ridiculed by characters whose hand-to-mouth thinking and behavior make a mockery of established form.

If Waugh's unique combination of daring, control, and side-glance

---

*"Evelyn Waugh: The Pillar of Anchorage House" first appeared in *Partisan Review*, vol. 10, 1943, no. 4. Reprinted here by permission of the journal and the author.

exercises has caused him to be classed merely with tightrope walkers, his subject matter, attitude, and choice of characters have been found equally damning. In a period that has rejoiced in solemnly attributing the most superficial accident to a basic historical condition, Waugh has preferred to indicate how a minor accident can render the important ridiculous. "[Basil] rejoiced, always, in the spectacle of women at a disadvantage: thus he would watch, in the asparagus season, a dribble of melted butter on a [beautiful] woman's chin. . . ." Where others have shown in a million ways the crushing effect of social forms on struggling individuals, Waugh, the lover of inanimate objects, has delighted in showing how valued material may be destroyed at a moment's whim by the wilful use of individual power. Candide is usually Waugh's central character—though his Candide may as easily be a house or a painting or a tradition as a man or a woman—and with the blandness of Goldsmith and the sophistication of Trollope he has liked to put rural innocence into the cruel hands of urban wise-guys, and to show, with sadistic pleasure, the helplessness of the intellectual confronted by the brute. Finally, in a period in which class tragedy superseded individual suffering, Waugh's sufferers and settings were stubbornly upper class. In the town it was Mayfair, in the country it was parkland; and the 'thirties were not a period which fostered aesthetic respect for both the young manhood of Studs Lonigan *and* the offspring of the landed gentry and new rich. The drip of butter on the face of beauty was inconspicuous against the monstrous social background.

But the ultimate fault was Waugh's. In the twelve years following his conversion to Catholicism, he produced a series of novels, short stories and travel books in which his satire and outrageous burlesque of English society changed, as Dunstan Thompson has pointed out, to kindly parody, of the kind *Punch* delights in. He showed clearly that his rebelliousness was to be that of the palace revolutionary—limited by England's palace walls. Father Rothschild S.J., the motor-cycling Jesuit who pulled strings of Cabinet policy with priestly dexterity, rode off on his machine in a cloud of pity for young aristocrats and never re-appeared. Never again did the Evangelist, Mrs. Ape, and her "angels" sing "There Ain't No Flies on The Lamb of God." Gone was the immortal Captain Grimes—believed by awed small boys to have lost in action a leg that had, in fact, been the victim of a drunken meeting with a Liverpool trolley car. Gone, too, were the ice-cold portraits of the easy, friendly society mother retiring to a hidden office to interview applicants for her secret houses of prostitution, and the extraordinary terror of the few terse lines in which a wellborn daughter, suddenly awaking to her fate, futilely begs her snobbish mother to help her escape from a socially desirable marriage to a man she despises. What Waugh wanted thereafter was to use the palace inmates as subjects for tragedy, not satire: but when he tried in *A Handful of Dust*, he failed because the field was too shallow. The nearest he came to success was in the short extract of an unpublished novel, which appeared in *Horizon* last year under the title "My Father's House." Here was a brilliant study of a Victorian painter watching his world crumbling about him: his huge canvases entitled "Agag Before Samuel" and "Feet of Clay" being pushed off the market by Gauguin's "disjointed negresses," his Victorian mansion becoming hemmed in by monster apartment houses panelled with green wood and infested with rats and prostitutes, his social status undermined when the politicians went into alliance "with the slaves." " 'We [the gentry] are extinct already, I am a Dodo,' he used to say . . . 'You, my poor son, are a petrified egg.' "

II

"My Father's House." It is the most meaningful of all Waugh's titles and, with its summons to lament the past, it could stand as an invisible title to everything Waugh has written. Houses, houses, houses—from the pages of *Decline and Fall, Vile Bodies, A Handful of Dust, Rossetti, Put Out More Flags.* Mostly they have been large country houses, often falling down or badly kept up. Sometimes they have been raped by vile bodies who have pulled them down and replaced them with modern horrors of chromium and colored slats. Sometimes they have been the individualistic creations of men like Rossetti and William Morris with massive, blackened furniture and immense appurtenances. Always the house has made the man; man has not existed apart from his roof any more than the rat has failed to swarm into the apartment house. And always the house has been a way of life for Waugh, desirable or detestable. He has dwelt on its driveways and park, the iron railings and stone walls that have stood between the house and the slaves; the carpets, busts and old priest-holes; the warm libraries where a dozing visitor is awoken by a padding maid with an afternoon tea in a silver pot surrounded by scones, relish, toast and cherry jam. For fifteen years Waugh has sung the house, and with it the precious furnishings he finds suited to it—the paintings that are not of disjointed negresses, the timbers that have been seasoned in estate barns, the owners who cherish it above themselves. And in this love of house, of continuous domicile and individual roof, Waugh appears for the defense in one of the most important struggles in English poetry and letters of the last 20 years. "My Father's House" (it would be "my Mother's" to many) is the starting point of England's recent literary past. It has shaped the intellectuals' outlook, their conduct, their England—indeed, the literary history of the 'thirties can be written with the house of childhood as its center.

The young men who have written English poetry for the last ten years have been mostly the men of Waugh's class, with gradations above and below. Their battle has been for self-emancipation; freedom, not from riches or love of grandeur but from the far more insidious influences of the houses of their birth and education. What appeared in their writings as a new faith in the proletariat and an enthusiasm for the urban under-privileged was, far more, an effort to purge the author's own personality of its upper-class preferences and trained acceptance of the old, rural order; to bring the lagging instincts into line with the advancing intellect. The bonds that held the heart in a setting of lawns, trees, cool drawing rooms and soft-spoken family friends were less evident but far more binding than the parallel ties of the public school. The intellectual pledged his new fidelity to the city, to the waste land that must [be] recreated; he entered the woods only by charabanc. In *New Signatures*, the poets' first public avowal of their determination to achieve self-conversion, one finds the whole intimate and painful struggle with past allegiances, phrased usually as an appeal to the non-fighters rather than a lyric expression of the writers' own dilemma. And the recurring center is "my father's house." In Spender it was a warning to young men that

> It is too late now to stay in those houses your
> fathers built. . . .
> It is too late to stay in great houses where
> the ghosts are prisoned
> — those ladies like flies perfect in amber

In Day Lewis it was the lament of a landed mother for her son:

> Warm in my walled garden the flower grew first.
> Transplanted it ran wild on the estate.
> Why should it ever need a new sun?
> (. . . One day) He crossed the frontier and I did not follow:
> Returning; spoke another language.

The strain is clear, too, in Auden's most famous sonnet:

> . . . Publish each healer that in city lives
> Or country houses at the end of drives;
> Harrow the house of the dead; look shining at
> New styles of architecture, a change of heart.

There was at issue a literal walking out from the paternal halls; Auden's "styles of architecture" were exactly that as well as symbols of the old and new in living. And in the new direction, there is clearly indicated the sharp line that had emerged to divide the intellectuals of the Left from such as Evelyn Waugh. Like these intellectuals Waugh saw the ghosts in the old houses, the flies lovely in amber; unlike them, he totally rejected the plea to "advance to rebuild." The ghosts must be materialized; or, if that were impossible, they must be preserved as the best available wraiths. In two brilliant satires (*Decline and Fall, Vile Bodies*) he had said what he thought of people who destroyed old houses; although his victims were of his own class, to say the least, he had pilloried them because they failed to see that their duty lay in preserving their country homes rather than in hell-raising in Mayfair. He had a clear idea of what England's house should look like, of the people that should live in it, of the art that should grace its walls. The people were to be the ones whom Lady Circumference of *Vile Bodies* found attending a reception at Anchorage House, one of the last of London's great town houses. They were not the bloated great, with their dubiously-acquired fortunes and reverberating soap-and-brewery titles. They were the relatively small fry:

> . . . a great concourse of pious and honorable people (many of whom made the Anchorage House reception the one outing of the year), their womenfolk well gowned in rich and durable stuffs, their menfolk ablaze with orders; people who had represented their country in foreign places and sent their sons to die for her in battle, people of decent and temperate life, uncultured, unaffected, unembarrassed, unassuming, unambitious people, of independent judgment and marked eccentricities, kind people who cared for animals and the deserving poor, brave and rather unreasonable people, that fine phalanx of the passing order, approaching, as one day at the Last Trump they hoped to meet their Maker, with decorous and frank cordiality to shake Lady Anchorage by the hand at the top of her staircase.

We know at once who these ideal souls are: they are the landed, and would-be-landed, gentry of England, the ones to whom "father" made his pledge of fidelity, though he professed to see them as dead as dodos, and their offspring as petrified eggs. They are that rigid backbone of England's rural constituencies — the conservative squirearchy (even when their houses are small) on whose paternalism the existence of millions of rural Englishmen depends.

What of the art that these squires should cherish? Waugh had chosen that in the first book he ever wrote: *Rossetti: His Life and Works.* His squire was to enliven his solidity with Pre-Raphaelite dreams of knighthood. The Pre-Raphaelite struggle against materialism — against the huge apartments "my father" hated, and industrialized living — Waugh made his own, ignoring Morris's socialism but accepting both the aesthetic and moral visions of the Pre-Raphaelite conception of medievalism, and relishing "the stimulus it gives to one's restiveness in an era of complete stultification." His world was not in negroid primitivism, but in such paintings as Rossetti's *Marriage of St. George*, and he quoted approvingly James Smetham's description of that odd hodge-podge of cluttered "medieval" objects: "One of the grandest things, like a golden, dim dream. Love 'credulous all gold,' gold armour, a sense of secret enclosure in 'palace chambers far apart'; but quaint chambers in quaint palaces, where angels creep in through sliding panel doors, and stand behind rows of flowers, drumming on golden bells, with wings crimson and green. . . ."

"English Gothic" Waugh called it and, in *A Handful of Dust*, he lamented its passing, exiling the Squire who tried to restore it to the jungles of Brazil — where he perished by the fiendish torture of reading aloud to a lonely maniac the novels of the industrialized Charles Dickens.

III

The friendly Alun Lewis, writing recently in the *New Statesman*, opposed himself to critics who considered Waugh a reactionary. "Romantic" he believed to be the proper description. But in the years before the war, Waugh's "romanticism" flowed smoothly into a contemporary mainstream of which so-called romanticism was no more than tributary. Visiting Ethiopia at the time of Mussolini's invasion, he wrote enthusiastically of the caliber of the invading armies, and condemned Englishmen who failed to see in this new colonial regime "inestimable gifts of fine workmanship and clear judgment" (*Waugh in Abyssinia*). A trip to Mexico shortly before the war led him to write *Robbery Under the Law* — more discreetly titled in good-neighborly America, *Mexico, An Object Lesson*. This violent diatribe of a converted Catholic was more than an indignant protest against the humbling of the Catholic church under the Cardenas government. It was also an intricate defense of unromantic General Franco. But perhaps most tragic to Waugh was the awful fate of Mexico's huge estates. "My father's house" had been virtually destroyed; the fate of the English manorial holdings was here in evidence on a huge scale. With bitter anger, Waugh demanded more "discipline" of the *peon* and inevitably saw Mexico's poverty as resulting from the country's lack of a landed gentry.

It was then that he published his unromantic Conservative Creed:

> I believe that man is, by nature, an exile. . . ; that his chances of happiness and virtue . . . generally speaking, are not much affected by the political and economic conditions in which he lives; . . . that the intellectual communists of today have personal, irrelevant grounds for their antagonism to society, which they are trying to exploit. I believe . . . that there is no form of government ordained from God as being better than any other; that the anarchic elements in society are so strong, that it is a wholetime task to keep the peace. I believe the inequalities of wealth and position are inevitable and that it is therefore meaningless to discuss the advantages of their elimination; that men naturally arrange themselves in a system of classes; that such a system is necessary for any form of co-operative work. . . . I do not think that British prosperity must necessarily be inimical to anyone else, but if, on occasions, it is, I want Britain to prosper and not her rivals. . . . I believe that Art is a natural function of man; it so happens that most of the greatest art has appeared under systems of tyranny, but I do not think it has a connection with any particular system, least of all with representative government, as nowadays in England, America and France it seems popular to believe; artists have always spent some of their spare time in flattering the governments under whom they live, so it is natural that, at the moment, English, American and French artists should be volubly democratic.

It must have seemed to him that the ceiling of the whole world was descending in blocks and splinters on the sagging roof of the paternal home. At least, on leaving Ethiopia, he had been able to view with pride the efforts of British gentlemen to live like squires in Kenya. But all Mexico could give him was the hardly surprising "trust" of members of the Catholic laity, some "good company in the Ritz bar," and "a bottle of magnificent claret in Mexico City." To return to an England on the verge of war under that epitome of unknightly rule, Neville Chamberlain, must have been the last straw. A world in which radicals were still vociferous, disjointed negresses still in vogue, playboys making their last bids, and the young squires held in their tents by industrialists in black coats — this was surely England's lowest decline from Waugh's high standard of glory.

When Tory salvation came in the form of the Churchill government, Waugh recognized it instantly. Returning from the Middle East he wrote *Put Out More Flags*. "A new spirit" was "abroad in the land," and in dedicating his work to the Prime Minister's son, Major Randolph Churchill M.P., of the 4th Hussars, Waugh apologized for the fact that he was not entirely contemporary in his approach. "These pages," he said, "may not be altogether acceptable to your ardent and sanguine nature. They deal, mostly, with a race of ghosts, the survivors of the world we both knew ten years ago . . . but where my imagination still fondly lingers. . . . These characters are no longer contemporary in sympathy; they were forgotten even before the war; but they lived on delightfully in holes and corners. . . . Here they are in that odd, dead period before the Churchillian renaissance."

Who are these neglected phantoms with a low standard of living, from whom Waugh dissociates himself with such tolerant superiority? Most of them appear from Waugh's own sleeve; they are his own literary creations invoked from the pages of his own novels. And, despite the nostalgic tone of Waugh's dedicatory words, we quickly find that these ghosts are highly contemporary; that while some are to be exorcised forever, others are to be re-embodied into active elements of the "Churchillian renaissance."

The old gentlemen are out. The doddering ghosts of aristocracy who spent their paternal vitality serving the tradesmen, pandering to the slaves, and betraying the younger squirearchy — they are through and will haunt no more. Not so the playboys. With Waugh's aid they do penance for their wasted ghosthood, conquer their dissipation and are entered, like gentlemanly *condottieri*, into the "new spirit" of the age. Readers of early Waugh may remember, for instance, Alastair Digby-Vaine-Trumpington. Alastair was distinctly a "vile body." But now, his wife Sonia tells us:

> . . . he was a much odder character than anyone knows. You remember that man who used to dress as an Arab and then went into the Air Force as a private because he thought the British government had let the Arabs down? . . . I believe Alastair felt like that. You see he'd never

done anything for the country. . . . I believe he thought that perhaps if he had done something perhaps there wouldn't have been any war. . . . He went into the ranks as a kind of penance.

As Alastair, saved from wraithhood by consorting with the lowest type of soldier, kneels in confession, he must note with some surprise that his literary creator has set on their knees beside him a row of reformed rakes. There is Sonia, bearing Alastair the child she could never conceive in her ghostly period. There is Peter Pastmaster, who mixed cocktails so expertly at the age of fourteen, and played "Pop Goes the Weasel" on the school organ. There is Angela Lyne, who took veronal under Chamberlain. There is even Angela's future husband, Basil Seal of *Black Mischief*, who carried self-interest to a sublime level of cruelty, and, before Chamberlain was ousted, conducted a virtually incestuous relationship with his sister while running a blackmail scheme based on the billeting of obnoxious slum children. The menfolk of this group of penitents are designed to join Waugh's own branch of the services, the Commandos—by Waugh's description a chummy sort of war club for reformed gentlemen. "Most of the war," explains Peter Pastmaster, "seems to consist of hanging out. Let's at least hang about with our own friends."

How well it has all worked out! These ghosts are ghosts no more; they have come through the hail of Spanish Loyalists, misguided intellectuals, decayed elder statesmen, enemies of the true faith, and are now ready to set a glowing seal on their creator's choice of life; to ride out of their English-Gothic castles—20th century Knight-Commandos going out to overthrow the ungentlemanly materialists of Nazidom.

Keeping their place till they return are the gentle Babbitts of the landed gentry. How near they came to ghosthood, those people of "decent and temperate life" we met ten years ago on the steps of Anchorage House! We saw them then in the London season; in *Put Out More Flags* they are back in their country homes, as though having caught the night train down. They are grooming "the splendid surface" of their lawns and devoutly working in the herbaceous borders; when "ice stood thick on the lily ponds . . . these good people fed the birds daily with crumbs from the dining-room table and saw to it that no old person in the village went short of coal."

The fate of permanent ghosthood is reserved for another group— England's younger intellectuals. These people have never before been mentioned in a Waugh novel; but they are Waugh's ghosts nonetheless, because the new signatures of most of them have stood on the wall to haunt him throughout his literary career. Now, the "Churchillian renaissance" has delivered them into his hands. The most opportunistic playboys—the men who drove the Gothic squire to his death in *A Handful of Dust*—may rise to the occasion in a time of crisis, but no radical is to be anything but a ghost beside the "new spirit." In prose that varies from childishness to a very high standard, Waugh throws his great capacity for savagery against the most thoughtful enemies of "my father's house." With Auden and Isherwood he plays with the happy cruelty of a slightly demented child, taunting them with Spain, reminding them in New York of their past devotion to contemporary happenings, recalling, for comparison, "Socrates marching to the sea with Xenophon . . . Horace singing the sweetness of dying for one's country." And to make sure the board is swept clean, Waugh rids England of the esthete, shown in the person of Ambrose Silk, one of Waugh's most able and cynical characterizations, combining low birth, Jewish blood, homosexuality and cowardice with decadent memories of Gertrude Stein, Cocteau and Diaghilev. Face to face with the aristocratic Commando, Basil Seal, Ambrose is utterly routed.

This is more than a parable of war. The conflict between the esthete and the man of action is Waugh's own conflict. For Ambrose, with his *Yellow Book* dreams, embodies so many of the anti-materialistic, esthetic elements that Waugh himself has advanced, and consequently there are moments in *Put Out More Flags* when Ambrose is more pitied than censured by his author. But the point is that estheticism is not in future to be sullied by such as Ambrose. In a typically Waugh scene we are shown Basil's mistress picking the monogram off the departed Ambrose's crepe-de-chine underwear, replacing it with a "B" for Basil.

IV

In *Horizon*, in a discussion of the sterility of "Puritan" poetry, Waugh presented his view of the proper function of the contemporary poet. "I think it is time," he said: "we made up our minds that poetry is one of the arts which has died in the last eighty years. . . . The men who write your 'poetry' seems [sic] to me to be trying to live on the prestige of a dead art. Shelley talked of poets as the legislators of the world, and they seem to have applied this to themselves without any justification at all. . . . Here we reach a deep cause of Puritanism — the poetic sense of responsibility. Let us tell the poets at once that no one need legislate who does not want to. . . . All we ask of the poets is to sing."

Horizon's editor rejects Waugh's charge that poetry is dead. But he tells us that "the sophisticated intellectual poetry of the 'twenties is exhausted," that poetry was "taken down a cul de sac to get away from the Georgians." The 'thirties gave it inadequate revival in "academic socialism." Now, "we are waiting for a new romanticism to bring it back to life." This will happen when "the tide of events sweeps round the lonely stumps on which our cormorants have been sitting and gives them a fishing ground." Meantime, editors must publish, among other things, "poems which reflect the lyrical influence of Lorca rather than the intellectual one of Auden, Eliot or Rilke." Only the "best work" of the best younger poets — Spender, Empson, Thomas, Barker, Rodgers, Vernon Watkins "must be encouraged."

These remarks, so valuable if they had been made in the '30's, are worrying at the present moment. Just what do they indicate? That the lyric poet, the domestic novelist and the literary essayist are to supersede writers whose only virtue is political propriety? Or, as seems more probable, that the editorial political narrowness of the '30's must give way to a new narrowness? In exchange for Puritanism are we to have, as Dali suggests, "an individualistic tradition . . . Catholic, aristocratic, and probably monarchic?"

The "Churchillian renaissance" is abroad in England. Behind its dashing skirts sit the pre-war industrialists, looking forward to the day when adventurous leadership will give place again to the 1922 Committee, and the demands of generals be as remote as reminiscent book reviews in the *Times Literary Supplement*. The call to poets to cease from legislating and to "sing," is invariably made loudest by men like Waugh, who cannot put pen to paper without legislating. And before we give Auden a military funeral and fire a volley into his grave, it will be well to look back at the lessons of the '30's and not throw the value out with the ignorance. The struggle to leave "my father's house" was no exercise in "academic socialism," however much it became inter-mixed with the sycophantic intolerance of fellow travellers. If, in the name of art and "singing," the intellectual is to sit passively waiting for the waters to bring him fish, the "romantic revival" is likely to be one-sided in the creels it fills. To fail to appreciate the Waughs of literature was a crime of the '30's; to accept their dicta as a way of life will be the crime of the '40's. In gloomier moments one pictures the abashed intellectuals returning like prodigals to the halls they abandoned, and singing as they polish their pedigrees. Gothic texts will line the walls where *New Signatures* once hung. To the cheers of his tenantry the reformed rake will return from the Commandos to take up his squireship of "English Gothic."

Never Apologize, Never Explain:
The Art of Evelyn Waugh   Edmund Wilson*

I did not read Evelyn Waugh at the time when he was first attracting attention. I never got started on him till a year ago, when I picked up a reprint of *Decline and Fall* and was so much exhilarated by it that I went on to *Vile Bodies*, and then read his four other novels in the order in which they were written. I may thus lay claim to a fresh impression of Evelyn Waugh's work — an impression, I believe, not much influenced by any

*Reprinted from Edmund Wilson, *Classics and Commercials* (New York: Farrar, Straus and Co., 1950), 140–46. Copyright 1950 by Edmund Wilson. Copyright renewed © 1977 by Elena Wilson. Reprinted by permission of Farrar, Straus & Giroux, Inc.

journalistic interest that work may have had, appearing at the end of the twenties, as a picture of the delirium of that period. Nothing can taste staler today than some of the stuff that seemed to mean something then, that gave us twinges of bitter romance and thrills of vertiginous drinking. But *The Great Gatsby* and *The Sun Also Rises* hold up; and my feeling is that these novels of Waugh's are the only things written in England that are comparable to Fitzgerald or Hemingway. They are not so poetic; they are perhaps less intense; they belong to a more classical tradition. But I think they they are likely to last and that Waugh, in fact, is likely to figure as the only first-rate comic genius that has appeared in English since Bernard Shaw.

The great thing about *Decline and Fall*, written when the author was twenty-five, was its breath-taking spontaneity. The latter part of the book leans a little too heavily on Voltaire's *Candide*, but the early part, that hair-raising harlequinade in a brazenly bad boys' school, has an audacity that is altogether Waugh's and that was to prove the great principle of his art. This audacity is personified here by an hilarious character called Grimes. Though a schoolmaster and a "public-school man," Grimes is frankly and even exultantly everything that is most contrary to the British code of good behavior: he is a bounder, a rotter, a scoundrel, but he never has a moment of compunction. He is supplemented by Philbrick, the butler, a graduate of the underworld, who likes to tell about revolting crimes. This audacity in Waugh's next book, *Vile Bodies*, is the property of the infantile young people who, at a time "in the near future, when existing social tendencies have become more marked," are shown drinking themselves into beggary, entangling themselves in absurd sexual relationships, and getting their heads cracked in motor accidents. The story has the same wild effect of reckless improvisation, which perfectly suits the spirit of the characters; but it is better sustained than *Decline and Fall*, and in one passage it sounds a motif which for the first time suggests a standard by which the behavior of these characters is judged: the picture of Anchorage House with its "grace and dignity and other-worldliness," and its memories of "people who had represented their country in foreign places and sent their sons to die for her in battle, people of decent and temperate life, uncultured, unaffected, unembarrassed, unassuming, unambitious people, of independent judgment and marked eccentricities."

In *Black Mischief* there is a more coherent story and a good deal of careful planning to bring off the surprises and shocks. There are descriptions of the imaginary black kingdom of Azania, which is the principal scene of the action, that are based on the author's own travels and would not be out of place in a straight novel. We note that with each successive book Evelyn Waugh is approaching closer to the conventions of ordinary fiction: with each one — and the process will continue — we are made to take the characters more seriously as recognizable human beings living in the world we know. Yet the author never reaches this norm: he keeps his grasp on the comic convention of which he is becoming a master — the convention which makes it possible for him to combine the outrageous with the plausible without offending our sense of truth. It is a triumph for him to carry from book to book the monsters of *Decline and Fall* and to make us continue to accept them as elements in later novels that touch us or stir us with values quite different from those of the earlier ones. There are two important points to be noted in connection with *Black Mischief*. The theme of the decline of society is here not presented merely in terms of night-club London: it is symbolized by the submergence of the white man in the black savagery he is trying to exploit. The theme of audacity is incarnated here, not in a Philbrick or a Grimes, but in a bad-egg aristocrat, who steals his mother's emeralds to run away from England, manipulates the politics of Azania by talking modern ideas to the native king and, forced at last to flee the jungle, eats his sweetheart unwares at a cannibal feast.

A *Handful of Dust*, which followed, is, it seems to me, the author's masterpiece. Here he has perfected his method to a point which must command the admiration of another writer even more perhaps than that of the ordinary non-literary reader — for the latter may be carried from scene to scene of the swift and smooth-running story without being aware of the skill with which the author creates by implication an atmosphere and a set of relations upon which almost any other novelist would spend pages of description and analysis. The title comes from T.S. Eliot's line, "I will show you fear in a handful of dust," but, except on the title page, the author nowhere mentions this fear. Yet he manages to convey from beginning to end, from the comfortable country house to the clearing in the Brazilian jungle, the impression of a terror, of a feeling that the bottom is just about to drop out of things, which is the whole motivation of the book but of which the characters are not shown to be conscious and upon which one cannot put one's finger in any specific passage. A charming woman of the aristocracy deserts a solid county husband and a high-spirited little boy to have a love affair with the underbred and uninterest-ing son of a lady interior decorator; the child is killed at a hunt; the husband runs away to Brazil and ends as the captive of an illiterate halfbreed, who keeps him for years in the jungle reading the novels of Dickens aloud. The audacity here is the wife's: her behavior has no justification from any accepted point of view, whether conventional or romantic. Nor does the author help out with a word of explicit illumina-tion. He has himself made of audacity a literary technique. He exempli-fies, like so many of his characters, the great precept of Benjamin Jowett to young Englishmen just starting their careers: "Never apologize, never explain."

The next novel, *Scoop*, is not quite so good as the ones just before and just after it, but it has in it some wonderful things. A quiet country gentleman, who writes nature notes for a big London paper called the

Daily Beast, gets railroaded, through a confusion of identities, to another of Waugh's Negro countries, where he is supposed to act as war correspondent. The story is simpler than usual, and it brings very clearly to light a lineup of opposing forces which has always lurked in Evelyn Waugh's fiction and which is now even beginning to give it a certain melodramatic force. He has come to see English life as a conflict between, on the one hand, the qualities of the English upper classes, whether arrogant, bold and outrageous or stubborn, unassuming and eccentric, and, on the other, the qualities of the climbers, the careerists and the commercial millionaires who dominate contemporary society. The story of William Boot comes to its climax when the grown-up public-school boy faces down the Communist boss of Ishmaelia, who is trying to get him off the scene while a revolution takes place: " 'Look here, Dr. Benito,' said William. 'You're being a bore. I'm not going.' " And the book has a more cheerful moral than any of its predecessors: William succeeds in holding his own against the barbarisms both of Africa and of London, and in the end he returns to the country, where they cannot get him again and where he continues to write his notes about the habits of the local fauna—though "outside the owls hunted maternal rodents and their furry broods." If this book is less exciting than the others, it is perhaps because the theme of audacity appears mainly in connection with the *Daily Beast*, with which the author cannot feel any sympathy.

Waugh's most recent novel, *Put Out More Flags*, written during and about the war, has an even more positive moral. Basil Seal, the aristocratic scoundrel who has already figured in *Black Mischief*, exploits the war to his own advantage by informing against his friends and shaking down his sister's county neighbors with threats of making them take in objectionable refugees, but finally he enlists in the Commandos, who give him for the first time a legitimate field for the exercise of his resourcefulness and nerve. Evelyn Waugh's other wellborn wastrels are already in the "corps d' élite," somewhat sobered after years of "having fun." "There's a new spirit abroad. I see it on every side," says stupid old Sir Joseph Mainwaring. "And, poor booby," says the author, "he was bang right." We see now that not only has the spirit of audacity migrated from the lower to the upper classes, but that the whole local emphasis has shifted. The hero of *Decline and Fall* was a poor student reading for the church, whose career at Oxford was wrecked by the brutality of a party of aristocratic drunks: "A shriller note could now be heard rising from Sir Alastair's rooms; any who have heard that sound will shrink at the recollection of it; it is the sound of the English county families baying for broken glass." And at the end he is addressed as follows by another and more considerate young nobleman: "You know, Paul, I think it was a mistake you ever got mixed up with us, don't you? We're different somehow. Don't quite know how. Don't think that's rude, do you, Paul?" But it is now this young man, Percy [sic] Pastmaster, and Sir Alastair Digby-Vaine-Trumpington and the English county families generally who are the heroes of *Put Out More Flags*. Evelyn Waugh has completely come over to them, and the curious thing is that his snobbery carries us with it. In writing about Harold Nicolson, I remarked on his fatal inability to escape from the psychology of the governing class, which was imposed on him by birth and office. The case of Waugh is the opposite of this: he has evidently approached this class, like his first hero, from somewhere outside, and he has had to invent it for himself. The result is that everything is created in his work, nothing is taken for granted. The art of this last novel is marvellous. See the episode in which Basil Seal blackmails the young married woman: the attractiveness of the girl, which is to prompt him to try a conquest, and her softness, which will permit his success (Evelyn Waugh is perhaps the only male writer of his generation in England who is able to make his women attractive), are sketched in with a few physical details and a few brief passages of dialogue that produce an impression as clear and fresh as an eighteenth-century painting.

Evelyn Waugh is today a declared Tory and a Roman Catholic convert; he believes in the permanence of the social classes and, presumably, in the permanence of evil. It has been pointed out by Mr. Nigel Dennis in an article in the *Partisan Review* that this would make him rather a dubious guide for England after the war. But, after all, he does not set up as a guide; and his opinions do not damage his fiction. About this fiction there is nothing schematic and nothing doctrinaire; and, though the characters are often stock types—the silly ass, the vulgar parvenu, the old clubman, etc.—everything in it has grown out of experience and everything has emotional value. *Put Out More Flags* leaves you glowing over the products of public schools and country houses as examples of the English character; but it is not a piece of propaganda; it is the satisfying expression of an artist, whose personal pattern of feeling no formula will ever fit, whether political, social or moral. For the savagery he is afraid of is somehow the same thing as the audacity that so delights him.

For Article on E. Waugh   George Orwell*

The advantages of not being part of the movement, irrespective of whether the movement is in the right direction or not.

But disadvantage in holding false (indefensible) opinions.

The movement (Auden etc.).

*Reprinted from "Extracts from a Manuscript Note-book" in *The Collected Essays, Journalism and Letters of George Orwell*, vol. 4, © 1968 by Sonia Brownell Orwell. Reprinted by permission of Harcourt Brace Jovanovich, Inc.

W's driving forces. Snobbery. Catholicism.

Note even the early books not anti-religious or demonstrably anti-moral. But note the persistent snobbishness, rising in the social scale but always centring / round the idea of continuity / aristocracy / a country house. Note that everyone is snobbish, but that Waugh's loyalty is to a form of society no longer viable, of which he must be aware.

Untenable opinions *cf* Poe.

Catholicism. Note that a Catholic writer does not have to be Conservative in a political sense. Differentiate G. Greene. Advantage to a novelist of being a Catholic—theme of collision between two kinds of good.

Analyse *Brideshead Revisited.* (Note faults due to being written in first person.) Studiously detached attitude. Not puritanical. Priests not superhuman. Real theme—Sebastian's drunkenness, & family's unwillingness to cure this at the expense of committing a sin. Note that this is a real departure from the humanist attitude, with which no compromise possible.

But. Last scene, where the unconscious man makes the sign of the Cross. Note that after all the veneer is bound to crack sooner or later. One cannot really be Catholic & grown-up.

Conclude. Waugh is abt as good a novelist as one can be (i.e. as novelists go today) while holding untenable opinions.

The Pieties of Evelyn Waugh

Donat O'Donnell [Conor Cruise O'Brien]*

Mr. Evelyn Waugh's seventh and most ambitious novel, *Brideshead Revisited*, was fortunate in earning the approval both of the reading public and of the theologians. In England, *The Tablet* saw in it "a great apologetic work in the larger and more humane sense," and in the United States, where it quickly sold over half a million copies, the critics of the leading Catholic journals concurred in this judgment. One, however, Father H.C. Gardiner in *America*, complained with justice that all the non-Catholic reviewers—including those who made it a Book of the Month Club selection—had missed the religious point of the book. It seems probable, therefore, that most of Mr. Waugh's readers, in America at any rate, did not know that they were reading a great apologetic work, and that, if they paid any attention to the Catholicism of *Brideshead Revisited* at all, they valued it as part of the general baronial decorations around a tale of love and high life.

*Reprinted from Donat O'Donnell [Conor Cruise O'Brien], *Maria Cross: Imaginative Patterns in a Group of Modern Catholic Writers* (New York: Oxford University Press, 1952), pp. 119–34, by permission of the author.

In this, of course, they were wrong, but their mistake was not entirely due to "secularist" stupidity and indifference. *Brideshead Revisited* is, in its author's words, "an attempt to trace the divine purpose in a pagan world"; men and women try to escape from the love of God, to find human happiness, but God destroys their human hopes and brings them back with "a twitch upon the thread." This is the central theme, austere and theological, but obscured (for those whose approach to religion is different from Mr. Waugh's) by bulky memorials of devotion to other gods. These alien pieties, some of them hardly compatible with strict Catholicism, were perhaps for Mr. Waugh the forerunners of a more articulated faith — as, in *Brideshead Revisited*, Sebastian Flyte's affection for a teddy-bear was the forerunner of a vocation. They appear in varying degrees and shapes in all his work and mingle with Catholicism in a highly personal system of belief and devotion, well worth analysis.

The main emotional constituent of Mr. Waugh's religion — using the term in a wide sense — is a deep English romanticism. His earliest work, *Rossetti*, betrayed a pre-Raphaelite affinity; and his first "serious" novel, *A Handful of Dust*, deals with the injury inflicted by modern flippancy and shallowness on a romantic mind. The hero, Tony Last, lives in a great ramshackle country house of nineteenth-century Gothic which he dearly loves, and which his wife's friends sneer at; his wife betrays him, and when he realizes the extent of her treachery, his disillusionment shows us in a blinding flash his imaginative world: "A whole Gothic world had come to grief . . . there was now no armour glittering through the forest glades, no embroidered feet on the green sward; the cream and dappled unicorns had fled. . . ."

We should, of course, be wary of too easily attributing similar fantasies to the author — although he takes his hero's side so bitterly as to mar what is in many ways his best novel — but it is significant that Captain Ryder, the hero of *Brideshead Revisited*, lives in the same sort of climate. "Hooper," he says, referring to a member of the lower classes, "was no romantic. He had not as a child ridden with Rupert's horse or sat among the camp-fires at Xanthus. . . . Hooper had wept often, but never for Henry's speech on St. Crispin's day, nor for the epitaph at Thermopylae. The history they taught him had had few battles in it. . . ." And Captain Ryder hoped to find "that low door in the wall . . . which opened on an enclosed and enchanted garden, which was somewhere, not overlooked by any window, in the heart of that grey city." This persistence and intensity of youthful romanticism are remarkable; so also is the fierce conviction that the romantic dream is directly menaced by some element in modernity. Tony Last's Gothic forest is withered by the cynicism of smart and up-to-date people in London; Captain Ryder's enchanted garden is crushed by the mechanized Hooper.

Closely allied with this romanticism is a nostalgia for a period of early youth. Tony Last is an adult, but his bedroom "formed a gallery

representative of every phase of his adolescence—the framed picture of a
dreadnought (a coloured supplement from *Chums*), all guns spouting
flame and smoke; a photographic group of his private school; a cabinet
called 'the Museum' filled with the fruits of a dozen desultory hobbies."
The only card game he can play is "animal snap," a bout of which is made
to occupy him during an evening of agony and suspense. Captain Ryder,
during part of his undergraduate life with the beautiful and charming
Sebastian Flyte, felt that he was "given a brief spell of what I had never
known, a happy childhood, and though its toys were silk shirts and
liqueurs and cigars, and its naughtiness high in the catalogue of grave sins,
there was something of nursery freshness about us that fell little short of
the joy of innocence." And amid all this he is conscious of "homesickness
for nursery morality." Sebastian himself is described as being "in love with
his own childhood." He carries with him everywhere a teddy-bear called
Aloysius, which he occasionally threatens to spank. Mr. Waugh's preoccupation with youth even permeates his more or less cynical comic novels
(*Decline and Fall, Vile Bodies*, et cetera). There is no display of emotion in
these, nor much analysis of states of mind, but sophisticated young people
play "Happy Families" (*Black Mischief*) and a Communist journalist
concentrates on working a toy train (*Scoop*). More important is the
schoolboy delight in cruelty which marks the earlier books especially, and
gives an almost hysterical tempo to their farce. One of the funniest scenes
in *Decline and Fall* deals with the brutal murder of an inoffensive old
prison chaplain. The convicts, in chapel, take advantage of the hymn-
singing to pass on the news:

> Old Prendy went to see a chap
> What said he'd seen a ghost
> Well he was dippy and he'd got
> A mallet and a saw.

> Who let the madman have the things?
> The Governor: who d'you think?
> He asked to be a carpenter,
> He sawed off Prendy's head.

> .   .   .   .

> Time like an ever-rolling stream
> Bears all its sons away
> Poor Prendy 'ollered fit to kill
> For nearly 'alf an hour.

Vile Bodies is rich in unregarded death: a drunken young woman kills
herself by swinging out of a chandelier; a titled gossip writer puts his head
in the gas oven; a Bright Young Thing expires after a lively party in the
room in the nursing home where she is recovering after a car accident. The

comedy of *Black Mischief* is ingeniously designed to lead up to a gruesome piece of cannibalism ("You're a grand girl, Prudence, and I'd like to eat you." "So you shall, my sweet, anything you want." And, as a result of later accidents, he does).

"In laughter," according to Bergson, "we always find an unavowed intention to humiliate and consequently to correct, our neighbour." One of the secrets of Mr. Waugh's comic genius is his keen interest in humiliation. Basil Seal, the adventurer-hero ("insolent, sulky, and curiously childish") of *Black Mischief* and *Put Out More Flags*, "rejoiced always," we are told, "in the spectacle of women at a disadvantage." Mr. Waugh is a great exploiter of human disadvantages, and his unscrupulous adolescent cruelty in this is the common quality of his two most obvious characteristics: his humor and his snobbery. Two of his comic novels, *Black Mischief* and *Scoop*, are based largely on a sly appeal to the white man's sense of racial superiority; much of the best fun in *Decline and Fall* comes from the exploitation of the manners of Captain Grimes, who, although he claimed to be a public-school man, was not really a gentleman and did not often have a bath; in *Put Out More Flags* the purest comedy lies in lurid descriptions of the appearance and behavior of three proletarian evacuee children. Examples of his deft use of the snob-joke could be multiplied almost indefinitely. It can be said indeed that if he were not a snob, if he were not the type of man who refers frequently to "the lower orders" (as he does in *Labels*) and objects to the presence of natives in first-class railway carriages (as he does in *Waugh in Abyssina*), he could not have written such funny books. This is an unpleasant fact; it means that the countless liberal, progressive people who have laughed over these books unconsciously share these prejudices. Mr. Edmund Wilson, in *The New Yorker*, condemned the snobbery of *Brideshead Revisited*, but he had swallowed with delight the snobbery implicit in the earlier novels, from *Decline and Fall* to *Scoop*. Snobbery was quite acceptable as an attitude: the critic objected only when it was formulated as a doctrine.

It is true that in his later books Mr. Waugh's snobbery has taken on a different emphasis. As he becomes more serious, his veneration for the upper classes becomes more marked than his contempt for his social inferiors. This almost mystical veneration, entirely free from any taint of morality, may be discerned in a slightly burlesque form in his early books. Paul Pennyfeather, the drab hero of *Decline and Fall*, was cast into prison through the fault of the woman he loved, Mrs. Beste-Chetwynde, the rich, beautiful, and aristocratic white-slave trader. He forgave her, however, because he believed "that there was in fact, and should be, one law for her and another for himself, and that the naive little exertions of nineteenth-century Radicals were essentially base and trivial and misdirected." *Decline and Fall* was, of course, published before Mr. Waugh's conversion to Catholicism, which took place in 1930; no doubt he would not now express his thought in the same way. But his almost idolatrous reverence for birth and wealth has not been destroyed by the Catholic faith; on the contrary *Brideshead Revisited* breathes from beginning to end a loving patience with mortal sin among the aristocracy and an un-Christian petulance towards the minor foibles of the middle class.

As might be expected, Mr. Waugh's political outlook is the expression of his social prejudices. In the introduction to his book on Mexico, *Robbery under Law*, he has set out his political creed in general terms: "I believe that man is by nature an exile and will never be self-sufficient or complete upon this earth . . . men naturally arrange themselves into a system of classes . . . war and conquest are inevitable." From these pessimistic premises he has drawn important practical conclusions: the propriety of strikebreaking, the justice of Mussolini's conquest of Abyssinia. As the title of his Mexican work indicates, his quarrel with the Mexican government concerned not so much their acquiescence in the persecution of the Church, as their encroachment on British oil interests. Taking Abyssinia from its Emperor is "inevitable" but taking Mexican oil from British investors is plain robbery. So phrased, the argument appears dishonest, but Mr. Waugh's sincerity is beyond all doubt. Indeed his conservatism is so intensely emotional that he is a sort of Jacobite by anticipation. In his imagination the class he loves is already oppressed; the King has taken to the hills. Already in *Decline and Fall* Lady Circumference and her friends were "feeling the wind a bit"; in *Vile Bodies*, the Bright Young People gad around gallantly, touched by the fever of impending doom, to be blasted in the final prophetic chapter by war and inflation. In *Black Mischief*, Basil's friends are impoverished by the Depression and in the later works the shadow deepens (brightened by the brief rally of the "Churchillian renaissance," 1940–41[1]) into the midnight of *Brideshead Revisited*. "These men," reflects Captain Ryder, contemplating the fate of some relatives of Lady Marchmain's, "must die to make a world for Hooper; they were the aborigines, vermin by right of law, to be shot off at leisure so that things might be safe for the travelling salesman with his polygonal pince-nez, his fat wet handshake, his grinning dentures." The Prison Governor in *Decline and Fall*, whose ideas on occupational therapy had such unfortunate consequences for the Chaplain, is, in Mr. Waugh's eyes, the typical reformer. He turns the full battery of his satirical power against "progressive" thinkers and workers, for he sees them as working to hand over power to a slavering mob of criminals, communists, and commercial travelers.

An interesting sidelight on all this is shed by the autobiography of his father, Arthur Waugh (*One Man's Road*, 1931). Mr. Waugh senior, a well-to-do publisher, recounts that Evelyn, as a little boy, "arranged theatricals in the nursery" and "marshalled a 'pistol troop' for the defence of England against Germans and Jews."[2] He edited a magazine about this troop, and his fond father was able to have it bound for him "in full morocco." *One Man's Road* also contains a photograph of the house in Hampstead in which Evelyn was reared, with the legend printed beneath: "No doubt it was never anything more than an ordinary suburban villa. But it was a great deal more to me."

The Gothic dream, nostalgia for childhood, snobbery, neo-Jacobitism — this whole complex of longings, fears, and prejudices, "wistful, half-romantic, half-aesthetic," to use a phrase of Mr. Waugh's — must be taken into account in approaching the question of Mr. Waugh's Catholicism. In Catholic countries Catholicism is not invariably associated with big houses, or the fate of an aristocracy. The Bordeaux of M. Mauriac and the Cork of Mr. Frank O'Connor are not Gothic cities or objects of wistfulness. But the Catholicism of Mr. Waugh, and of certain other writers, is hardly separable from a personal romanticism and a class loyalty. Is Lord Marchmain's soul more valuable than Hooper's? To say in so many words that it was would be heresy, but *Brideshead Revisited* almost seems to imply that the wretched Hooper had no soul at all, certainly nothing to compare with the genuine old landed article. And *Brideshead Revisited* is the most Catholic of Mr. Waugh's novels. His religion, even before his conversion, abounded in consolation for the rich. That obliging and ubiquitous priest, Father Rothschild, S.J. (of *Vile Bodies*), refuses to censure the goings on of the Bright Young People: ". . . it seems to me that they are all possessed with an almost fatal hunger for permanence. I think all these divorces show that. People aren't content just to muddle along nowadays. . . . And this word 'bogus' they all use. . . ." The paradoxes of the wealthy Jesuit are not perhaps intended to be taken seriously, but the same sort of spiritual consolation, this time with no perceptible trace of irony, may be derived from *Brideshead Revisited*. Lady Marchmain confesses that once she thought it wrong "to have so many beautiful things when others had nothing," but she overcame these scruples, saying: "The poor have always been the favourites of God and his saints, but I believe that it is one of the special achievements of Grace to sanctify the whole of life, riches included." In Mr. Waugh's theology, the love of money is not only not the root of all evil, it is a preliminary form of the love of God.

After the publication of *Brideshead Revisited* in America, a certain Mr. McClose, of Alexandria (Va.), wrote a postcard to Mr. Waugh, saying: "Your *Brideshead Revisited* is a strange way to show that Catholicism is an answer to anything. Seems more like the kiss of Death to me." Mr. Waugh in an article in *Life* (8 April 1946) dismissed this criticism with a sneer about halitosis. And yet it is much more to the point than are *The Tablet*'s eulogies. The deathbed conversion of Lord Marchmain is the decisive crisis of the book; the death of an upper class and the death of all earthly hope are two of its principal themes. The lovers are forced apart by a sense of sin; the house is deserted; the family scattered; the only child that is born is dead. Mr. Waugh's political forebodings and the form of his private myths (of which a sense of exile is the main constituent) make his Catholicism something that is, in earthly affairs, dark and defeatist, alien to the bright aggressive Catholicism of the New World, as well as to the workaday faith of the old Catholic countries. Out of all the tragedy, and justifying it, one good is seen emerging—the conversion of the narrator. In Brideshead chapel he has seen "a beaten copper lamp of deplorable design relit before the beaten doors of a tabernacle," and he rejoices; but when he leaves the chapel, he leaves it empty of worshippers.

This rearguard Catholicism is not indeed "an answer to anything," nor is it intended to be, any more than Tony Last's Gothic city or Proust's rediscovered time is an answer to anything. The funeral is strictly private, and salvation also. There was once an Irish priest who refused to pray for the conversion of England, and Mr. Waugh, I fear, might refuse to pray for the conversion of Hooper.

And just as snobbery and adolescent cruelty gave edge and tension to his early work, so now the intense romantic and exclusive piety of his maturer years gives him strength and eloquence. The clear focusing of remembered detail, the loving reconstructions of youth, and the great extension of metaphor in *Brideshead Revisited* all recall Proust more than any living writer, and the texture of Mr. Waugh's writing is both finer and stronger than is usual in Proust.[3] Mr. Waugh has evidently read some Proust—indeed in *A Handful of Dust* he twice pays him the tribute of misquotation—and there are passages in *Brideshead Revisited*, notably the opening of Book Two, that seem to paraphrase parts of *Remembrance of Things Past*. "My theme is memory," says Mr. Waugh, "that winged host that soared about me one grey morning of war-time. These memories which are my life—for we possess nothing certainly except the past—were always with me. Like the pigeons of St. Mark's, they were everywhere, under my feet singly, in pairs." He continues in this strain for much longer than I can quote, and we recall Proust, whose theme was the same, whose metaphors equally exuberant, and who developed his theme from a recollection of feelings, under his feet, two uneven paving-stones in the baptistry of St. Mark's.

The resemblance is neither accidental nor merely superficial and it has nothing to do with plagiarism. The outward lives of the two men are very different—one can hardly imagine Proust in the Commandos—but their mental worlds are, up to a point, surprisingly similar. Proust was tenacious of childhood, with a feverishly romantic mind capable of turning a common seaside town into an enchanted city. This romantic sensitivity to names, and perhaps also his social position (he belonged, like Mr. Waugh, to the upper middle class), led him to a veneration for the aristocracy. For him the name of the Duchess of Guermantes could evoke the Patriarchs and Judges on the windows of the cathedral of Laon, as well as the ancient forest in which Childebert went hunting, and it was in pursuit of these things that he entered the salons of the Faubourg St. Germain. There he acquired a sense of social distinction as marked as Mr. Waugh's, and much more delicate. So far the resemblance is striking, but there it ends. Proust never raised a political or religious superstructure on these foundations. Once he remembers wondering, in a fashionable restaurant, "whether the glass aquarium would always continue to protect the banquet of the marvellous beasts," but he does not make an issue out of it. He shows Parisian society decaying and breaking up under the pressure of the war, but he writes as a spectator, even as a connoisseur, not as a partisan. More than this, his mind is able at last to disentangle the Duchess of Guermantes from Childebert's forest, and to regard fashionable snobberies as not different in kind from disputes on precedence among greengrocers' wives. Mr. Waugh has not yet taken this decisive step. And Proust's religious experience, if we may call it so, is confined to the discrepancies of mortal life in time. He never took Mr. Waugh's decisive step, from romanticism to the acceptance of dogma.

The difference between the two men may in part be explained by their historical setting. Proust lived and wrote at a time when the upper classes were menaced, but not severely damaged. They had suffered an infusion from the classes below, but their money was still safe enough. It was easy for Proust—especially as his health was bad—to feel that "society" would last his time. As he had no children and did not believe in immorality, he did not have to worry about what happened after that. He could therefore cultivate an easy and speculative detachment. In our time, however, the upper classes, even in England, are not merely menaced; they have been gravely damaged. They feel not merely frustrated or irritated but actually oppressed by the high level of modern taxation and they see their equals leveled all over Europe. Proustian detachment and sense of nuance tend to perish in this atmosphere, and the wistful romantic easily develops, as Mr. Waugh has done, into an embattled Jacobite.

It would, however, be a simplification to insist too much on the direct influence of economic history. Even if the two men had been born contemporaries, their evolution would have differed widely because of the great difference in the manners of their education. The efforts of Proust's parents to "harden" him were neither consistent nor successful, and no one else seems to have made the attempt at all. This easy upbringing did not produce an ideal citizen or soldier, but it did ensure a continuity of emotional life, with, in this case, a certain lucidity and calm. The young Waugh, on the contrary, was subjected to the discipline of an English public school, and a religious one at that. Captain Ryder speaks sadly of "the hard bachelordom of English adolescence, the premature dignity and authority of the school system." Mr. Waugh endured these things and emerged an English gentleman, with slight symptoms of hysteria. Cream and dappled unicorns clearly have no place at a public school, and an inner life that includes such creatures will feel itself menaced. If it does not die, it will take on a new intensity, becoming a fixed intolerant mythology. Such is Mr. Waugh's private religion, on which he has superimposed Catholicism, much as newly converted pagans are said to superimpose a Christian nomenclature on their ancient cults of trees and thunder.

The hero of *Scott-King's Modern Europe*, the first of the satires which Mr. Waugh has published since *Brideshead Revisited*, "found a peculiar relish in contemplating the victories of barbarism," and so, undoubtedly, does his creator. Both *Scott-King* and its successor, *The Loved One*, contemplate not without relish, aspects of victorious barbarism, the first in Europe, the second in America. The relish in both cases is satirical: the bitter delight of the aristocrat who finds the rabble living down to his worst expectations.

The European satire is much the less successful of the two. It is set in a *lieu vague*, Neutralia, which might be Spain without the clergy or Yugoslavia without the Communist party. The idea behind this is presumably that of the uniformity of modern totalitarianism, the two-aspects-of-the-same-bestial-visage theory of Miss Odette Keun. Unfortunately the visages of Communism and Francoism, bestial though they be, are quite separate and sharply distinct, so that a satire assuming the identity of the two degenerates easily into querulous confusion. The troubles of Scott-King, a middle-aged classics teacher who accepts an invitation to take part in cultural celebrations in Neutralia, are as many as those of Candide but neither so terrible nor treated so lightly. He becomes involved in the insolence and delays of air travel; the grandeurs and miseries of totalitarian entertainment; obstruction by a Second Secretary at the British Embassy who wears pencils in his breastpocket and behaves like "a clerk in the food-office"; finally the black underground, and return via illegal immigrant ship. After undergoing these scourges of modernity he goes back to teach the classics, refusing to take up any more practical subject, on the ground that "it would be very wicked indeed to do anything to fit a boy for the modern world." This tale has its amusing moments, but it fails; indignation is diffused over miscellaneous objects, some of them more worthy of the attention of the club bore than of the satirist; the style itself, still touched by the elegiac afflatus of *Brideshead*, is blown about at times between the pompous and the mock-heroic: "To even the Comic Muse, the gadabout, the adventurous one of those heavenly sisters, to whom so little that is human comes amiss, who can mix in almost any company and find a welcome at almost every door—even to her there are forbidden places."

The Loved One, which immediately followed *Scott-King*, throws such prudery to the winds and invades forbidden places—the mortuary and the cemetery—in a spirit of atrocious levity. This time the satire is precisely aimed—through the great burial place of Southern California, Forest Lawn Memorial Park—at the materialist civilization of America. When he visited Hollywood, Mr. Waugh was powerfully impressed by Forest Lawn. In what is possibly the only article ever to have appeared both in *Life* and in *The Tablet*, he gave a factual account of that incredible necropolis, with its zones, (Slumberland, Inspiration, Hope, Babyland), its concealed radios giving out popular songs, its mausoleum, columbarium, and non-sectarian churches, and its slumber-rooms, decorated in satin, where the newly dead, in new suits and with elaborately painted faces, await burial. He showed, with quotations and illustrations, how Forest Lawn substitutes for the old morbid conceptions of death its own sunny eschatology which guarantees eternal bliss for all clients (Negroes and Chinese excluded) and inspires 300 smiling acres studded with curvilinear statuary. Not content, however, with mere description, he set himself to capture "the Spirit of Forest Lawn" — a deity often invoked by the proprietors of the cemetery — in a short novel entirely devoted to funereal affairs. Dennis Barlow, the hero of *The Loved One*, is an unsuccessful young film writer who gets a job in a pets' cemetery, "The Happier Hunting Ground," and falls in love with a mortuary cosmetician, Aimée Thanatogenos, who works in "Whispering Glades" (Forest Lawn). In his wooing of Aimée, Dennis becomes the rival of the senior mortician of Whispering Glades, a Mr. Joyboy. This gentleman, who regards the profession of embalming as a high and solemn vocation, conducts his courtship in terms of his work. His is the science of adjusting the expression of corpses, with the aid of little pieces of cardboard and according to such categories as "serene and philosophical," "radiant childhood," "judicial and determined," and, as a lover, he turns his skill to good account on the dead that go to the cosmetic room: "Of recent weeks the expressions that greeted Aimée from the trolley had waxed from serenity to jubilation. Other girls had to work on faces that were stern or resigned or plumb vacant; there was always a nice bright smile for Aimée."

Love among the slabs and kidney bowls moves its predestined course to a grotesque catastrophe. Aimée, torn by the contradictions of the mortician's code, kills herself and her body is disposed of, to avoid scandal, in the incinerator at the pets' cemetery. Dennis makes an entry in the register of that institution so that, in accordance with a custom whereby the owners of deceased pets are annually consoled, "tomorrow and on every anniversary as long as The Happier Hunting Ground existed a postcard would go to Mr. Joyboy: '*Your little Aimée is wagging her tail in heaven to-night, thinking of you.*' "

And Dennis leaves sunny California to return to his "ancient and comfortless shore."

In its calculated outrageousness *The Loved One* is one of the most effective stories Mr. Waugh has ever written. Sober and economical in language, neat and coherent in structure, it makes every blow tell, both on the reader's nerves and on the civilization it condemns. A lesser artist might have found Forest Lawn pathetic, worthy of no more than a passing and fastidious remark — such as Mr. Aldous Huxley's refined treatment of it in *After Many a Summer*. Mr. Waugh is neither compassionate nor refined. The central jest of *The Loved One* is cruel, the story itself is cruel and abounds in cruel embellishments, variations, and subordinate episodes, from the scene near the beginning dealing with the humiliation, suicide, and embalming of an elderly film writer to the final humiliation, suicide, and incineration of the hero's fiancée. Beneath the unemotional language and casual timing which give the twist of wit to these horrible events, there is a perceptible undercurrent of sheer delight. It is this delight — Mr. Waugh himself speaks of "over-excitement with the scene" — that makes the pages of *The Loved One*, in contrast with *Scott-King*, so electrically alive.

Delight in what? There is no simple answer to this. It is partly the professional satisfaction of the satirist in range of a colossal target, partly a reactionary rejoicing in the imbecilities of modernity. At a rather deeper level it is that delight in cruelty for its own sake which has always been a mark of Mr. Waugh's best work; the incineration of Aimée Thanatogenos is a brutal variant on the scene in *Black Mischief* where Basil Seal eats his fiancée. More important than these sources of excitement, though mingling with them, is a complex feeling that might crudely be described as a natural affinity with lunatics. The hero falls in love with Aimée because of the "rich glint of lunacy" in her eyes. He almost falls in love with Forest Lawn for the same reasons: "Whispering Glades held him in thrall. . . . In a zone of insecurity in the mind where none but the artist dare trespass, the tribes were mustering. Dennis the frontiersman could read the signs."

The tribes . . . the frontier. . . . We are brought back to the picture of that interior nostalgic castle holding out against the barbarians. These sharp divisions and dramatic pictures belong to a youthful imagination which Mr. Waugh has jealously and vividly retained, and which is the true key to his work. Inwardly the sensitive adolescent with his Gothic dream, to be guarded from his brutal companions; outwardly the rowdy schoolboy, organizer of cruel pranks, picturesque adventurer. The first of these personalities is dominant in *A Handful of Dust* and *Brideshead Revisited*; it inspires also, less happily, *Helena*, a shapeless and sentimental piece of historical fiction about the piety of a British lady in the age of Constantine, epoch of the conversion of the upper class. The second, the personality of Basil Seal, rules over all the earlier novels and now reappears in *The Loved One*. In so grotesque a setting and in the safety of satire, the great Catholic writer, who also happens to be a beleaguered Jacobite, can let his natural irresponsibility have free rein. The result is a foray disciplined in its tactics but anarchic in its aim; the sack not merely of Forest Lawn, but of adult dignity.

So fantastic a mind is hardly qualified to make great contributions to Christian thought, or to render balanced judgment on the political issues of the day. It is, however, pre-eminently well equipped for artistic creation. An indomitably childish imagination, which refuses equally the sway of modernity and of middle age, is Mr. Waugh's incalculable force.

Notes

1. This is the period reflected in *Put Out More Flags*. A review of that novel in *Partisan Review* (Summer 1943) gave an interesting survey of Mr. Waugh's political development, but exaggerated its symptomatic importance for England.

2. He also "placarded Boscastle harbour with home-made labels championing 'Votes for Women.'" This is less easy to reconcile with his later activities.

3. This is not to imply that *Brideshead Revisited*, as a totality, comes within measureable distance of Proust's achievement in *Remembrance of Things Past*.

The World of Evelyn Waugh   Stephen Spender*

The group of Evelyn Waugh's novels from *Decline and Fall* to *Brideshead Revisited* can be read almost as one developing narrative. This is not to be explained simply by the fact that some of the characters, like Lady Metroland, Peter Pastmaster, and Basil Seal, occur in several volumes, while others, like Ambrose Silk and Anthony Blanche, have such a strong family resemblance as to seem the same person under different names. Nor is it that several of his scenes are laid either in extremely sophisticated or extremely primitive surroundings; nor even that the Evelyn Waugh of his travel books, though invisible there, is very much a felt presence in the novels.

The real reason for this unity in diversity is that the novels are all essentially concerned with the same situation: the contrast between an England still dreaming of its past greatness, whose memory is evoked by country houses and the countryside, and an England of the 1920s and early 1930s in which people live their lives as though they were part of another, and absurd, dream. Beyond these two dreams of the old England and the Bright Young Things, there is the awakening of the will into a nightmare reality beyond which there lies yet another dream: of the renewed greatness of England.

Evelyn Waugh and many of his characters belong to a generation old enough to have passed their childhoods before the First World War, though not old enough to have fought in it. They have memories of pre-war or islanded-from-war country childhoods where hunting and the nursery are the centres of a ritual of idyllic country life. At Brideshead, visits are made to the top room, where Nanny Hawkins lives, by the members of the Marchmain family, for whom she remains a symbol of wisdom. In *Put Out More Flags* when Basil Seal and his sister Barbara are

*Reprinted from *The Creative Element: A Study of Vision, Despair and Orthodoxy among Some Modern Writers* (London: Hamish Hamilton, 1953), 159–75, by permission of the author.

alone together they lapse into nursery conversation which is slightly sinister:

> "Basil, you're up to something. I wish I knew what it was."
> Basil turned on her his innocent blue eyes, as blue as hers and as innocent; they held no hint of mischief. "Just war work, Babs," he said. "Slimy snake."
> "I'm not."
> "Crawly spider." They were back in the schoolroom, in the world where once they had played pirates. "Artful monkey," said Barbara very fondly.

English upper-class childhood, on a knife-edge between incredible innocence and incredible sophistication, is amongst the deeply felt experiences of these books. Such an upbringing has surely never been described with more objectivity and yet with more intensity than in the portrait of a small boy — John Last — in *A Handful of Dust*. And the boys — especially Beste-Chetwynde — at Llanaba Castle, where Augustus Fagan presides in *Decline and Fall*, are sharply observed.

Waugh's feeling for class is rooted in childhoods of people simply unaware that members of any other social class exist, except to wait on them as nannies and grooms. Apart from Nanny Hawkins, Captain Grimes and Paul Pennyfeather are among his few sympathetic portraits of characters not gentlemen: and of course Grimes is a joke, but a kindly one and therefore meant to be more than a joke. Money plays almost as much part in these novels as class: Waugh is as unfashionably uninhibited about the need of it if you haven't got it, and the beauty of it if, like the Marchmains, you have, as most contemporary novelists are about sex. Although there is a good deal of mockery of the titled and the rich, this is never directed from the point of view of those who are below. It is partly satiric observation of manners directed at the Bright Young Things of the 1920s, and partly satire directed from above, from the past, and from beyond, against the contemporary and the decadent.

A paragraph in *Decline and Fall* is the gauge whereby Mr. Waugh measures England. These thoughts of Paul, although used here to produce the irony of anticlimax, none the less express his Romanticized vision of old England:

> The temperate April sunlight fell through the budding chestnuts and revealed between their trunks green glimpses of parkland and the distant radiance of a lake. "English spring," thought Paul. "In the dreaming ancestral beauty of the English country." Surely, he thought, these great chestnuts in the sun stood for something enduring and serene in a world that had lost its reason and would so stand when the chaos and confusion were forgotten? And surely it was the spirit of William Morris that whispered to him in Margot Beste-Chetwynde's motor car about seed time and harvest, the superb succession of the seasons, the harmonious interdependence of rich and poor, of dignity, innocence,

and tradition? But at a turn in the drive the cadence of his thoughts was abruptly transected. They had come into sight of the house.

"Golly!" said Beste-Chetwynde. "Mamma has done herself proud this time."

The car stopped. Paul and Beste-Chetwynde got out, stretched themselves, and were led across a floor of bottle-green glass into the dining room, where Mrs. Beste-Chetwynde was already seated at the vulcanite table beginning her luncheon.

This has that poetic lushness which is too dense in parts of *Brideshead Revisited*, where it is introduced without irony. But it contains the main theme of these novels: the contrast between dream and nightmare, the heavily charged, idealized vision of the past with the garish present.

Evelyn Waugh is a serious comedian, but his seriousness is difficult to analyse. It does not lie in any one quality. For instance, although his novels contain many touches of satire, they do not have the deadly aim and intellectual grasp at the roots of a subject which makes satire effective. He is best when he is satirizing the Bright Young Things or Amy Macpherson and her co-religionists, subjects in themselves ludicrous, weakest when (as in the satire of modern European states in *Scott-King's Modern Europe*) an analytic grasp of a situation is required. But if he has too high a reputation as a satirist, his mastery of the comedy of manners perhaps passes unnoticed under his extravagant fantasy. I have mentioned how clearly and vividly he portrays the small boys in *Decline and Fall*. The portraits of Miss Runcible and the Bright Young People in *Vile Bodies* only *seem* exaggerated: really it is their accuracy that is astonishing. Basil Seal is surely one of the best-drawn characters in modern fiction. Like Charlus or any other great character, although completely defined within the novels where he appears, he retains that mysterious quality of unexpectedness which seems to exist in a dimension of the imagination the novelist only suggests: so that when we have closed *Black Mischief* or *Put Out More Flags* we are left wondering, and imagining, what Basil is up to now.

It is this depth of observation of manners which distinguishes Waugh from the merely funny writers, and makes his comedy *serious*. It moves from the farcical to the comic, and from the comic to the tragic upon the axis of the truth of his observation of manners. As with Chaplin, we can weep with the comedian when he is being tragic and sympathize with this pathos, because we move from mode to mode of a true character portrayed. What we can least accept, though, is the sententiousness which Waugh, like Chaplin, sometimes assumes when he is being "serious."

The underlying seriousness of Waugh's novels lies not in their opinion-atedness but in their narration of a *search*. To read several of his novels through within a few days, as I have recently done, is to feel oneself at times in the presence of a disguised spiritual autobiography. The search is religious and preoccupies the reader all the more because it is not his characters who are involved in it, but the writer himself. Perhaps one of the things which makes Evelyn Waugh primarily a comic writer is that, with all his observation of manners and behaviour, he is unable success-fully to project his own spiritual struggle into a character. He creates most successfully the kind of characters whom the writer loves but despises. When he attempts a sympathetic character like Charles Ryder or Julia in *Brideshead Revisited*, he falls into the wrong kind of absurdity. He sees people from the superior point of view of one who has always his own opinions, his own very definite conceit of himself. It is he who knows what is right and wrong and good and bad; and the moment he tries to project this knowledge into the mouth of one of his characters, the situation becomes false. It is Mr. Waugh who delivers Father Rothschild's little homily in *Vile Bodies*; who gives the lecture on what is the best brandy and what are the best glasses out of which it should be drunk in the scene in the Paris restaurant in *Brideshead Revisited*; and it is he who puts Basil Seal on the side of the angels at the end of *Put Out More Flags*. These are solemn matters, we are made to feel, too solemn for these characters, so Mr. Waugh takes over.

The search begins, as it were, from the Garden of Eden, in *Decline and Fall*. The title of this novel refers, of course, to the misadventures of Paul Pennyfeather, habitually punished for crimes committed by his betters, from the moment when he is sent down from Scone College for indecent behaviour after his debagging by Lumsden of Strathdrummond to his imprisonment in Egdon Heath Penal Settlement for participating in the White Slave Traffic—an offence in which Margot Beste-Chetwynde has involved him. But the title has also a subtler irony; for *Decline and Fall*, like the novels of Ronald Firbank, deals with a world where there is in reality no Fall, no Sin, no Retribution.

No crime in *Decline and Fall* "counts," and no one suffers for his offences. His four weeks of solitary confinement "were among the happiest in Paul's life." Captain Grimes epitomizes his own life story in one of those confessions which immediately acquits him in the court of the Republic of Love: " 'Funny thing, I can always get on all right for about six weeks, and then I land in the soup. I don't believe I was ever meant by Nature to be a schoolmaster. Temperament, said Grimes, with a far-away look in his eyes—'that's been my trouble, temperament and sex.' "

The headmaster, Dr. Fagan, says "Grimes has been convicted before me . . . of a crime—I might almost call it a course of action—which I can neither understand nor excuse." However, immediately after saying this, he announces that Grimes will marry his daughter Flossie, "He is *not* the son-in-law I should readily have chosen. I could have forgiven him his wooden leg, his slavish poverty, his moral turpitude, and his abominable features; I could even have forgiven him his incredible vocabulary, if only he had been a *gentleman*. . . ."

Grimes, like Paul, goes through many vicissitudes, but he always turns up. What he symbolizes is rather heavily underlined. We are told he is "of the immortals. . . . Surely he had followed in the Bacchic train of distant Arcady, and played on the reeds of myth by forgotten streams, and taught the childish satyrs the art of love?"

Really, though, Grimes inhabits a world of a Christian or Old Testament myth of life before the Fall, rather than of Greek innocence. The joke of his life is that of a "child of nature" playing a game against man and human institutions, and sharing the secret of his innocence with God.

This is one of the best and oldest of the jokes of the Christian—pre-eminently the Catholic—world. It is the joke of Rabelais and Cervantes, and we feel it whenever we love a villain. It is pre-eminently a Catholic joke, because Catholics, with the secrecy of the confessional, separate more sharply than do Protestants the law of God from that of man.

But *Decline and Fall* (1928) was written, I believe, before Evelyn Waugh's conversion to Catholicism. He was received into the Church in 1930. And it might have been the Bible of Agatha Runcible and the other Bright Young Things in his second book, *Vile Bodies* (published 1930).

The Bright Young Things of England in the 1920s, who are now middle-aged, correspond to the young Americans of Hemingway's Paris. They differ from Hemingway's characters in their brittle determination not to take themselves or anything else seriously. Hemingway's Brett and her friends lead seriously unserious lives, drinking, making love and travelling, but prepared at any moment to look into their cups and discover an unhappy love or a broken heart or some other symptom of . their belonging to a "tragic generation." What is really so attractive and seductive about the Bright Young Things is their refusal to be tragic. They are genuinely frivolous, real sneerers and jeerers who raise what is after all an important moral question: Is anything worth taking seriously? This question should only be answered in the negative by those who are able to treat love lightly, always maintain a certain gaiety, and never under any circumstances show the slightest trace of self-pity.

When Adam Fenwick-Symes gets off the boat-train, after the Channel crossing in which Miss Runcible is so shamingly "gone over" by the Customs officials, he suddenly remembers that he is engaged to be married to Nina Blount. The telephone conversation which follows ("Oh, I say, Nina, there's one thing—I don't think I shall be able to marry you after all." "Oh, *Adam*, you are a bore. Why not?") sets the tone of their relationship, which is spent in Adam getting, and throwing away, the financial opportunities for marriage. When Miss Runcible crashes in the racing car, she dies in a nursing-home room, where her delirium is indistinguishable from the delirium of her life:

> She was sitting bolt upright in bed, smiling deliriously, and bowing her bandaged head to imaginary visitors.
> "*Darling*," she said, "how *too* divine . . . how are you? . . . and how are *you?* . . . how angelic of you all to come. . . ."

The novel ends with a prophetic glimpse of Adam sitting "on a splintered tree stump in the biggest battlefield in the history of the world." The Garden of Eden of *Decline and Fall* has given way to the false dream of the Bright Young People from which there is the awakening into the nightmare of the Third World War.

Halfway through *Vile Bodies* a conversation takes place between Father Rothschild, the Jesuit priest (who until now has been a figure of fun), Lord Metroland, newspaper proprietor, and Mr. Outrage, the Prime Minister:

> "Don't you think," said Father Rothschild gently, "that perhaps it is all in some way historical? I don't think people ever *want* to lose their faith either in religion or anything else. I know very few young people but it seems to me they are all possessed with an almost fatal hunger for permanence. . . . My private schoolmaster used to say, 'If a thing's worth doing at all, it's worth doing well.' My church has taught that in different words for several centuries. But these young people have got hold of another end of the stick, and for all we know it may be the right one. They say, 'If a thing's not worth doing well, it's not worth doing at all.' It makes everything difficult for them."

A little later the Prime Minister asks, "Anyway, what do you mean by 'historical'?"

"Well, it's like this war that's coming."

So the Bright Young Things are perhaps justified in their refusal to take life seriously, since in the 1920s it has no serious cause to offer them. However, the refusal in Waugh goes deeper than theirs, and Catholicism has not enabled him to assume an attitude towards modern life in which the severest criticism is based on charity and sympathetic understanding. Finally it becomes a refusal of everything except a return to the old England, a land of knights equipped with machine-guns, if not clad in shining armour. In the dedicatory letter to Randolph Churchill which precedes *Put Out More Flags*, he seems to have discovered such a grail in what he terms the "Churchillian Renaissance." But the concluding sentences of *Scott-King's Modern Europe* (published in 1947) seem to reflect not so much a mood of despair as a feeling that the only intelligent attitude towards the modern world is one of total rejection and insistence on complete unreality.

Scott-King, after his return from modern Europe, says to the headmaster:

> "I think it would be very wicked indeed to do anything to fit a boy for the modern world."
> "It's a short-sighted view, Scott-King."
> "There, headmaster, with all respect, I differ from you profoundly. I think it the most long-sighted view it is possible to take."

This is petulantly negative, because there is nothing in *Scott-King's Modern Europe* to suggest what kind of a world a boy should be equipped for. The satire is directed from a point of view which, perhaps deliberately, has no possible application to the Europe that is being satirized. And although one may sympathize with the complete rejection of modern Europe, the only alternative Evelyn Waugh seems to have to offer (a deliberate cultivation of scholarship which is known not to be worthwhile) seems trivial. Not just the life satirized but the satire itself is frivolous.

In *Black Mischief*, the macabre nightmare which underlies the lives of Waugh's characters bursts at the end into the terrifying scene when Basil Seal, at the funeral feast of the Emperor Moshu, whom he has served so egregiously, discovers that he has eaten Prudence, the daughter of the British Ambassador, who was his mistress in the capital of the Azanian Empire. Waugh adds to his more and more clearly defined nightmare of the modern world a metaphor, also to be found in T.S. Eliot and Dr. Edith Sitwell: that the decadent life of an over-civilized society falling into unreality resembles the cannibalism of savages. Dr. Edith Sitwell's *Gold Coast Customs* draws a parallel between the life of London salon society and the customs of savages. The dialogue of *Sweeney Agonistes* suggests the cannibal instincts of Eliot's modern characters.

Black Mischief is Waugh's most poetic, besides being perhaps his most amusing, book, in which the need for moralizing asides is least felt. The behaviour of the Azanian Emperor and of the British and French Embassies at his capital are managed with a satire closer and more incisive than in any other of his novels. Despite the satire, one believes in the reformist zeal of the Emperor Seth, the politics of his opponents, the intrigues of the French Ambassador and the apathy of the British, much as one believes in Stendhal's Duchy of Parma. Nor is Basil Seal's conversion into a capable administrator incredible, for given sufficiently grotesque circumstances, one can believe that he would act with a zealousness of which he is incapable in England.

Basil Seal shows exceptional energy and initiative for an Evelyn Waugh character. John Beaver, in *A Handful of Dust*, is far more typical. He might be described as a kind of corrupt Candide, a colourless, rather passive young man, to whom things happen, and who is transformed by events into a cold-blooded financial, sexual, and social opportunist. Paul Pennyfeather is the most attractive of this tribe, to which Adam Fenwick-Symes also belongs (Mr. Scott-King is a particularly dim specimen). John Beaver, the son of a go-getting interior-decorating mother, is the least attractive of all Evelyn Waugh's heroes.

Mean, and a hanger-on whom everyone dislikes, he is taken up by Brenda, whose husband, Tony Last, spends all their income on keeping up his Victorian Gothic house, which Brenda detests. In his tepid way, John Beaver becomes her lover. Out of this essentially comic relationship, Mr.

Waugh creates a situation close to tragedy. He does so with an admirable astringency, without sentimentalizing his main characters, who are both detestable and real. In their different ways, Beaver, Tony Last, and Brenda are all selfish and self-absorbed. What Mr. Waugh succeeds in making us realize is that despite their hardness, two of these characters — Tony and Brenda — really suffer. But the tragedy is borne by their son, John, when he is killed in a hunting accident.

Mr. Waugh shows in this novel that within a situation where people act ruthlessly and selfishly, tragedy, as it were, may be distributed over their lives, though each may be incapable of feeling its intensity. John is the most sensitive and alive person among these rather dead people. When Brenda first hears of his death, involuntarily she exclaims "Thank God," and one feels that perhaps this attitude of hers has allowed him to die. Mr. Waugh's novels show very well that within a heartless comedy of manners there is incipient tragedy — on this level of true observation his comedy fuses with tragedy. The ending of *A Handful of Dust*, where Tony Last is lost in the Amazonian forest and falls into the hands of an elderly Englishman, to whom he reads the novels of Dickens, and who will not release him, is an admirable excursion into what in contemporary France would be called "the absurd."

After *A Handful of Dust*, little is added in *Scoop* and *Put Out More Flags*. But *Brideshead Revisited* is both a recapitulation of all the between-wars material, from Oxford until 1940, and an entirely new departure. It is a revolution in Waugh's whole approach to the novel which gives one something of the shock which the introduction of the "talkies" gave to those accustomed to the silent film. In *Brideshead Revisited* he brings his novel-writing into line with that of Graham Greene, whose principal theme is the contrast between sin and sanctitude, according to the Catholic view of life as it exists in the minds of English converts.

When a comedian turns serious, one has to ask whether this consciously serious manner really says more than the unconscious seriousness of his comedy. As a comedian, Waugh has been preoccupied with serious jokes, jokes that deal with fundamentals of life and death, jokes which put the values of a God with a sense of humour above those of human institutions. His comedy can bring us face to face with hideous realities.

His serious humour has, moreover, great diversity. There is the Before-the-Fall joke of *Decline and Fall* which makes sinners sinless and every punishment let everyone off. A development of this is the forgiven, lovable sinner joke, which fuses the spirit of comedy with that of charity: for the sharpness of his observation and his parody should not allow us to forget how much affection he shows even for his most diabolical characters. Then there is the Candid Camera joke: for the real funniness of the conversation of the Bright Young Things and of characters like Ambrose Silk is in their being photographically exact. Waugh has the gift, rare among novelists, of recording conversations and scenes from real life which seem too fantastic to be real. He does not, like Forster, create the idiom of a character so convincingly that his words seem to be the invention of his behaviour, but he can imitate very well the idiom of certain types and individuals. Lastly he has the powerful imagination which can invent situations as poetically true as the endings of *A Handful of Dust* and *Black Mischief*. His weakness — which spoils his satire — is the tendency towards crude exaggeration. For instance, in *Scott-King's Modern Europe* there is an account of the formalities necessary for leaving England at the end of the war, which is inexact without being fantastic. A satirist may caricature, but he should not simply distort facts, or — like anyone else with a grievance (satire is essentially complaint) — he loses the sympathy of his audience.

Comedy often consists in saying what — if said seriously — would seem almost unsayable. Evelyn Waugh's sympathy with characters like Basil Seal who are not merely sinners but devils is an example of this. To take Basil Seal seriously is either to condemn him (as Anthony Blanche and his set, more or less, are condemned in *Brideshead Revisited*) or to excuse him, as Basil is, in fact, excused by becoming a "reformed" character at the end of *Put Out More Flags*. Still more unsayable are those views which when stated comically affect us as social criticism, but when stated seriously are social anachronism. There is something of anachronism about the whole situation of the very aristocratic, very rich Marchmain family in *Brideshead Revisited*. The novel contains too many scenes like this (when the narrator, Charles Ryder, arrives in Venice to visit Lord Marchmain, the father of his friend Sebastian Flyte) which read like involuntary caricature:

> Plender [Lord Marchmain's valet] led us to the waiting boat. The gondoliers wore green and white livery and silver plaques on their chests; they smiled and bowed.
> "*Palazzo. Pronto.*"
> *Si, Signore Plender.*"
> And we floated away.
> "You've been here before?"
> "No."
> "I came once before — from the sea. This is the way to arrive."
> "*Ecco ci siamo, signori.*"

This is, of course, realistic dialogue and description. Yet it reads like a parody of the effect of discreet but none the less vulgar glamour which surrounds the Marquis of Marchmain and his family in the mind of Charles Ryder.

Yet in *Brideshead Revisited* Evelyn Waugh adds to his nostalgic descriptions of English life what is probably the best account of Oxford in the late 1920s. The first part of the book is spent by Charles in watching his fellow-undergraduate friend Sebastian Flyte become a drunkard.

Sebastian grows distrustful ˜of this ˜friendship, since he comes to suspect that Charles has been taken into the confidence of Lady Marchmain, who is charming, sensitive, and insidiously domineering. The second half of the novel is concerned with Charles falling in love with Sebastian's sister Julia who is married to a brash Canadian business operator.

The purpose of the novel is to show the Catholic pattern woven through the lives of the characters. Despite their folly, failure, and disorder, their religion is capable of saving them and it gives their lives significance. As Julia explains to Charles when she is trying to break away from her own marriage (and therefore also from her faith, which forbids her to marry him):

> "I've been punished a little for marrying Rex. You see, I can't get all that sort of thing out of my mind, quite — Death, Judgment, Heaven, Hell, Nanny Hawkins, and the Catechism. It becomes part of oneself, if they give it one early enough. And yet I wanted my child to have it. . . . now I suppose I shall be punished for what I've just done. Perhaps that is why you and I are here together like this . . . part of a plan."

The presence of their faith in the lives of this family, sometimes clear, sometimes obscured, is vividly felt. That the Catholic characters are imperfect, dissolute, and even — like Lord Brideshead — wooden and pompous is artistically right. All the same, since none of the characters — unless perhaps Nanny Hawkins — represents the faith burning within the pure life, it is all the more necessary that in the course of the action certain ambiguities should be cleared away and the reader should feel the plan of God as a pattern distinct from a kind of spiritual glamour mingled with a good deal of worldliness which attracts Charles Ryder to the Marchmains. The distinction between the love of God and the love of man (also the subject of Graham Greene's novel *The End of the Affair*) has to be made and made clearly. For, to start off with, there is a good deal of doubt in the reader's mind whether Charles Ryder is in love with Sebastian's family on account of their style of living, or the attractiveness of Sebastian, or the aura of their religion.

The purpose of the narrative is to make clear this distinction. The great revelation is in the scene which describes Lord Marchmain's death. To prepare the reader for the full extent of this illumination, Charles Ryder is made (this is a serious artistic flaw) more obtusely and outspokenly anti-Catholic in the latter half of the book than in the first half. To some extent this may be explained on the grounds that he wants to marry Julia and that he feels her religious conscience opposes the marriage. All the same, the explanation does not hold. If Charles really cared for Julia or had any understanding of her psychology in her position, surely the last thing he would do would be to ridicule the Catholic religion to her, and least of all at the time when her father is dying. He has not been portrayed as that kind of blunderer in his relationship with her brother Sebastian.

The crisis of the novel is when Lord Marchmain returns to Brideshead to die, after the death of Lady Marchmain. Shortly before his death, he sends away the priest who has come to visit him with these words: "Father Mackay, I am afraid you have been brought here under a misapprehension. I am not in extremis, and I have not been a practicising member of your Church for twenty-five years. Brideshead, show Father Mackay the way out." Lord Brideshead interprets this to mean that in the event of his being *in extremis* Lord Marchmain would not refuse the priest. "Mumbo-jumbo is off . . . the witch-doctor has gone," comments Charles Ryder, who now behaves like the caricature of a stupidly insensitive person, to Julia. Besides being unsympathetic, he is also crudely interfering. He obtains from the family doctor the opinion that if Father Mackay, against Lord Marchmain's wishes, is brought to see him again, the shock might well prove fatal. In fact the behaviour of Charles Ryder, who is presumably meant to represent the non-Catholic attitude, is of a kind to make the non-Catholic (and perhaps also the Catholic) reader wonder why Lord Brideshead does not ask him to leave the house.

At the end, despite the wishes of Charles (who is not a member of the family), Father Mackay is brought to Lord Marchmain's death-bed. Lord Marchmain, who has fallen into a coma, recovers consciousness, and makes the sign of the cross. Charles is deeply moved and the change in his attitude is presumably a preliminary to conversion: "Then I knew that the sign I had asked for was not a little thing, not a passing nod of recognition, and a phrase came back to me from my childhood of the veil of the temple being rent from top to bottom."

This scene is affecting, and we are convinced that the attitude of Charles is changed. However, even here the absolutely clear distinction between the presence of the divine and the human is not made. There is nothing to distinguish the reaction of Charles from that of a man who has been made to realize that he has shown a stupid disrespect for another man's profoundest belief and who now feels sorry for it. And when, immediately after this, Julia explains to Charles that she cannot marry him, the distinction is still less clear. It is difficult to see how she could do so, after his behaviour of the past few days.

The real failure of *Brideshead Revisited* is not confined, however, to these concluding scenes. It really lies in the character of Charles Ryder. Within his sensibility is the meeting of the minds of his Catholic friends and the agnostic views he supposedly represents. His development should record the emergence of the pattern of the true religion from the unsatisfactory lives of the Marchmains, and also from his own agnosticism.

Charles Ryder lacks the character for such a role. Despite his rationalism, he is a bigot of a rather insignificant kind. He is a painter, but considers modern art "great bosh." He is a snob, not only in his relations at Brideshead, but in most things. He is lacking in charity. He is incapable of remaining more than faintly interested in Sebastian after his friend has become a drunkard.

Three-quarters of the way through the book we are suddenly confronted with the *fait accompli* of Charles's marriage to a lady whom he does not love, and to whom we are first introduced when he and his wife are on board ship, leaving New York for England. On board, there is also Julia, with whom Charles starts having a love affair. The reader is expected to sympathize with Charles's dislike of his vapid and pushing wife. But the assumption that the character of a person to whom one is married is an excuse for loathing her would seem as unchristian to some readers as it seems essential to the Catholic pattern of Evelyn Waugh.

For Charles Ryder to be brought to see that Lord Marchmain received spiritual comfort from Extreme Unction does not therefore convince the reader of the transcendence of God's Catholic plan. Nor does his separation from Julia shortly after this revelation, on the grounds of her religion. After all, separation from someone he loves is only a negative decision, made less impressive by the reader's suspecting that Charles Ryder loves no one. If there were an indication that by this separation Charles recognized the duty of loving his own wife, and Julia hers of loving her husband— both of whom have been portrayed as completely unlovable—then we might be convinced of a miraculous change. The lesson of God's and Nanny Hawkins's plan might be that it is your duty to love someone to whom you are bound by solemn ties; or at least charity might demand that you see no one as completely hateful. But to Julia and Charles their marriages only have the significance of sacred obstacles which prevent their marrying one another. The "plan" of marriage in *Brideshead Revisited* looks very like a trap sprung by God to prevent people who love one another from marrying. For it appears to be a rule of Mr. Waugh's world in this novel that the married couples detest one another. Julia and Charles hate their respective partners, and Lord Marchmain hates Lady Marchmain.

The ethics of *Brideshead Revisited* are, indeed, puzzling to the uninitiated. If you are, like Sebastian, a hopeless drunkard, God according to Lord Brideshead (who despite his wooden pomposity is an authority on these matters) particularly loves you. The sentimental friendship between Sebastian and Charles is romanticized, and the Catholics, who are always passing judgment, have nothing against it: indeed, Cara, who, although Lord Marchmain's mistress, is devout, seems to bless it as a "phase." As in some of Graham Greene's novels, the one offence which brings eternal damnation is getting a divorce from someone to whom you do not want to be married in order that you may marry someone you love.

However, the lack of sense of moral proportion in *Brideshead Revisited* is probably artistic rather than religious. It comes from trying to state comic seriousness—which can accept the idea that all marriages are unhappy and yet one is not allowed to marry the person one loves—as didactic moralizing, and the absurd as sober truth. When he is seriously unserious Mr. Waugh is charitable — and that, of course, is what makes his comedy serious. He caricatures his characters without failing to observe their truth, and he condemns no one. As he admits in the prefatory letter which introduces *Put Out More Flags*, he finds more food for thought in the follies of Basil Seal and Ambrose Silk than in the sagacity of the higher command. The "higher command" might here be taken to refer to more than the military. It is when he identifies his prejudices with a moralizing religion that qualities anachronistic and absurd in his view of life — intolerance, bigotry, and self-rigteousness — work against his talent, and even tend to caricature the very ideas he is supposed to be supporting. When he is solemn, his work provides an extravagant example of faith without charity. One can understand and respect the reasons which made him abandon the personal vision of the earlier novels. Yet there was more love among the innocent savages of *Decline and Fall* and the cannibals of *Vile Bodies* than we find among the Marchmains or in Charles Ryder.

[From "Huxley and Waugh: Or I Do Not Think, Therefore I Am"]   Sean O'Faolain*

Waugh's detachment, while having its own shape of ambiguity, is much more genuine than Huxley's. He is detached by hardness of mind, hardness of thought about people — not about affairs, or ideas, for he is not in any sense an intellectual; he is, or rather was in his great satirical period, a man of fashion with Joyce's trick of suddenly leaving the company to take satirical notes on his cuff in the wash-room. Where this toughness springs from God (quite literally) alone knows: it was one of those inexplicable natural gifts like genius or personality.

It must have helped that he early became a Roman Catholic. (Many critics who do not warm to the Catholic feeling in *Brideshead Revisited* seem to forget that Waugh had become converted to Catholicism in the year of the publication of his second novel.) For to be a Catholic in England is to be detached by many degrees from the main English tradition.

> The aesthetic appeal of the Church of England [Waugh himself wrote] is unique and peculiar to these islands. . . . In England the . . . mediaeval cathedrals and churches, the rich ceremonies that surround the monarch, the historic titles of Canterbury and York, the social organization of the country parishes, the traditional culture of Oxford

*Reprinted from Sean O'Faolain, *The Vanishing Hero: Studies in the Novelists of the Twenties* (Boston: Atlantic, Little, Brown, 1956), 50–69, by permission of the author and Curtis Brown, Ltd. © 1957 by Sean O'Faolain; renewed 1985.

and Cambridge, the liturgy composed in the heyday of English prose-style—all these are the property of the Church of England, while Catholics meet in modern buildings, often of deplorable design, and are usually served by simple Irish missionaries.

Does one imagine a note of nostalgia, which would imply attachment-detachment, and promise sympathy and understanding? I cannot help recalling Newman after his conversion saying sadly to a fellow-convert that his new friends had never known the world in which he, in memory, still lived.

Then there is the class-difference. A critic once described him as a snob and he replied: "I think perhaps he is right in calling me a snob; that is to say, I am happiest in the company of the European upper classes." Happy, but possibly also all the more objective about them by not having been born into them. His grandfather was a country doctor from Somerset; his father, after Sherborne and New College, became a reader to Kegan Paul, later chairman of Chapman and Hall, a prolific editor of the English classics. It is, in the good French sense, a bourgeois background. When Evelyn Waugh passed through Lancing and Hertford College he moved into a wider world, a step which it is not so easy to take in France as in England; unless one can equate the Jockey Club with St James's and Buck's—Waugh's clubs—as open doors to the life of "the European upper classes"?

And there was his formative period, with its critical attitude of life in general and English life in particular. Had he been born fifteen years earlier or later he might have been led to join the Labour Party. (It may not sound likely; but one remembers that Wellington, Balliol and the Foreign Office could lead so sceptical a mind as the Hon. Harold Nicolson's that way.) The kind of party that attracted Waugh's contemporaries led him to *Vile Bodies*.

Masked parties. Savage parties. Victorian parties, Greek parties, Wild West parties, Russian parties, Circus parties, parties where one had to dress as somebody else, almost naked parties in Saint John's Wood, parties in flats and studios and houses and ships and hotels and night clubs, in windmills and swimming-baths, tea parties at school where one ate muffins and meringues and tinned-crab, parties at Oxford where one drank brown sherry and smoked Turkish cigarettes, dull dances in London and comic dances in Scotland and disgusting dances in Paris—all that succession and repetition of massed humanity. . . . Those vile bodies. . . .

Even this brief run, culminating in the title of the novel, so characteristic of Waugh's style in its eclectic adjective, proposes a very different kind of mind to Huxley's, for though it inveighs it does it with gusto, and one reads it not in admiring glee at the destruction wrought but with an amusement unalloyed by contempt for its victims. The adjective alone might put us at our ease, like a reliable name on an aircraft; we feel we are taking off with a good company in good company. *Vile* has no sour connotations. It is not depressing, it is not moral, it is young and lively and it is also old and reputable, a blend of Shakespeare and slang; it suggests a sort of hopeless, good-humoured scorn of fate, chance or folly like a man who has gone for a long tramp in vile weather with a leaking mackintosh, and will describe his misfortunes afterwards with a blend of resignation and derision which does not exclude the suggestion that he enjoyed the adventure he reviles. Attachment-detachment again?

The effect of this genuine but ambiguous detachment of Waugh's is that the laughter his first six novels evoke is our happy tribute to the delicate balance he strikes between his detachment from his characters which allows him to satirise them and his affection for them which allows him to pity them. Surely we all remember *Vile Bodies* as much for its compassion as its bite? Recall, for example, how generously he handles those two vile bodies Adam and Nina. They are a foolish young couple and he does not spare them the exposure of their folly, but he never suggests that they are wicked, and he does not moralise over them. They did anticipate their wedding-night, but they loved one another truly; and as if to alleviate their unorthodox behaviour Waugh so arranges things that Adam intended to anticipate lawful wedlock only by one night, and that Nina yielded to him only because she was so touched by his silly dance of joy over the cheque he had extracted from her dotty father that she could not bear to point out to him that her papa had signed it with the name Charlie Chaplin. He grants them virtues, however foolishly applied, as when he allows them to visit the sick Miss Runcible — though so boisterously that their kindness helps to polish her off. He does not spare them their choice of friends. Peter Pastmaster drinks like a fish and sleeps with negresses; Lady Metroland is a high-class procuress; Miles Malpractice is a homosexual; Mrs Panrast is a Lesbian. But these are minor characters in the romance of Adam and Nina, and no society has ever been free of such aberrants. He makes Adam try to earn a living on which to marry Nina, though because he is an incompetent young fool he must be dogged by bad luck and always look like a silly young mug. Adam is entirely faithful to Nina and when he marries her we are to presume that they live happily ever after. Indeed, the unique thing about *Vile Bodies* is that this satire by an undeceived contemporary has achieved so much benevolence without an iota of sentimentality.

But then, Waugh is sometimes charged with unnecessary cruelty towards his characters? Mr Donat O'Donnell, for example, writes in his interesting study of a group of Catholic novelists, *Maria Cross*:

> Mr. Waugh is a great explorer of human disadvantages, and his unscrupulous adolescent cruelty in this is the common quality of his two most obvious characteristics: his humour and his snobbery. Two of his comic novels, *Black Mischief* and *Scoop*, are largely based on a sly

appeal to the white man's sense of racial superiority; much of the best fun in *Decline and Fall* comes from the exploitation of Captain Grimes who, although he claimed to be a public school man, was not really a gentleman and did not often have a bath; in *Put Out More Flags* the purest comedy lies in the lurid descriptions of the appearance and behaviour of three proletarian children.

One must agree that Waugh does, frequently, indulge in pointless cruelty, and that when he does so it is a mistake and a blemish. In *Black Mischief* Mr Youkoumian treats his wife with such persistent and callous brutality that instead of laughing at her misfortunes we protest at them. But this is not usual with Waugh, and I think Mr O'Donnell has here missed two points, one essential to an understanding of Waugh; and I can only hope that it may make him feel a little uncomfortable to recall that G.K. Chesterton, who thought that the disasters piled on the innocent head of the hero of *Decline and Fall* were merely "distressing," would be entirely on his side.

First: while it is true that the misfortunes of Mrs Youkoumian are not funny, one must understand the analeptic mechanism of the sort of laughter they can produce. Some years ago a multiple murderer named John Christie was arrested, tried and hanged in London. He had enticed women into his flat, in the sort of quarter which would have been suitable for a Graham Greene or a Simenon crime story. He had strangled the women and stacked them up in a cupboard like coats on coat-hangers, one in front of the other. Others he had buried. I have heard this case discussed not only by intellectuals but by ordinary, good-living, decent Irish people with peals of laughter. In Dublin he was commonly referred to as Corpus Christie. Before that a man named Haigh had melted down several women in barrels of acid so that nothing was left in the bottom of the barrels but their false teeth. It was the only way by which one victim was identified. In the effort to escape the gallows Haigh not only pretended lunacy but declared that he drank his own urine. This also I have heard discussed with the utmost gaiety. Surely this sort of laughter is like a man who has drunk poison tickling his throat with a feather to make himself vomit the evil thing. Waugh is not, I feel, in his scenes of apparently gratuitous cruelty laughing at humanity, or laughing with humanity. His laughter is a horrible cathartic laughter. He invents a scapegoat who suffers the cruelty of life for us. We identify ourselves with the sufferer. We laugh it off. This does not make it funny. It does make it bearable. We have considered, faced-up to cruelty and borne it by proxy in some form, to some degree.

But Waugh's cruelty is more often a deliberate and well-pointed and wholly admirable part of his technique, and if it is double-edged, it is for sound reasons. This is where Mr O'Donnell has not only missed a point but completely failed to understand what Waugh is generally driving at in his satires. True, the loathsome Mr Basil Seal does make money during the war by packing dirty and destructive refugees into the gracious, well-loved, much tended country homes of his neighbors, later withdrawing them for handsome bribes. But what is Waugh's purpose in this? Basil Seal is a type consistently despised by the Twenties; a man without an iota of the admirable Epicurean private virtues they admired, and he is therefore clearly presented as a crook. On the other hand, the soft-headed, soft-boiled mugs whom he defrauded and tormented were largely the people who, by their soft-headed goodness, had brought all the trouble on the world in 1914; just as in the postwar decade they would be going around, still mugs, still soft-headed, asking people to sign peace pledges; just as later, in the Thirties these same people would be reading Auden, and Isherwood, and Spender, and Koestler and all the Pylon boys who were the intellectual vanguard of the Socialist revolution which would go far to wipe out the bourgeoisie completely—and would have done so if there were not in even the soft-headed British bourgeois some tough residue of the strain of Hampden and of Pym that not even the half-baked Liberalism of the nineteenth century and the inhuman humanism of the first decades of the twentieth could wholly destroy. Waugh could not possibly have been on the side of these deluded souls, even against Seal. He regarded them much as a sergeant-major might regard a thoroughly hopeless set of raw recruits; and he let them "have it."

Besides, the Basil Seals of the world had at least three virtues in the eyes of the Twenties: he was clever; and amusing—"amusing" is still a popular word among English intellectuals, applicable to anything from Byzantine Art to Boston Baked Beans—and he was not contributing to the complacency of the stupid good. He was therefore a useful Attila, a Scourge of God to lash the stupid good and carry off his wickedness in scornful laughter. It is almost always so in Waugh's novels. His hard-bitten scoundrels surpass his heroes and heroines: Basil Seal, Margot Beste-Chetwynde who becomes Lady Metroland, Captain Grimes, Solomon Philbrick. Virtuous innocence is his laughing-stock, personified by any of Seal's pathetic victims, or Paul Pennyfeather, or Adam Symes, or old Prendergast, or Cedric Lyne, or Tony Last whose only fault was that he was a dull husband who did not know the ropes, and lived in an innocent (but to Waugh dangerous) dream of Gothic Worlds with dappled unicorns on the lawn, and childish toys sentimentally preserved in the bedroom cupboard—just the sort of fellow who would become a hero in a silly war like that just finished in 1918. . . .

. . . But the really important unmasking is that of the life of the young people of his decade whom he presents not so much with paternal bitterness as with brotherly exasperation, always assuaged—or so one may feel—by his honest memory of how much he enjoyed their company while the going was good. For all through his work the sub-audible implications suggest certain foiled desires, certain ideals, a certain norm which, he feels, their lives denied, so that one gradually begins to see that his way of presenting them involves what music-hall comedians call the Double Take. We laugh, and then the rubber-band slaps back in our faces and we realise that the laugh is on us. While he is making us laugh over the follies of these young people, even inducing in us some sympathy with their rebellion against their elders, their general disillusion, their dissatisfaction with what Miss Elizabeth Bowen has called the "edited" life of conventional society, we begin to realise that Waugh is also revealing that he is disillusioned over their disillusionment and rebelling against their revolt. He is seeing through them just as clearly as he insists on seeing through a garish make-up. He sees that their revolt is negative, their lives are prodigal, they are just as incapable of any clear concept of a desirable image or way of life as their fathers against whom they are in revolt. That scene in which Miss Runcible dies while all her gay friends sit around her bed cracking jokes, exchanging gossip and drinking champagne, unaware that she is sinking into oblivion, could be taken as a symbol of Waugh's basically moral criticism of the Twenties, whose kiss is death.

It is not that there is anything much that is positively wrong about them; it is that their lives are fatally negative. As we watch them we may feel side-by-side with Hemingway in *The Sun Also Rises* which comments in the same spirit on the American expatriates in Paris and Spain between 1918 and the Depression. These amusing, often delightful young people of Waugh's satires were not without their own earnestness, their own longings, their own idealism, but, to borrow from Camus's *L'Homme Revolté*, they can only gyrate in the realm of rebellion, incoherently, emotionally, without ever advancing into the realm of those ideas which belong to a creative revolt. So they waste life, managing it so loosely. Their damnation is a deprivation, an absence, a vacuity, like Marlowe's hell. In those wild days and nights of the Twenties it must have sometimes occurred to Waugh as it did to Lawrence that they were all "done for," that at any moment the clock would strike and the chorus come in chanting to the jazz-drums of falling bombs and clattering ack-ack, "Cut is the branch that might have grown full straight / And burned is Apollo's laurel bough."

In his early and, I think, best books Waugh said none of this — he was much too finely equilibrated a humorist to utter explicit statements, and so long as he could imply his norm he apparently felt no urge to project a positive hero to represent it. This reticence delighted his generation and continues to delight us, as it will probably delight every generation to come. It is the mark of the moral satirist who, like all universal moralists, has detached himself from the accidentals of life by withdrawing to the remote ground of principles so general that . . . they could be equally acceptable to people of another nation, and of another time.

This admirable detachment disappeared with the publication of *Brideshead Revisited* in which Mr Waugh changed ground. Ceasing to be a moral satirist he became a writer of romances. We, his devoted readers, had to make, and were not always able to make, a rapid adjustment of our expectations, and, if we were his critics, were called on to apply totally different standards. At this distance it is easier to do both things; to recognise that this is not (to understate) another funny book, that it is solemn and serious, romantic and nostalgic, exclusive and personal, and, far from being general in its application, relies to a most disturbing degree on its appeal to our interest through accidental and irrelevant detail. It is this last point which strikes one the most forcibly; as may be seen at once if we retell the story without the accidentals.

One Charles Ryder meets a young man named Flyte, and through him his family. The father and mother have separated. They had both been religious-minded people, the mother being specially pious, but the father abandoned his religion when he left his wife to live with his mistress. The mother dies midway through the book. There are four children. Young Flyte and his sister Julia have reacted from their mother; his brother and sister remain close to her. Flyte becomes a dipsomaniac, driven to drink, one might say, by the insistent morality of his mother. Julia marries a thrusting Canadian, outside the church of her origin, has an affair with somebody unnamed, falls in love with Ryder and proceeds to divorce her Canadian husband. When the father ultimately returns home to die, Julia is so affected by seeing him, at the point of his final coma, bless himself that she refuses to marry Ryder, breaks off the proposed marriage, and, we are to understand, returns to the religion of her parents. Ryder, an agnostic, is impressed and begins to take an interest in religion. When the war breaks out the old home is taken over by the military. A rather conventional romance.

Such a summary, like all summaries, cannot, of course, even remotely suggest the manner in which Waugh has treated his story, or the sort of life he has infused into these bare bones: it does help to define a subject which a dozen writers might treat in a dozen different ways. But Waugh has written his story in a mood of such nostalgic heart-ache for old things passing or passed away, in a style so tender and fondling, given his chief characters such picturesque backgrounds and so much inherited wealth and traditional grace that one could not quarrel, even while one winced, with Miss Rose Macaulay's choice of the word "lushness" to describe the general effect of surfeit. It would be unjust not to say that he also showed that he possessed hitherto unexpected technical resources for the handling of extended scenes and complex moods: to give only one instance, the swift sketching-in of Ryder's relationship with his wife, and the unstated but clearly felt suggestion of his own state of mind at the beginning of Book Two is a masterly development of the old quickie technique of disconnected snapshots. Indeed the chief development in this novel is from disjunction to smoothness — perhaps too much smoothness. Yet, technique apart, how much of his treatment of the essential subject amounts to unessential trappings! It is quite irrelevant, to give a dozen examples, that

young Flyte is Lord Sebastian Flyte; that he is a lovely, epicene young man
of the Nineties with engagingly eccentric ways, such as his devotion to his
teddy-bear Aloysius; that he and Ryder meet amid the golden glories of
Oxford; that his father is a marquis, his home a beautiful country house,
and that he lives now with an Italian mistress in a Venetian palace; that
Julia is Lady Julia, or that she marries 'a man who becomes a Cabinet
Minister; that her love affair with Ryder begins aboard a liner, First Class,
during a storm, in the environment of roses, masseuse-oil and champagne;
that Lord Sebastian becomes a dipsomaniac not among the pubs of
Camden Town but in the low dives of Fez. All this is romantic embroidery;
a harmless pleasure for the reader, just as it is a pleasure to listen to well-
bred people talking in a well-dressed play about something else besides the
mist that does be on the bog, or fish-and-chips or Rearmament, moral or
otherwise. But when we have passed through these accidentals to what
seems at first sight to be the core of the novel, its insistently pervasive
Catholicism, it is with a shock of dismay that we gradually realise that this
is the most irrelevant accidental of all. In fact, if I may be permitted to
give my own personal reaction to the novel as a professing Catholic
(adding in all humility that there may be something wrong with my idea
of Catholicism), I fail to see why the book could not have been equally
well written — admittedly with a very different setting — by a fervent
Congregationalist. Had, for instance, the author of *Mark Rutherford's
Autobiography* written *Brideshead Revisited* as *Tanner's Lane Revisited*
we might not only have been just as impressed, but perhaps more deeply
impressed had he done with it what he did with the *Autobiography*, that
is, turned the accidental or immediate subject of his inherited faith into
the universal theme of any man's struggles and tensions with any religious
dogma whatsoever. This seems to be the essential question. Does Waugh
universalise his theme, or does he move within an enclosed and exclusive
circle of very limited appeal?

What is his theme? If it is that there is no happiness on earth without
God no member of any theistic religion would deny it. If it is that God
lures us back to him by ways obscure and strange a Mohammedan would
not deny it. If it is the "twitch on the thread" which can pull men back
from the ends of the earth, from the deepest jungles of indifference and
vice to the ways of virtue, the validity of the observation is almost
devastatingly universal. It applies to so many pulls, such as patriotism and
love. It may, for all one knows, work powerfully with the Salvation Army.
Any novel dealing with any of these themes, and they all occur in
Brideshead Revisited, must, if it proposes to show how they operate inside
one particular religion, throw a piercing light on the specific quality,
power and appeal of that religion, or show them operating in such a way
as to impress equally an atheist, an agnostic or a member of any Church in
the world. Otherwise, obviously, its appeal is not universal. My feeling is
that Waugh has not fully succeeded in doing either of these things, and for

the reason I have stated—that he has abandoned his detachment, to which I would here add that he has abandoned it through an excess of loyalty. For the first, would, say, a Mohammedan reading the novel understand the power and the appeal of Catholicism? He would certainly have to acknowledge its power, since it is so clearly stated—which is not the same thing as to understand it. Its emotional appeal he could not possibly understand. Even I, who happen to be a Catholic, fail to see the appeal of any such religion as is here depicted, if for no other reason than that it has brought the minimum of happiness to the maximum number of people; and I do not speak of happiness in a wordly sense. Nor can it be argued that the lives of the Marquis, Lord Sebastian or Lady Julia show that if Catholics are unhappy it is only because they do not practise their religion. The mother is a devout Catholic: she appears throughout as a most melancholy woman who is hated by her husband and who has driven her son to drink. Her elder son, Brideshead, also a devout Catholic, is as sombre a figure as one would willingly take a day's march to avoid. To Cordelia, the younger daughter, religion is indeed a tower of strength and consolation and our Mohammedan reader must feel that a faith so powerful to console and bestow inner joy is something to envy. But the most contented person of all is Cara, the mistress of the Marquis, who has learned in the light-hearted Italian way to wear her religion easily and rely on the infinite goodness of God. If Mr Waugh were writing propaganda for the Catholic church she is the woman most likely of all to convert our heathen friend. (Why does everybody who writes about religion concentrate on being miserable abut it?)

The theme, as we have seen, is universally valid; the treatment is not. In effect it is reduced from godliness to obedience. Consider the turning-point in the whole story, which is centrally the story of Charles Ryder and Julia Flyte. It occurs when Brideshead is telling Ryder and his sister of his intention to marry a Catholic widow; referring to his sister's marriage, outside the church, to the divorced Canadian Rex Mottram, he says roughly that his future wife would not possibly live in the same house as Julia: "It is a matter of indifference whether you choose to live in sin with Rex or Charles or both—I have always avoided inquiry into the details of your *ménage*—but in no case would Beryl consent to be your guest." The result of this bombshell is a harrowing emotional outbreak from Julia in a long speech delivered to Ryder, alone, on the subject of her sin:

> "All in one word, too, one little flat, deadly word that covers a lifetime.
>
> " 'Living in sin'; not just doing wrong, as I did when I went to America; doing wrong, knowing it is wrong, stopping doing it, forgetting. That's not what they mean. That's not Bridey's pennyworth. He means just what it says in black and white.
>
> "Living in sin, with sin, by sin, for sin, every hour, every day, year in and year out. Waking up with sin in the morning, slipping diamonds

to it, feeding it, showing it round, giving it a good time, putting it to sleep at night with a tablet of Dial if its [sic] fretful.
"Always the same, like an idiot child carefully nursed, guarded from the world. 'Poor Julia,' they say, 'she can't go out. She's got to take care of her little sin. A pity it ever lived,' they say, 'but it's so strong. Children like that always are. Julia's so good to her little, mad sin.' "

Then her speech rises to a wild threnody for Christ dying with her sin, over the bed in the night-nursery, in the dark little study at Farm Street with the shining oil-cloth, in dark churches where the charwoman's brush is raising dust and one candle burns; and so on to the thought of a never-to-be-comforted Christ, a Christ never given shelter, always hanging there, outcast, a Citizen of the bare stone and the dust and the smouldering dumps, thrown away there, poked at after nightfall by an old man with lupus carrying a forked stick, "nameless and dead, like the baby they wrapped up and carried away before I had seen her." The scene ends with her lashing her agnostic lover across the face with a switch because he has said something that she thinks stupid and lacking in sympathy and understanding. It is a painful and impressive scene. Yet, what was this frightful sin? To everybody except to Roman Catholics or High Anglicans divorce is specifically a Roman Catholic sin; a sin of disobedience; a theological sin; a sin against the Council of Trent; a sin argued about over many centuries; an institutional sin; a club sin. They will feel deeply for Julia, but they will also feel like outsiders looking in. They must feel this even more during those long, professional arguments, at the end, when Marchmain is dying, about the efficacy of Extreme Unction for a semi-conscious, if not virtually unconscious, man.

A religious theme given institutional treatment is always liable to get lost in the embroidered folds of ecclesiasticism; and so is the author. The old detachment is sold to loyalty, and while one admires loyalty there is no place for it in art, just as there is no place for it in philosophy — or for that matter in mathematics. The team-spirit breeds loyalty, but artists and philosophers (and mathematicians) do not work in teams. In reading *Brideshead* one wrings one's hand when Waugh's loyalty to the aristocratic spirit makes him say of the family history given to Ryder by Lady Marchmain — a "family history typical of the Catholic squires of England": "These men must die to make a world for Hooper; they were the aborigines, vermin by right of law, to be shot off at leisure so that things might be safe for the travelling salesman, with his polygonal pince-nez, his fat wet hand-shake, his grinning dentures" — Hooper being the harmless representative in this novel of the cruder post-war world nowadays satirised by writers like Mr John Wain and Mr Kingsley Amis. The point is not that one disagrees or agrees with Waugh abut the superiority of the Catholic squires of England to the non-Catholic salesmen of England; the point is that this is not the snarling way for any man of letters, least of all for so gifted a satirist, to make any point whatever. One must only feel that in *Brideshead*, whether dealing with Church or class, Waugh has allowed himself to be drawn into the whirlpool of his subject. He became his own Undine, killing with a kiss. The moralist, losing his detached standpoint, died, and so did his satire. Where the changeling Waugh went to nobody knows, but he cannot really be far away: he has returned with *The Loved One* and some splendid sequences in his last two novels.

Yet, here again loyalties dominate, and he is again arguing against himself. His natural, instinctive, inherited position was that those same times which destroyed the traditional nobility eliminated the traditional hero. Hungry for both, he has concentrated in *Men at Arms* and *Officers and Gentlemen* on the professional hero (as in *Brideshead* on the professional Catholic) who is, it is quite true, a well-known and highly-valued type in the British Army: the well-bred, utterly loyal, utterly fearless Catholic public-schoolman. Apart from the fact that the area is once again as enclosed and circumscribed as a Henty novel, Waugh's loyalty in response to loyalty is seen to be patiently excessive and destructive of detachment by the fact that all his wealth of satire is reserved for commoners and there is not a glimmer of humour in his picture of Guy Crouchback, who by a shift of angle, such as Stendhal commanded, must appear as a character with endless comic possibilities. It does not even seem to occur to him that from the point of view, and in the language of Crouchback's fellow-officers and superiors, he must have often appeared as a pain-in-the-neck. It must be although there is room and room enough for humour on the subject of loyalty, humour is another one of those pursuits in which there is no room for loyalty. But few humorists have a sense of humour about everything. Most have no sense of humour about themselves.

Waugh is a writer of a purely brainless genius, which he has amplified by the possession or development of enormous technical skill. He was born with the natural gift for satire. His satires will probably live as long as literature lasts. And he has written seven of them! What an achievement that is one may realise by trying to think offhand of seven other comic novels by seven other individual English writers. Being a man of genius he should never, under any circumstances, have opinions, for whenever he has written out of his opinions it becomes all too plain all over again that imagination is a soaring gull and opinions no more than a gaggle of ungainly starlings, chattering angrily on a cornfield. Opinions breed anger, nourish hate, ossify the heart, narrow the mind.

> An intellectual hatred is the worst,
> So let her think opinions are accursed.
> Have I not seen the loveliest woman born
> Out of the mouth of Plenty's horn,
> Because of her opinionated mind

Barter that horn and every good
By quiet natures understood
For an old bellows full of angry wind?

He has what Yeats wished for his daughter, a "radical innocence . . . self-delighting, self-appeasing, self-affrighting." He did not receive it from ancestry, or from this class or that, from church or university; he did not build it out of ideas, or theories. It is one of Nature's primal gifts. But it can be lost, and it can commit suicide. It can poison itself. Thinking is pure poison to innocence. Huxley who never knew innocence thrives on thought. Waugh? One recalls what Cocteau said of Mistinguette, that she magnificently reversed Descartes's *Cogito, ergo sum* into *Mais je ne pense jamais! Donc je suis!*

The Wall and the Jungle: The Early Novels of Evelyn Waugh

Alvin B. Kernan*

In Evelyn Waugh's novel *Helena*, Constantius, father of the future Roman emperor Constantine, rides with his bride Helena, later St. Helena the discoverer of the true cross, along the rough Roman wall which separates Gaul from Germany, forming the outermost defense of the City of Rome. He explains to Helena the meaning of the wall: "Think of it, mile upon mile, from snow to desert, a single great girdle round the civilized world; inside, peace, decency, the law, the altars of the Gods, industry, the arts, order; outside, wild beasts and savages, forest and swamp, bloody mumbo-jumbo, men like wolf-packs; and along the wall the armed might of the Empire, sleepless, holding the line. Doesn't it make you see what the City means?" On one side of a guarded wall, barbarism, on the other, civilization; on one side animals, on the other social man; on one side the jungle, on the other The City; on one side chaos, on the other order. This speech renders in geographical terms a master image of life which underlies most of Waugh's novels. In this hard-headed, classical view of life the powers which threaten civilization are ineradicable, and the opposing forces are distinctly separated, barbarism and chaos on the outside, civilization and order on the inside, with the ceaselessly manned wall in between. But in the postwar England of the '20s and '30s, the basic scene of Waugh's first four satiric novels—*Decline and Fall* (1928), *Vile Bodies* (1930), *Black Mischief* (1932), and *A Handful of Dust* (1934)—the walls have already been broached and the jungle powers were at work within The City.

*Reprinted from the *Yale Review* 43 (1963 / 64): 199–220, by permission of the journal, © Yale University.

Decline and Fall, his first novel, opens with a night brawl in the quadrangle of Scone College, Oxford. High up in the walls of the College sit the remaining defenders of order, education, and tradition — the Junior Dean, Mr. Sniggs, and the Domestic Bursar, Mr. Postlethwaite. Their lights are extinguished so that they will not be seen by the rioting members of the Bollinger Club holding their annual meeting. From below in the darkness comes the shrill sound of the "English county families baying for broken glass," and out into the quad dressed in bottle-green evening coats rush the members of the Boller, "epileptic royalty from their villas of exile; uncouth peers from crumbling country seats; smooth young men of uncertain tastes from embassies and legations; illiterate lairds from wet granite hovels in the Highlands; ambitious young barristers and Conservative candidates torn from the London season and the indelicate advances of debutantes." Savagely drunk, they break up a grand piano, smash a china collection, throw a Matisse into a waterjug, and have "great fun" with the manuscript of a Newdigate Prize Poem found in an undergraduate's room, and round off their evening by debagging and throwing into a fountain a passing student whose school tie happens to resemble that of the Bollinger Club. Above, the two dons creep to the window, peer out, and anticipate huge fines, which will provide a week of Founder's port for the senior common room. The Junior Dean, hoping for even larger fines, prays, "Oh, please God, make them attack the Chapel," but unfortunately the members of the Boller begin to get sick and pass out. Next day authority reasserts itself with all its pomp and ceremony: in solemn assembly the officers of Scone fine the undergraduate members of the Bollinger Club, insuring Founder's port for the high table, and send down the young man who was debagged for indecent behavior with the awesome words, "That sort of young man does the College no good."

Nearly every scene in Waugh's satirical novels is built on the pattern of the Scone College scene. When an actual wall appears, its form and history betray its inability to hold out the forces of barbarism. The machiolated, towered, and turreted wall — with workable portcullis — around Llanabba Castle in *Decline and Fall* was built by unemployed mill workers during the cotton famine of the 1860s. The ladies of the house were upset by the thought of the men starving and went so far as to hold a charity bazaar to raise money for relief; the husband, a Lancashire millowner influenced by the Liberal economics, was equally upset by the thought of giving the men money "without due return." Sentimentality and enlightened self-interest were both neatly satisfied by putting the men to work on the wall. "A great deal of work was done very cheaply," and the Victorian taste for the romantic was satisfied by the neo-Gothic character of the construction which transformed plain Llanabba House into Llanabba Castle. The shabby, self-satisfied, and self-glorifying attitudes which caused the wall to be built were merely degraded remnants of older, more meaningful beliefs in such values as work and responsibility toward one's workers and fellow men. Already well along the way toward barbarism themselves, these Victorian attitudes offer no real resistance to the forces of destruction, and the wall they built is overwhelmed in the next century when the house becomes a boy's school which shelters every kind of greed, ignorance, and savagery.

While actual stone walls are not always present in Waugh's scenes, the immaterial walls of culture are. The traditions, the social institutions, the ritual language, the buildings, the manners, the morals, the codes of service, the esthetic values, "all that seemingly solid, patiently built, gorgeously ornamented structure of Western Life," are for the classicist like Waugh the walls protecting sense, order, and meaningful life from riot and savagery. One of the major effects of Waugh's writing comes from the ceremonial fullness with which these values are voiced and acted out. Dignified judges speak with timeless authority of the right of society to repress ruthlessly those "human vampires who prey upon the degradation of their species"; earnest custom officials meticulously sift all incoming books to exclude any writings which might affect the moral welfare of the English people; His Britannic Majesty's ministers are sent to far-flung and savage lands to protect truth and justice and show the more unfortunate peoples of the earth the way to civilization; the children destined to rule the nation are sent to ancient public schools where their minds and characters are carefully formed; the inquiring mind presses forward to the discovery of new truths about man and his universe; and social gatherings are enriched with names evoking ancient glory and service, "the fifteenth Marquess of Vanburgh, Earl Vanburgh of Brendon, Lord of the Five Isles and Hereditary Grand Falconer to the Kingdom of Connaught."

All this is, of course, a magnificent, hilarious sham. The judge who defends society with such sonorous certainty is condeming an innocent, powerless man and letting the real criminal go free. The earnest custom officials ferret out and burn Dante with the solemn warning that "if we can't stamp out literature in this country, we can at least stop its being brought in from the outside." The Envoy Extraordinary to Azania has forgotten how to speak all foreign languages, even French, and spends his time in the legation bathtub playing with rubber animals. A new master at a public school who asks what he should try to teach the boys is handed a heavy stick and told, "Oh, I shouldn't try to *teach* anything, not just yet, anyway. Just keep them quiet." Scientific inquiry continues its onward march with such inventions as the Huxdane-Hallay bomb, "for the dissemination of leprosy germs," and the spirit of Mill and Darwin descends to the sociologist Sir Wilfred Lucas-Dockery, the warden of Blackstone Gaol, who theorizes that men become criminals because of thwarted creative instincts: putting his theory to practice he provides a mad prisoner with a set of carpenter's tools, which the victim of thwarted creative instincts at once uses to cut off the Chaplain's head. The

Hereditary Grand Falconer to the Kingdom of Connaught turns out to be a gossip columnist for *The Daily Beast*.

Waugh has frequently been accused of being a snob and deadly conservative, but in fact he treats the representatives of the old order as savagely as he does the new barbarians. He defends tradition, not the *status quo*; social order, not the establishment. The standards against which his fools are measured and found to be fools is not, in his early novels, located in any individual but in the values and social forms to which his characters without knowing what they are doing still give voice. Waugh is ultimately, like the chief character of *Brideshead Revisited*, a painter of old houses, an architectural painter who arrives to fix in paint the stately old houses of England just before the auctioneer and the demolition crew go to work to make room for shops and modern two-room apartments. And like Charles Ryder, Waugh finds his ultimate values in building, "holding it to be not only the highest achievement of man but one in which, at the moment of consummation, things were most clearly taken out of his hands and perfected, without his intention, by other means." Individual men, on the other hand, are less important, "something much less than the buildings they made and inhabited . . . mere lodgers, and short-term lessees of small importance in the long fruitful life of their homes."

In Waugh's England there is no possibility of eradicating the powers of savagery and dullness which are destroying the old houses and social traditions they symbolize, for the powers are rooted in life itself; and by their very nature they continue to press against the walls and creep between the building stones of old houses as persistently as the lush vegetation of jungle — to which they are frequently compared — edges in to tear apart the building stones and choke the streets of abandoned cities. The most fundamental of these powers is a deeply ingrained, apparently indestructible tendency in man himself toward disorder, anarchy, and violence — toward those tendencies which Pope summed up as dullness. At times these dark powers appear undisguised in cannibal feast, jungle dances, savage riots and battlefields. But even in the great cities of the West the sounds of this ancient anarchy are always in the background, like the jungle drums which always beat in the hills just outside the city of Debra Dowa where the Emperor Seth in *Black Mischief* attempts to create a modern state. It appears, only slightly disguised, as the insane and murderous carpenter. It is the epileptic royalty, savage lairds, and ruthless politicians of the Bollinger Club. Or it may take shape as the random sexuality of Brenda Last or the charming ruthlessness of a "howling cad" like Basil Seal, the brutality of a Colonel MacAdder or a General Strapper, the deviations of Miles Malpractice and Mrs. Panrast, and the far-flung operations of the Latin American Entertainment Company, Ltd., Lady Metroland's efficient chain of South American brothels. Nature is seldom more beneficent than man, and the destructive powers in humanity have their natural correspondents in the nervous horse which kicks to death a small boy on his first hunt, the battering sea which the travelers cross at the opening of *Vile Bodies*, and the malarial mosquito which destroys Tony Last's chance of escape from the jungles of Brazil in *Handful of Dust*. Waugh's world is, in short, one in which life and order are threatened constantly from within and without.

No one who lives in this world takes it for anything other than familiar, secure Old England. But the pretenses are stripped away, unknowingly of course, by the Christmas sermon of an addled minister who somehow forgets that he is no longer the chaplain of a regiment on foreign service:

> "How difficult it is for us . . . to realize that this is Christmas. Instead of the glowing log fire and windows tight shuttered against the drifting snow, we have only the harsh glare of an alien sun; instead of the happy circle of loved faces, of home and family, we have the uncomprehending stares of the subjugate, though no doubt grateful, heathen. Instead of the placid ox and ass of Bethlehem . . . we have for companions the ravening tiger and the exotic camel, the furtive jackal and the ponderous elephant. . . ."

The clergyman speaks with a peculiar kind of emptiness created by the absence of both heart and mind. The emptiness first appears in Waugh's novels as an extreme form of traditional English reticence, then expands to the point demanded by caricature; great voids are gradually opened up behind the foreheads and in the hearts of the dramatis personae. They have no private minds, no intense feelings whatsoever; no personality, no individuality—whatever we call that reality of self which has been the subject of most of the writing of our age. As we encounter character after character of this kind, the world of the satiric novels slowly fills with automatons composed of ready-made, fashionable phrases. Their names tell us all there is to know about them: Lady Circumference and her son little Lord Tangent, the Earl of Pastmaster, Paul Pennyfeather, Lord Maltravers, the Minister of Transportation, Basil Seal, Agatha Runcible.

The use of type characters is, of course, common in satire, for the satirist is never interested in deep explorations of human nature. His characters are merely personifications of the particular form of dullness to which he wishes to give visible shape. But what in some satirists is an artistic device for getting dullness out into the open by disentangling it from the complexities of real character becomes in Waugh realism of sorts. He sings the rich, the powerful, the fashionable, and the fortunate; and he shows them to be as stiff, empty, and mechanical as fictive abstractions. On the rare occasions when there are hints that a character is feeling or thinking it comes as a great surprise to both character and reader. Who would have thought that the butterfly Agatha Runcible in *Vile Bodies* had any mind to lose? Or that Simon Balcairn, the aristocrat turned gossip columnist in the same novel, could have felt enough despair to make suicide necessary? Even when such actions establish a rudimentary mind or heart, the thought and emotions which emerge have a primitive, childlike quality, as if the owners were completely unused to such functions as thinking and feeling.

This all-pervasive simplicity and mindlessness is the principal cause of the trouble in Waugh's satiric world. What hope for the future when the full exercise of intellect in one of the leading politicians of the country, Lord Metroland, results only in such "hand-to-mouth thinking" as this? He has been told at a party that the mad antics of the younger generation result from a "radical instability" in the country. Somewhat puzzled and concerned he returns to his mansion to find his drunken stepson, Peter Pastmaster, fumbling with the lock. To his greeting Peter's only answer, repeated several times, is "Oh, go to hell." Seeing a tall hat on the table by the door, Metroland concludes that it belongs to his wife's lover, Alastair Digby-Vaine-Trumpington, and goes into the study because "it would be awkward if he met young Trumpington on the stairs." Once in his study he surveys the familiar details: the businesslike arrangement of the furniture, the solid green safe with the brass handle, and the rows of comforting books which promise knowledge and security: *Who's Who*, the *Encyclopedia Britanica, Debrett, the Dictionary of National Biography*. These reassure him greatly, and when he hears Trumpington leaving he says to himself, "radical instability indeed," and goes upstairs to his beautiful aristocratic wife, whose wealth comes from the operation of a chain of South American brothels.

Such vacuity—and Metroland is a *thinker* compared to most of Waugh's characters—justifies Waugh's unstated but insistent argument that a meaningful society can only be one which follows and defends strenuously some traditional pattern of belief and value. If people cannot reason clearly or feel deeply—and there is no indication in Waugh's novel that the majority of them ever could—then their only hope of a full and valuable life is to follow the traditions evolved during the long course of trial and error which is human history. Leave man, individual man, to decide on his own values, throw him into a relativistic world in which nothing is certain, corrupt the traditional institutions and ways of doing things so that no honest man can believe in them, and the result will be, as Waugh regularly shows, confusion, self-defeat, the grotesque distortion of human nature, and frantic but meaningless activity.

It is the arrangement of incidents and the overall pattern of events—plot—which ultimately establish the "meaning" in Waugh's novels. Like most satires, they lack a conventional story, intricately contrived and carefully followed. The sporadic attempts of two young people to get married, a picaresque ramble through English society, occasional references to the decay of a marriage, these and other such devices loosely bind the incidents together. But the books are not constructed around these plot lines, for what in more conventionally constructed novels would be the main story appears only now and then. When it does the situation will often have changed considerably since its last appearance, but no explanation is offered of how these changes came about. The effect is of something "just happening," of a discontinuity through which some unknown and unidentifiable power is working to force matters to a disastrous conclusion.

The major portion of the satires is composed of a series of brief and apparently unrelated episodes which flash on the pages in the manner of scenes from a newsreel. A scene in a fashionable London restaurant will be followed by a meal in the African or Brazilian jungles; a business journey will be interrupted by a long, carefully reported conversation between two women — neither of whom we have ever seen before or see again — about a recent scandal at Ten Downing Street. Events at a boys' school will give way to a discussion of modern architecture by a Professor Otto Silenus. Even when Waugh follows for a considerable length of time the adventures of the same characters, they will move at random from watching a movie being made, to a party, to an automobile race, stopping along the way to have a number of drinks, look for a hotel room, drive through a slum in the industrial Midlands. Then the scene flickers to another setting and we are watching the ridiculous pretensions of a sister in a fashionable nursing home, listening to a gossip columnist telephone his editor, and hearing about a young boy who fell out of an airplane.

By some standards Waugh would appear to have put his novels together very badly, but he is, of course, reproducing in his arrangement of scenes and his handling of time the chaotic, frenetic, disconnected movements of modern life. Only a true culture, not a disintegrating one, can have an Aristotelian plot in which one event follows inevitably from another and the whole is composed of a beginning, a middle, and an end. But randomness and disorganization are only surface effects. Each of the episodes is thematically related to the others with which it is in sequence. All show in different terms the assault of appetite and stupidity, the ravening tiger and the ponderous elephant, on the old beliefs and ways of life, and the consequent meaninglessness. The scenes are carefully arranged so that one scene defines its neighbors: an episode of polite savagery in London is juxtaposed to a scene of overt savagery in the jungle, or a description of an ultra-modern house built for machines rather than men borders on a party scene in which fashionable men and women move in a pattern of conditioned responses and respond to every new situation with the predictability of a machine.

Satire regularly offers not a still, quiet world but a busy, bustling one in which crowds of men race furiously about pursing some *ignis fatuus*. In Waugh's satires railway lines are thrown across primitive wastes, huge business empires are in ceaseless movement creating new products and searching for new markets, busy factories cover the landscape, and cars race madly about the roads. Solemn, serious politicians, educators, clergymen, financiers, and men of affairs move confidently forward on the path of change, progress, and enlightened self-interest. The disillusioned younger generation rushes restlessly about in search of pleasure and something new in life. Amiable rogues endlessly move on looking for new amusements and more profitable deals. This is, on the surface, the humming, vigorous world of the twentieth century, the era of ceaseless change and inevitable progress. But all this movement is illusory, for in Waugh's world, as in Carroll's Wonderland, "it takes all the running you can do to keep in the same place."

What in fact happens in Waugh's novels is that all the running produces only circular movement — the second of the patterns Swift shows to result from self-delusive flights, overreaching fancy, which go "like one who travels the East into West; or like a strait line drawn by its own length into a Circle." The circle has been in the past a figure of perfection, but it has also been, as it is in Dante's *Inferno*, the figure of empty, meaningless movement, of eternal hunger which never finds satisfaction or rest. It is in the "infernal" sense that circularity appears in Waugh. It is the pattern of aimless, self-defeating life, the natural movement of the jungle and the savage:

> Dancing was resumed, faster this time and more clearly oblivious of fatigue. In emulation of the witch doctors the tribesmen began slashing themselves on chest and arms with their hunting knives; blood and sweat mingled in shining rivulets over their dark skins. Now and then one of them would pitch forward on to his face and lie panting or roll stiff in a nervous seizure. Women joined in the dance, making another chain, circling in the reverse way to the men. They were dazed with drink, stamping themselves into ecstasy. The two chains jostled and combined. They shuffled together interlocked.

The English spectator at this dance draws back dazed from the heat of the fire, the monotonous sound of the drums, and the mind-obliterating circular movement of the dance; but the man of the future, the hypercivilized Professor Otto Silenus, who looks forward to the day when men will be as functional as machines and houses as simple in design as factories, finds the circle the only true image of life:

> "It's like the big wheel at Luna Park. . . . You pay five francs and go into a room with tiers of seats all around, and in the centre the floor is made of polished wood that revolves quickly. At first you sit down and watch the others. They are all trying to sit in the wheel, and they keep getting flung off, and that makes them laugh, and you laugh too. . . . the nearer you can get to the hub of the wheel the slower it is moving and the easier it is to stay on. There's generally someone in the centre who stands up and sometimes does a sort of dance. Often he's paid by

the management though. . . . Of course at the very centre there's a point completely at rest, if one could only find it. . . . Lots of people just enjoy scrambling on and being whisked off and scrambling on again. . . . Then there are others . . . who sit as far out as they can and hold on for dear life. . . . the scrambling and excitement and bumps and the effort to get to the middle, and when we do get to the middle, it's just as if we never started. It's so odd."

The jungle dance and the wheel at Luna Park are the two extremes which meet, primitive past and primitive future, the blood-crazed circling of the stone-age savage and the mechanical construction of a technologically advanced civilization without humane direction. These are the two great images of the hopeless circle in which existence moves in Waugh's world, but the circular pattern appears everywhere. Politics is a circular game. The Right Honourable Walter Outrage M.P. is in one week as Prime Minister and out the next, and it is an attentive man who can tell at any given moment whether Outrage is in or out. The bright young things in search of amusement go to an endless series of parties, parties in hospitals, parties in hotels, masked parties, savage parties, parties in stately old houses, parties in bed, but all parties turn out to be the same party where one hears the same talk and sees the same faces. Waugh's trick, deriving from Thackeray, of having the same people with the same ridiculous names pop up again and again in the most unlikely places makes it appear that it is impossible to break out of this circle of familiars. And when these people do pop up they are always doing the same old things. Lady Metroland is always suggesting to attractive young girls that if they are dissatisfied with their present situation a position can be found for them as entertainers in Buenos Aires. Lord Monomark is still surrounded by several perfect beauties and several sycophants listening to him talk about his latest fad diet. Peter Pastmaster is still drunk, Alastair Digby-Vaine-Trumpington is still drinking, and the mysterious Toby Crutwell — sometime cat burglar, war hero, and M.P. — has still left the party just before we arrived. *The Daily Excess* and *The Daily Beast* are still getting the news wrong, the older generation is still worried about the younger, Parsnip and Pimpernell are still writing left-wing poetry and issuing manifestoes, and Basil Seal is still managing to get money out of someone. . . .

In his description of the revolutionary government of Mexico in the 1930's, *Robbery Under Law*, Waugh remarks that he does not believe that there is any one God-given form of government, but that a government consistent in its principles and dedicated to keeping order is necessary because "given propitious circumstances, men and women who seem quite orderly, will commit every conceivable atrocity. The danger does not come merely from habitual hooligans; we are all potential recruits for anarchy. Unremitting effort is needed to keep men living at peace; there is only a margin left over for experiment however beneficent." Lacking *consistent* principles and failing to keep the peace results in those meaningless, endless circles around which his characters run in his novels. Once the boundaries, the rules, and the markers are destroyed, as they are at the Llanabba races, then the rational judgment no longer has a framework within which to locate and identify things, and the purpose of human effort is lost. Cupidity, pride, stupidity, and cunning are loosed to complete the wreckage of order and obliterate the meaning of any dimly remembered purpose. However, running round and round until tea time and the arrival of the most important guest was no doubt the best possible training for boys about to enter the giddy whirl of Waugh's world where all rules are off, all the markers gone, all races shams because there is no longer any sense of being a "creature with a defined purpose."

Quelling the Riot:
Evelyn Waugh's Progress   Herbert Howarth*

The critics who lit with pleasure at Evelyn Waugh's earliest novels anticipated a rake's progress; he gave them a pilgrim's. Their praises became a little rueful; and he listened without self-deception. Introducing a new edition of A Handful of Dust thirty years after its first appearance he remarked, "This book found favour with the critics who date my decline from it." Much as they admired the grim pages they mourned the extinction of the iconoclastic inventions and the quick, exhilarating prose of its predecessors: "You grow correct, that once with Rapture writ, / And are, besides, too moral for a Wit." Decline and fall, indeed! But did Waugh's contemporaries see his work quite clearly? A year or two after his death it already looks different. This essay is an attempt to retrace his path, to understand certain conditions of his journey, and to honour the persistence with which, against recurrent problems, he stuck to his course.

In rebound from a war a society jettisons the values of the world which produced and permitted the holocaust. The twenties were years of rebound. In Germany they were years of brilliant riot (creative but eventually disastrous). In England something less. The mood, says Ford Madox Ford, remembering the maroons which signalled the armistice of autumn, 1918, was "No more respect . . . For the Equator! For the Metric system! For Sir Walter Scott! For George Washington! Or Abraham Lincoln! Or the Seventh Commandment!" It was a mere foretaste of the Berlin-rivalling England to ensue on the Second World War (brilliantly

*"Quelling the Riot: Evelyn Waugh's Progress" by Herbert Howarth was reprinted from The Shapeless God: Essays on Modern Fiction, Harry J. Mooney, Jr. and Thomas F. Staley, editors. Published in 1968 by the University of Pittsburgh Press. Used by permission.

creative, in peril of disaster; to be saved, we hope, by a ballast of sanity). But a group of wealthy and titled fledglings, beaux and sylphs, in London, Oxford, and Cambridge, made a bid for a semblance, a lustrous fake, of anarchy. And in the arts there briefly flourished an attempt like theirs to thrive without an interior, to be rippling surface. Examples are the social-occasion stories with which Eliot and Vivienne Eliot experimented in the *Criterion*; the early novels of Aldous Huxley; and Evelyn Waugh's first two novels, which came at the end of the decade and only just in time before the masquing lost momentum and a new seriousness arrived.

Early Waugh is elegant as Pope, grotesque as Smollett, morning-brisk as Prokofiev. *Decline and Fall* is Waugh's *Rape of the Lock*: it mocks the follies of the crush, yet is bright with the privilege of participation. Liberated by the day's madness, the freebooter overplot sprints forward; is checked, in parody of the eighteenth-century novelists, by a fantastic narration, but this is rapid too; and sprints forward again. Dialogue and commentary are close-pruned. Recall the tale after twenty years, and you may think that Waugh indulges himself here and there: that he saunters *andantino grazioso* from Berkeley Square up Hay Hill to Dover Street. Refresh your memory from the text, and you find that the effect is accomplished with five direct sentences, four of them factual. Out of taut prose Waugh distils a lyric suggestion that life is gay—liable to abrupt punctuation, but gay.

In a book where fantasy runs free it is easy to find Waugh's "permanent images." Montaged over Paul's reflections in prison—his half-regret at taking the rap for Margot Beste-Chetwynde, his half-satisfaction—is Waugh's image of beauty. Margot is beautiful. Would Paul have wished to see her scrubbing in the prison-laundry for the sake of mere justice? "As he studied Margot's photograph . . . he was strengthened in the belief that there was, in fact, and should be, one law for her and another for himself, and that the raw little exertions of nineteenth-century Radicals were essentially base and trivial and misdirected." In 1928 this seemed a youthful caper, part of the anti-value riot, a squib under the throne of humanitarianism. It firmed into an attitude: beauty is a joy forever; beauty must come first; all things broken and ugly and all people broken and ugly, must be swept out of the way. Preserve Marie Antionette, and let the mob starve. I assume that we know all that can be felt and said against this. But we may respect the man who comes out fighting for it. Waugh fights for it: — against our humanitarian phalanx, and against an opposition he may dread more: the teaching of his Church. This is one of the problems of his journey.

The air of *Decline and Fall* is astringently sunlit. In *Vile Bodies*, for all the piquant episodes, there is a darkening: crepitation of storm, London fog, the coming war. Eliot, whose poems had seized Waugh at Oxford, whom he repeatedly quotes or echoes, and with whose path his journey crisscrosses, has said that under the sheen of the parties and ragtime lay a corrosive ennui. "*What a lot of parties*," Waugh now says, "... all that succession and repetition of massed humanity. . . . Those vile bodies." The nausea and shadow are symptoms of an invading moral sense.

In 1930, three years after Eliot, harried by freedom, took sanctuary in the Anglican Church, Waugh was received into the Roman Catholic Church. In England the Roman was for three centuries an oppressed Church; and her English members still have the awareness of a minority, and the pride, to which they are entitled, of having borne and outstayed the years of disadvantage. Waugh, by nature addicted, and by Oxford encouraged, to lonely causes and the joy of fighting against odds, yet conservative, and dismayed by fragmentation and chaos, found a double fulfilment in conversion: as a Roman Catholic he fused with a world-body and became concentric and at peace, and as an English Roman Catholic he appeared to family, friends, and to that public whom he regarded as the Mob and whose faces he hardly distinguished, as eccentric and militant.

The next novel, *Black Mischief* of 1932, is a battleground between two Waughs: the man with a new Catholic life; another unregenerate Waugh, the fiercer for the submission of his counterpart. Not that the Catholic Waugh overtly presents his faith, in this extravaganza. There is only one momentary manifestation of the "neo-Catholic novel": a Canadian priest, muscular, red-bearded, cigar-smoking, straight-talking and "occupied in shaking almost to death the brigade sergeant-major of the Imperial Guard." He is a tentative towards the new image of the Roman priest, such as Ford Madox Ford had beautifully sketched in Father Consett in *Parade's End* and Graham Greene was to perfect in several variations (an image to erase and replace the fearsome image of Rome current among nineteenth-century English non-Catholics). The plot, however, is shaped to serve the faith. Barbaric Azania, void of loyalty, cannibalistic, is the type of the world without a Western Church. But movements from the deep drive against the flow of the story. Inmost Africa — which, like Gide and Malraux, like Greene and van der Post, he has gone exploring (let Eliot read Frazer at home and scent the ritual in Stravinsky's theatre, these have taken their anthropology on their own hides) — is an inmost part of Waugh. Penitent at Rome, Augustan at his desk, he yet sits in the drumming circle and dips into the cauldron, consumes the scrap of marrow and digests the victim's mana. Basil Seal, who comes into literature with this book, is an amphibian from the undertow of Waugh's psyche. A "corker" in good looks and masculine endowment, hard-drinker, brawler, manipulator of many languages, every etiquette, every know-how, Basil Seal is the continuation of the world-anarchy of the twenties and Waugh's personal anarchy: an aggressive, ruthless, refusal to conform which is at the core of his nature, and which lashes out of the depths in sudden farcical fury at his conscious obedience to a civilizing Church.

His truculent and wilful resistance to the norms of his day, and a special pleasure in offending the liberal and the humanitarian, find some outlet in almost every book. A phrase in *Black Mischief* will illustrate. Out of the hills, where, reversing the expectations into which the first chapter has decoyed us, he has won Seth's battle, and therefore at this moment a kind of hero, comes General Connolly. He was a stocky Irishman, says Waugh, and then tosses his curriculum at us: ". . . service in the Black and Tans. . . ." Name of obloquy! Approve it or not, Waugh seems to challenge, toughness makes a better man than *bonne volonté*. There is more than a touch of Kipling in the paragraph. Where everyone else has conspired to sell or desert Seth, the white General has stood fast. Waugh deliberately dons imperialism and other untimely codes, and wears them with defiance.

But with the writing of *Black Mischief* and the nightmare of "The Man Who Liked Dickens," the protesting anarchists in him were for the while played out and placated. He turned to a moral work. *A Handful of Dust* is one of those searingly anaphrodisiac dramas to which Eliot's *Waste Land* gave rise (and the genealogy is the clearer for Waugh's title). It lists the whimsical and unnecessary steps by which Brenda Last gets into adultery, the absurdity of her interest in a clod, his predatory motives for getting in, and then for getting out, the spiralling of her passion till, at the apex of Waugh's predication (which is nothing but succinct reporting), she thanks God that her child is dead and not her lover. The terseness heightens the horror, suggests the concentrated strength of that disgust at vile bodies which stirred in the phrase of 1930. The bodies of 1934 are his friends of 1928 and 1930; they play their adulteries in the restaurants, parties, and flats where he formerly found amusement. There is no perfume in Metroland for the Waugh of this book.

Delight has moved to the country. Tony Last is "madly feudal." His roots — with all the organic vitality of that metaphor — are in his family home, Hetton. His thoughts and his money are devoted to maintaining it, to maintaining its servants and pensioners, to keeping it intact for the family in the future. From the aberrant Brenda he accepts every injury and imposition until he learns that she requires him to sell Hetton. Then the worm turns. Waugh has deployed his pieces, as a novelist traditionally may, so that the reader, up to this moment enraged by the accumulating successes of adultery, is elated that the adulterers get their come-uppance and is lifted on the wave of sentiment we call "wanting to cheer." But: *we are glad that Tony Last defends himself; Waugh* is glad that he defends *the house.* Waugh has adopted what will henceforward be a principal position: the great English house, which, if it is not now a Catholic house, must have been so in the past, is both the embodiment of beauty and the repository of tradition and faith.

As a social ideology, in fact as "Young England," feudal England has been the habitat of some good writers for a hundred and twenty five years since Disraeli by a sense of opportunity and an imaginative flare-up plied the reveries of Lord John Matters into *Coningsby* and *Sybil*. Against the avaricious competitive commercialism of his day, and the hard-heartedness of the Liberal creed of work, Manners dreamed of a stable noncompetitive order: the classes graded, but the grades interdependent; and the higher a man's rank the more onerous his responsibilities to the ranks below. In his plan men would relate not to the distant capital city but to a great house, the manor of the mediaeval organization; and the lord or magnate must live constantly in his house, *visibly* fulfilling his duties to his district and radiating life from his central presence. This legend, this doctrine (it is more than the one and less than the other), burgeoned in minds well aware that the Middle Ages were sweetened by distance and Sir Walter Scott, but in love with the idea of reciprocal decency. It has intertwined, though not by any official cultivation, with the thought of the revived Roman Church in England. It is an important constituent of the neo-Catholic novel, present in the most refined practitioner, Ford Madox Ford, as in the most popular, G.K. Chesterton. When Waugh describes himself in the strenuously crusty opening pages of *Pinfold* as an idiosyncratic Tory, he is slightly mistaken. His Toryism is not idiosyncratic. He is one of the remarkable group descended from Young England. *A Handful of Dust* signals his allegiance. *Brideshead Revisited* and the war trilogy confirm it.

After predication, a nimble turn back to Africa and farce. With *Scoop* at their disposal, it is hard to decide why the critics accused, accuse, Waugh's comedy of dessication. *Scoop* is a spectacular lampoon on the Press and the politicians. It is grotesque in Waugh's Smollett vein, and is counterpoised in Smollett's way by Smollett's sort of insular sentiment. The protagonist, Boot of Boot Magna, is the sentimentalist's English country-gentleman: naive, unworldly, self-effacing, but, once roused by injustice, resolute in retaliation. Tapping out his famous cablegram to smash Dr. Benito and avenge Kätchen, Boot is a light-hearted version of Tony cutting up rough to save the feudal system.

Insular sentiment? Waugh is insular, again and again. It is a part of the reactionary pose (it accords well with the repertoire of attitudes struck by the marvellous father in *Work Suspended*). But just discernible is another Waugh with an extra-insular sensibility. Kätchen's story shows that, even before the forties, when everybody began to hear of statelessness, Waugh knew a little of the out-Europeans, who make their way across the world with no passports but courage and wit. In Graham Greene's hands Kätchen and her prospector husband would have grown to figures of unforgettable pathos. But Greene's special art lies outside Waugh's range; and even if graced with the resources Waugh would not have disturbed the balance of his comedy. But he says just enough, as he works with quick strokes, to lay bare a nerve and infer another tale, a more acrid mood.

Work Suspended, the first two parts of a novel interrupted by the outbreak of war, has a keen beauty. He appears to have been working towards a full-length study of love. The pages in some respects anticipate *Brideshead*; but into *Brideshead*, when the time came to write it, different tones crept, for by then many bridges had been destroyed by war.

Waugh gave up his novel to enlist. Like Guy Crouchback he felt the satisfaction of the opportunity to strike back at "the Modern Age in arms"; and the Basil Seal, the "tough nut," in him saw the chance to emerge cloaked and daggered and live with royal licence the "exhilarating days" of which the dedication of *Officers and Gentlemen* speaks. Though he had suspended a good novel when the events of August 25, 1939, broke up an epoch, and though he could never revert to it, he formed new literary projects within a year. Physical work fertilizes a writer. His brother Alec found it easy to complete a novel during active soldiering in the First War, and easy again when he was with his regiment at the outset of the Second. Evelyn Waugh wrote throughout his service with the Marines and the Commandos.

Put Out More Flags, a sketch-book of England adapting to the struggle during the first year of sparring, is organized on Waugh's favourite binary plan. One object is to graph the first eddies of a new spirit in Britain. The playboys who were tarring Mercury or debagging Paul Pennyfeather, and running the dirigible party or reeling to the Old Hundredth, now one by one find their way to the Commandos. Qualities which had lain unelicited, or which Waugh had not been ready to notice, appear in them. Basil Seal comes to the help of Angela Lyne, drinks chivalrously with her to guard her from over-drinking alone. He marries her with an attractive non-avidity for her wealth. Besides the guts, which we always knew him to have, the appalling Seal discloses a fundamental stratum of decency. That is one tide of the novel. And the counter-tide? Boobyism. Waugh dramatizes the smugness, folly, and blobs of official-dom and its bevy of Sir Josephs. In the earlier books he had occasionally jeered, in *Vile Bodies* at the Premier benignly and the censorship-bent Home Secretary less benignly, in *Scoop* at the sale of titles. He and his friends probably regarded this spoofing as merely convivial. The spoofing of *Put Out More Flags* is, not more purposeful, for it is unlikely that Waugh expected his victims to be changed by it — in fact, the seriousness of the matter shows most in his cynicism, he doubts whether any change can be accomplished — but more deeply-felt: the nation may bumble along in peacetime, but in the emergency of war sanity should take over; whereas he sees insanity and complacency on the loose. To say so, with a fitting hyper-fantasy, is the job of a satirist ". . . So proud, I am no Slave: / So impudent, I own myself no Knave: / So odd, my Country's Ruin makes me grave." In the tracks of Pope Waugh has graduated from pleasure to anger. An angry ridicule drives the counter-tide of *Put Out More Flags*;

and it is renewed in the trilogy when Waugh looks back at the six years of military crisis and judges them as a whole.

In the middle of war he turns his gaze to the past, which looks lovelier for the contrast. Parting company now from the Eliot who declared the years of *l'entre deux guerres* largely wasted, he writes *Brideshead Revisited* to commemorate a period of delight; but also to justify its passing. He finishes his manuscript in a mood of authorial bliss. In Algiers he sits before Diana Duff Cooper, as if he were Basil sitting before Sonia, and tells her that he has written his masterpiece. It is evident, from the carefully-conventional similes stitched across the narrative, that he aimed at epic: the epic of the twenty years of social transition to which he was witness.

Later Waugh revolted against the book. Is it not included, and condemned, in the piece of literary history which he slips into *The End of the Battle?*—not quite Ludovic's "very gorgeous, almost gaudy, tale of romance and drama," but almost certainly one of those "books which would turn from drab alleys of the thirties into the odorous gardens of a recent past transformed and illuminated by disordered memory and imagination." And, certainly, Waugh wrote nothing more in the *Brideshead* style. He recoiled to speed and pungency. Evidently he felt that there was fulsomeness in *Brideshead's* nostalgic tone and baroque ornamentation, and that its conservative rhetoric, though apparently proper in a chronicle which describes, and makes us like, the conservative art of Ryder, was peacockish. And he may have felt that sentiment had broken out of its containing form.

At this point a word may be said on Waugh's sentiment in general. Sentiment is not always so vicious as the academies suppose. The Victorians, from Dickens to Louisa May Alcott, did very well with the conglomerations of event and emotion which makes us "laugh and cry." Waugh sometimes practices their sequences, in his own fashion. So does Joyce. Joyce kept in sight a rule of that anti-Dickensian Meredith: "The sentimentalist is he who would enjoy without incurring the immense debtorship for a thing done." Intended as a stricture, the sentence implies, as Joyce saw, a positive corollary: pay the immense debt and you are entitled to the enjoyment. Joyce paid with a lifetime of labour, the intellectuality of his architecture, his own health and his family's (losing parts while he wrote, like Captain Carpenter dropping limbs while he rode). Waugh paid with stylistic severities, structural economy, a ruthless demeanour and illiberal inventions like the Connolly children, by which he made himself to some a public enemy and to himself a poor representative of his religion ("Why does everyone except me find it so easy to be nice?" groans Pinfold). Having paid, he permitted himself a lachryma, a tableau, a carillon, an arabesque of paling stars, but at distant intervals and briefly. They were indulgences which, though he had worked for them honestly, he eyed sternly. He struggled, lifelong, to keep his sentiment prisoner and earn its parole. In *Brideshead* the sentiment ran free and wild. Or so it seemed to him when he eventually looked at the print. Never again!

It is bad taste to like *Brideshead.* I like it. For all its blemishes, the soft places, the pompous antitheses in the Churchill mode, the incredibly unoriginal "epic similes" of kingfisher and Chinese ivory, it moves with a compelling flight. It records a social change, and Waugh's pain for the slipping past, his disgust with a present "where wealth is no longer gorgeous and power has no dignity." It takes up the questions of *A Handful of Dust* again: reconsiders and praises again the great-house and responsible-family values of Young England; resumes and extends the moral study, this time, however, not with a sombre and Puritanical condemnation of Frivolity, but with a voluptuous catalogue of the beauties of house and fountain, wines and food, men and girls, and a testimony to the sweetness of these first gods of his, in virtue of which his renunciation becomes the greater. As Sebastian's story, the subject of *Brideshead* is the making of a saint, and it has a place beside other books of the first half of our century which have the same subject: Ford's *Fifth Queen* and his Tietjens series, Eliot's *Cocktail Party,* Greene's *Power and the Glory* and *A Burnt-Out Case.* As the story of a house and a family, it is a parable of the struggle of England (in whose skies, said the Fifth Queen, the angels weep) for the end of infidelity and the reconnection with faith. As Ryder's story, it is the drama of the artist—George Herbert's drama, for instance, as well as Waugh's—pulled between Beauty and God.

It is horrible and excellent by its repudiation of love. After her marriage to the coarse Rex Mottram and one or two will-o'-the-wisp affairs Julia Brideshead finds passionate love with Ryder. It is a joy. She fights to keep it. She gives it up on the edification of her father's unpredictably religious death. She sends Ryder away. Sends him away because she loves him and while she admits that sooner or later she will be in bed with someone else. But a "jolly-up," as Waugh's Mayfair slang puts it, is superficial and venial. Love for Ryder, standing between her and God, is indefensible. Graham Greene plots *The End of the Affair* in a similar way. In contradistinction to the romantic and market-place dogma, according to which carnality is sanctioned by sincere love, the neo-Catholic novel says that lust does less harm than love, which induces forgetfulness of God. But where there is love, the lover will sooner or later be confronted with a crucial opportunity to foreswear it. Julia lays hold on the opportunity. Ryder leaves Brideshead, telling Julia in his grim to-the-point style that he hopes her heart will break. But he learns that she made the right choice, by which, as the epilogue implies with a neat restraint, he too is directed to God. This is a peculiar twisting of the old concept of the Christian Platonists that beauty and love are a ladder: The *scala al Fattor.* They may be; but on condition that they are sacrificed.

Is love one of Waugh's aversions? A choric paean in *Work Suspended* does obeisance to "love that delights in weakness, seeks out and fills the empty places and completes itself in its work of completion." *Brideshead*, his fullest study of passion, praises and deplores it. His other stories are busier with the pleasures of fornication in which emotions never play or only lightly. Whereas Greene talks in almost every novel about the ambush and pathos of love.

In *Brideshead* Waugh's binary pattern is lop-sided: much more attention is given to figures of affection and honour than to figures of inanity and malevolence. But there is a studied attack on the Modern Age that takes the great house over and deforms it. Waugh projects the modern spirit in two persons: the raw Hooper, dealt with in a few strokes; Rex Mottram, drawn more exactly to catch the insentience, the gaping lacuna, beneath the bombast. Mottram has a virtue: the enterprising courage with which he made his first ten thousand pounds. But his enterprise aims at crude ends by rotten means. His ear is alert for news of "mortal illness and debt." He has no curiosity about meaning, no sense of tradition, responsibility, or the charities. It is a gloomy paradox of the war that Mottram becomes a Cabinet Minister. A victory with and for him may be a defeat. This point, thrust into the last pages of the book, adumbrates Waugh's profound pessimism: there will never be much decency in the res publica, never much relief from folly and violence.

Waugh is honest. Whether he likes a thing or not, he reports it; whether we are going to like it or not, he reports it. *Brideshead* is an honest political chronicle. Ryder participates in the General Strike of 1926. He volunteers, as Waugh had volunteered, to patrol the streets of London in a self-appointed posse of playboy deputies and cudgel the workmen, whom he expects to see storming some Bastille and letting riot loose. For Ryder and Waugh working-people and democracy mean the sansculottes and the mob, and the mob means the sacking of order and beauty and the death of Christ. But that is in the streets of the imagination. In the streets of London Ryder is surprised by normalcy, his team gets no "good battle," and its sole victim is, by the muddle of these occasions, a man of peace. Yet when the Strike is called off he feels "as though a beast long fabled for its ferocity had emerged for an hour, scented danger, and slunk back to its lair." Such is his nightmare. On the other hand, he catches the nullity of the aristocratic strike-breakers in a dozen lines of drunken dialogue. More significantly, he shows Lord Brideshead refusing to rally to his caste: "Brideshead had refused to take any public service because he was not satisfied with the justice of the cause." As a man Brideshead is pedantic and absurd, but as a Catholic he is incorruptibly serious. Eighteen years after 1926 Waugh admits, what he could not have admitted then, that to a religious man who tests every act of his life and every public event by the principles of his faith, the ancien régime is sometimes wrong, the people sometimes right. For a moment he makes touch with the actively egalitarian Catholicism, which was heard in Chesterton (consider his sonnet, "I Know You") and is heard often today. The plot of *Brideshead* moves through a sequence of change comparable to the change which took place in Waugh's art across his thirty-five writing years. The charm of Ryder at Oxford yields to the leanness of the later Ryder, the ripple of beauty to the solemnity of conviction, the sunniness of morning to a darkness centuries old, world-wide, lit by a lamp. In the latter half of this book, and perhaps hardly anywhere else in Waugh, unless in the rather different *Helena*, the religious sensibility is allowed expression in a poetic modulating of the prose, in a dark flickering, in bars of diapason. There is some intuition of the continuity from Judaism to Christianity: " 'You've never been to Tenebrae, I suppose?' 'Never.' 'Well, if you had you'd know what the Jews felt about their temple. *Quomodo sedet sola civitas. . . .*' " There are suggestions of the "catholicism" of the Church: "All over the world people were on their knees. . . ." ". . . *Quomodo sedet sola civitas* . . . I had heard that great lament . . . sung by a half-caste choir in Guatemala." Over-rich, Waugh afterwards felt, and did it no more. But good that he did it once!

By two post-war sallies, *Scott-King's Modern Europe* and *The Loved One* (Dennis Barlow's Modern California), Waugh proves to himself that he is not lost in his emotions: that he can still write rapidly. He demonstrates the feat of reducing a novel to a novella. He had once complimented his fictitious Ambrose Silk on "a story which a popular writer would have spun out to 150,000 words; Ambrose missed nothing; it was all there, delicately and precisely, in fifty pages." He enjoys his own prowess.

Both tales are rejections of the modern world, to fit a boy for which "would be very wicked indeed." Both performances are equally expert. *The Loved One* has eclipsed *Scott-King* only because its mortuary details evoke that lugubrious public giggling which increases as the formal religions disintegrate, or, as Ludovic would claim, with our "death-wish."

Elaborated with the same economy, *Helena* is an offering: a Catholic's offering to the Church which received him; a pilgrim's offering to the saint who travelled from the Home Counties to Jerusalem; a middle-aged man's offering to the boy who went to Oxford as a History Scholar; an Englishman's offering to Britain. He chooses, for this history of the making of a saint, a British saint, and suggests with a free fancy and a spice of convinced enthusiasm that England has contributed not only to the roll of saints but to the traditions and outlook of the Church. Helena found in Christianity what no other creed of her time could offer, the history of a man who lived, taught, and died, and rituals which involved the Christian in the experience: this is His body, this is His blood. She embraced a religion intelligible to her British pragmatism; and by seeking and finding the Cross she helped to confirm and perpetuate the three-dimensional realism of the Church. And she brought British humour to Roman gravity, the fresh-air dash of the hunting-field and the tenacious British equestrians to the recovery of relics and the Catholic temper, the earthiness of the Colchester stables to a faith born in a stable. Waugh knows how far too far he is going; but it is a piece of English humour to make a wholly genuine, wholly humble oblation with these impossible flourishes. He offers, in fact, a toy. At the close he invokes the Magi: they were late-comers, and are therefore patrons for a convert, and they brought exotic toys as their gifts, and are therefore patrons for artists and lapidary writers: "pray always for all the learned, the oblique, the delicate. Let them not be quite forgotten at the Throne of God when the simple come into their kingdom."

In small but not negligible part *Helena* is also a satire on Roman politics; and the lurid gibes enable us to see more clearly into Waugh's novels and the man. We understand the name of Prime Minister Outrage. We understand why Pinfold has never voted in a Parliamentary election, and why he has even abstained from the Catholic efforts to go from the rock to the forum and redeem the times. Waugh believes that political life has always been polluted. Mottram had his counterparts in the Roman warlords, climbing to the purple over strangled competitors and bartered wives. If "history" means "the sequence of politics," then Waugh says, as Helena says to her heedless son, "Keep out of history" — words in tune with the Joycean "History is a nightmare from which I am trying to awake." The Empire, the City, the Bureau, all collective undertakings, are contaminated. Pull out to a Dalmatian farm or a house in the Cotswolds. This political dismay is not unique, but Waugh's cry of retreat is. Among the English writers in general, and the neo-Catholic writers certainly, the tendency is to regard politicians as corrupt (landsmen scoundrels, growled Conrad), yet to hold it the staple of honour to remain engaged and struggle with corruption. Ford knew the facts of politics, was near the pre-1914 Establishment when scandal battered it, later saw the profiteers in the lunch-cars of the wartime trains and wrote his angry verse-commentary, *Footsloggers*; but he persevered with the notion of a clean society; and he recalls in *Parade's End* not only the viciousness of his rulers but the goodwill he has sometimes encountered in them. The High Tory Tietjens and the Radical Cabinet Minister (modelled on C.F.G. Masterman) get together over a beer and agree "on two fundamental legislative ideals: every working man to have a minimum of four hundred pounds a year and every beastly manufacturer who wanted to pay less to be hung." Graham Greene, who took his inspiration from Ford, combs politics to find good men in Sodom and finds them: Dr. Magiot in Haiti, and the Wisconsin Presidential Candidate, and the Candidate's wife: by whose constancy the world may be redeemed. Eliot urged that, while the first problem is to learn the right theology, the next is to apply it to the cleansing of the State and the struggle, not to be refused though the end is beyond achievement, for the City of God on earth. So Waugh stands apart from the predecessors and contemporaries who otherwise are nearest to him.

But he is in touch with a different tradition. He has one prescription for the improvement of the world: cultivate. Helena tells her son to do the work she has done on her lands: "clearing and draining and planting. That is something better than history." Swift, amid his furious indictment of man's misconduct and madness, rather similarly said: "whoever could make two ears of corn or two blades of grass to grow upon a spot of ground where only one grew before, would deserve better of mankind and do more essential service to his country than the whole race of politicians put together." We may also think of Lord Munodi in Balnibarbi, or Pope's tribute to Bathurst.

A disappointment at its first appearance, *The Ordeal of Gilbert Pinfold* now begins to seem a little masterpiece, and is an indispensable source for any study of Waugh. He must have known how it could be used to analyse him. But it was a drama lived in him, given to him complete, and, with his artist's sense of the relevance of the object, he would not abjure it. The experience was medical and religious (is there any difference?). In an old language: Pinfold is possessed by demons. In the current language: impulses suppressed under the carefully-practised persona of the Cotswold Tory demand a hearing. A "hearing" is the exact word. Pinfold's hallucinations are aural. The anarchists and rioters, whom Waugh once evoked as performers on his page and who seemed satisfied with that *Lebensraum*, now rebel against some insufficiency from his pen and speak, with thoroughly-realised identities, as if in a neighbouring but impenetrable room, or over a radio which he cannot switch off. They accuse him of the faults his prejudices and convictions most resent. He stands blazoned as his own enemy, his own victim. *Pinfold* is a *Dorian Gray*, but the conception is truer, the execution more naturalistic, the purpose a scrupulous fact-finding.

Across the span of the fifties Waugh composed a trilogy in which he brought together his several modes, informative reporting, comic fantasy, angry satire, sentimental admiration, and a nostalgia which is carefully moderated to avoid the *Brideshead* baroque. And the trilogy is more than a mosaic of styles. In this final sustained effort the impudent inventions of his farces and the pudor and predication of his moralities are blended.

The trilogy is the story of Guy Crouchback's quest for the reason of his creation, the story of the making of his soul. It is also — and the mating is superb — the story of his War: why he enlisted; what he hoped; what he suffered. *Men-at-Arms* begins in a mood of promise, almost of soaring. Guy has spent the thirties in comfortable but pointless isolation and sloth, for which he blames himself, and from which the War, surely a Crusade against the shames of the modern world, brings release. He hurries to England to play his part, and is accepted by the Halberdiers. For two hundred pages of pleasant fantasy and neat reporting Waugh describes his "love-affair" with the Army, his initiation into Halberdier etiquette, oddities, and decencies. Then, in the last five chapters, a slow reversal begins: on an African beach Guy leads his first raid competently, but gets a reprimand instead of a citation. Within a month his friendly gift of whisky accelerates Apthorpe's death, and he gets a rocket. We are descending to the dark mood of the second novel of the trilogy.

Officers and Gentlemen is a book of anger. Though there is a glimpse of Churchill, a Waugh hero, cutting through disorder with robust commonsense, it is a-typical. By and large, the tale is of the termites— incompetence, nest-feathering, and something like treason—which tunnel official structures. There is the mess and malice of the real Crusades, little of the chivalry of the Crusades of legend.

The nouns of the title ring satirically. We have been thinking of Waugh, he has thought of himself, as a champion of caste. He springs surprises. Not in Trimmer, who is Waugh's New Man as we might have expected him to be, guileful, cheap, and oafish. But in some of the minor characters who rave and madden through his pages. In Ludovic, the New Writer. Ludovic is out of the mould of the Admirable Crichton. He has the skills of the Barrie—Wodehouse butler, rooted in the resourcefulness of primitive man. He has the butler's deference. Break through the deference, and you may hear a snarl. For Pinfold Waugh there is nothing nastier than "the underdog's snarl." Waugh of the trilogy is ambivalent. When the friction between the vicious overdog, Major Hound, and the underdog Ludovic comes to ignition-point in a cave in Crete, Ludovic's deferential voice ("after what's happened, Sir, don't you think it will be more suitable") suddenly turns from its plummy to the plebeian key ("to shut your bloddy trap"). Waugh immediately throws in an image of bats bursting down from the vault of the cave, reminiscent of the "beast" of the General Strike. But Ludovic's bite at the hound has already set us cheering; the bats hardly frighten us; and we remain cheerful when the Mob in the shape of Ludovic guillotines Authority in the shape of the Major.

Less vivid but curiously significant is the case of Ivor Claire. Waugh's introductory picture of this officer, elegant, quiet and contained, impeccably taking his horse over jumps, suggests that he is to be a symbol of aristocratic dependability and that the Allied triumph will be a triumph of blue blood. Guy looks at him and perceives "quintessential England, the man Hitler had not taken into account." But Waugh is preparing a turnabout that no reader of his previous novels would have dared to predict. Quietly and adroitly Claire rats in Crete. He leaves his troops and brother-officers to fall prisoner and makes a comparatively cosy evacuation. It is one of the disillusions with which Waugh conducts Guy's sentimental education. And the next? The Establishment rallies round Claire, covers his disgrace, and ships Guy, who might have given evidence against him, by slowest transport home. The Angry writers have written, of course, more boisterously and blisteringly against the Establishment, but these rapid pages of *Officers and Gentlemen* sharply expose its *mores* and manoeuvres; and they have the value of in-criticism: Waugh lams his own group at the bidding of fact and justice. This is the positive side of his cult of eccentricity. When the Establishment says "Hush," he's damned if he'll hush.

All the same, Waugh likes Claire — and what he stands for — too much to leave him in permanent disgrace, and, reverting to an Imperial convention, he arranges for him to win back his spurs in Burma. Here and elsewhere the trilogy quivers under the oscillation between a mature and an immature Waugh. (This is not a literary fault. An unstable position may be fearfully interesting.)

The title of the British edition of the third novel of the trilogy is *Unconditional Surrender*, of the American, *The End of the Battle*. It is a pun in both languages: the enemy "unconditionally surrenders," Guy conforms to the will of God; the war ends in a victory, Guy's inner struggle ends in reconciliation with God. Throughout the pages Guy continues to suffer the sour defeats that the world thrusts on a good man. Like Tietjens in *Parade's End*, which in several respects is the War I equivalent of this War II trilogy, he finds that anything brave, competent, or humane he does in his crusading goes down on the official dossiers to his discredit. Is it possible to remain uncorrupted by disillusionment? Under the volley of perplexities Guy learns, like the tragic heroes, to know himself and others. He learns that war and its attendants come when everyone in some measure wills them; and that even the man who welcomes war for an honourable reason, to drive off his own sloth in driving out an evil system, is among the guilty. " 'God forgive me,' said Guy, 'I was one of them.' " He also finds his way, like a comic hero, to success: a religious success, for this is a religious comedy. He performs the "small service which only he could perform, for which he had been created." He belongs to a distinguished Catholic house. The gallantry of gentlemen and the courage of martyrs is represented in its annals; it stands for courtesy, humility, and charity. He is the last heir and has no child and his wife is estranged. Now his wife becomes pregnant, but not by him: by Trimmer, the representative of democracy, "the people's war," and push. Guy remarries her in full knowledge of the circumstances. Commonsense and fair play, in the person of his Scottish friend, Kerstie, try to stop him: " 'You poor bloody fool,' said Kerstie, anger and pity and something near love in her voice, 'you're being *chivalrous* — about *Virginia*. Can't you understand men aren't chivalrous any more and I don't believe they ever were.' " Guy makes his choice with a Young England chivalry and a Catholic care for the soul that transcends questions of dignity or pedigree. His father has taught him, in a letter which is the heart of the book, that "the Church . . . doesn't strike attitudes and stand on its dignity. It accepts suffering and injustice." There may be danger in this non-militant doctrine. But how beautifully Waugh presents and applies it! The invention of the parable of Virginia's child and Guy's acceptance is Waugh's unconditional surrender. He has fought the modern world, hated the people in their raw emergence. But now he accepts the crossing of the strains and takes the child of the sans-culottes into the gentle heritage. The old England accepts the new England. It is a sacrifice; Waugh has made Trimmer unmitigatedly gross so that no reader can call the decision less than a sacrifice. The immolation of Waugh's dream of past and caste is Isaac burned: intolerable, magnificent.

Lonely socialite, grim gay-dog, curmudgeon of the gospel of mercy, Waugh loved the stance of the Retrograde, sulkily barring his Church from its heartening resumption of the social tasks of Christianity. But as we read him we are likely to find, to our surprise, and, were he here, to his, and to our pleasure, but it would not have been to his, that he was a nicer man than he thought. On the evidence of the trilogy we must say at the very least, that if he was too much of a snob to accept redbrick England like a gentleman (old Mr. Crouchback would have done better, and Jimmy Porter's father-in-law did better), he was religious enough to take it as his Cross.

"The men loved him. He made them laugh." Graham Greene writes this epitaph for Jones—who is almost Apthorpe. *The Comedians* is, indeed, finely sprayed with reminiscences of Waugh's fiction, and seems to say that in a world of grit and violence (and Greene generally has embodied the grit and violence much better than Waugh) comedy represents and begets courage and sparkles with consolation (and Waugh generally has animated and consoled the world better than Greene). If there were nothing else in Waugh but the absurd inventions, the wit, the slang poetry, he would command our affection and gratitude. But there is more: the reporting of his time, the fierce individual reaction to it, the struggle with a conscience strengthening against his will, the resolute moralizing of his tale at the cost of popularity. And there is the tenacity with which he laboured to make his light novels works of art. He *was* an artist. He wrote because he must—because his imagination stepped beyond the permitted into unpermitted zones. But even the authentic writer who writes because he must may write carelessly. Waugh wrote as trenchantly as he could. And "if he pleased, he pleased by manly ways." We are in his debt alike for his comedy, for the moralities which are the annals of the civil war in his soul, and for his craftsmanship.

[From Evelyn Waugh and the Upper Class Novel"]

Terry Eagleton*

. . . The humour of Waugh's early satire works, in general, by a bland externality which reduces violent, grotesque and nightmarish events to the status of casual asides. The consequence of this is interestingly paradoxical. At first glance, it gives the impression of a kind of control: the novel remains serenely unruffled by the violent fantasies it records, filtering them through a level, dispassionate tone which creates a comic tension between substance and form. In some ways, this tone is the equivalent, at a literary level, of a quality common to Waugh's characters: an inability to be surprised or disoriented by experience which is partly the sophisticated Englishman's bland self-possession, partly a sense that nothing that happens is ever real enough to warrant significant response. The two attitudes interact in the subject-matter of the novels, so that bored sophistication comes very close to a more troubling sense of blank futility and dispossession; but they interact also in the novel's own approach to this subject-matter. For the scrupulous neutrality which implies a kind of control on the novelist's part is really an illusion: it is essentially a way of concealing a more deep-seated lack of control, an inability to interpret, evaluate and understand the experience recorded. It is therefore difficult to determine whether the novels present a deliberately external attitude to what is in some sense "real" experience, or whether they merely register the inherent externality of unreal events. On the one hand there is this, familiar device in *Decline and Fall*:

> "She is the honourable Mrs Beste-Chetwynde, you know — sister-in-law of Lord Pastmaster — a very wealthy woman, South American. They always say that she poisoned her husband, but of course little Beste-Chetwynde doesn't know that. It never came into court, but there was a great deal of talk about it at the time. Perhaps you remember the case?"
> "No," said Paul.
> "Powdered glass," said Flossie shrilly, "in his coffee."
> "Turkish coffee," said Dingy.

This is merely gratuitous: there is no "real" event to be responded to, since the related incident exists wholly at the level of language. It is just a piece of opportunism, on a level with the casually reported amputation of Lord Tangent's leg, to inject a momentary, uninterpreted sensationalism into the narrative. On the other hand, there is the outcome of Paul's trial: "His sentence of seven years' penal servitude was rather a blow. 'In ten years she will be worn out,' he thought as he drove in the prison van to Blackstone

*Reprinted from Terry Eagleton, *Exiles and Emigrés: Studies in Modern Literature* (London: Chatto & Windus, 1970), 46–69, by permission of the author and publisher.

Gaol." The humour of this depends at least in part upon our taking the prison-sentence seriously — as "real" — and then contrasting it with Paul's understated response; the violence which was merely abstract in the case of the powdered glass suddenly assumes a more sinisterly concrete form. This, indeed, is the irony: the violence and fraud which amused us at a distance now enter the foreground of the novel, to catch us unawares.

Yet is is difficult to believe that Paul's experience in prison is really very different in quality from the amputation of Tangent's leg or the clichéd fantasy which surrounds the butler Philbrick. The prison is really a joke, the processes of law are "preposterous," and Paul finds his weeks of confinement to be among the happiest of his life: "there was no need to shave, no hesitation about what tie he should wear, none of the fidgeting with studs and collars and links that so distracts the waking moments of civilised man." So the novel is ambivalent in its attitude towards Penny-feather's incarceration: on the one hand it is the unexpected eruption of a violent undertow of reality into an unreal social world; on the other hand, it shares in the fantasy qualities of that world, and so can offer no genuine criticism of it. The most it does is poke gentle fun at cuff-links.

There is a similar ambivalence about the crime and fraud within the upper-class world itself. Its point is to suggest the real depredations and brutalities which underlie the glittering surface Paul finds attractive, but the sharp edge of that criticism is blunted by the grotesque enormity of the crimes themselves: white slave traffic, poison, conspiracy. These forms of corruption are so extreme as to be unreal: they reflect less a considered satiric criticism than an uncontrolled sense of nightmare and absurdity. In order to achieve a standpoint of "moral" criticism on the experience it presents, the novel needs to resort to a flamboyant and wholly incredible set of images, which merely share in the unreal quality of the society itself, and so are less effective as genuine criticisms in proportion to their monstrousness.

Decline and Fall, then, sets the keynote for many of Waugh's later themes. There is, to begin with, the conflict between morality and style, reflected in the vicissitudes of Pennyfeather's career. Pennyfeather, like Tony Last in *A Handful of Dust*, is a colourlessly honourable man in a stylish world of sharp operators; but although, like Last, he therefore represents the focal-point of a kind of social criticism, he resembles Last also in being too passive, unrealised and inarticulate to make that criticism tell with any acuteness. The blankness which leads him to the role of victim also prevents him from reacting effectively against that role, and a radical questioning of an exploitative society is thus neatly avoided. The stylish world is predatory, but it has a verve and insouciance which is admired, in contrast to the monkish honesty of Pennyfeather himself. "Morality" is not rejected, but it cannot survive relevantly within the realm of style; to be moral is to withdraw, perhaps rightly, from the world, but so to leave it invulnerable to one's criticisms. Endorsing and rejecting attitudes cancel each other out here, as they do elsewhere in the novel: Dr Fagan's educational commercialism is satirised, but so also are the progressive educational notions of Potts; both liberal and conservative responses to prison-reform are held up to ridicule; Negroes and racialists are found equally amusing; Potts the moral reformer is as absurd as the vices he hopes to abolish.

The upshot of all this is that upper-class values are satirised but not dismissed; they are fraudulent and hollow, but there is really nowhere else to turn. So the cool externality of the style is not, at root, a "placing" externality at all: as a mode of perception, it is part of the world it sees. This fact is most evident in the garishly violent events of the novel, which find their epitome in the episode where Mr Prendergast is carved up with a handsaw. Like most of Waugh's grotesquely violent scenes, the incident is reported rather than presented, and this is itself significant: the imagery of violence is needed, as a shocking intimation of breakdown, but it must be enjoyed vicariously, through the accounts of eye-witnesses, so that it will not load the casually distanced reportage of the novel with a pressure it could not sustain. The surface-texture of flippant observation must be kept intact, but "deeper" forces at the same time exposed. Yet "exposure" implies a sort of controlled objectivity which is hardly there at all: the Prendergast incident, like other such occurrences in Waugh, is really a mixture of disturbance and indulgence. It is disturbance in so far as it indicates, not any significantly "objective" reality in the novel (thematically, the event is wholly pointless), but an uncontrolled reflex of fantasy on the part of the novelist; it is indulgence in so far as it signifies a quite gratuitous sensationalism, done entirely for its own sake. In both ways, the neutrality of presentation is deceptive: it suggests a control which is not there. Paradoxically, Waugh's distance from the subject-matter of his satirical novels only goes to show how intimately a part of them he is: he resembles his characters most evidently in this inability to belong to his own experience.

Waugh's second novel, *Vile Bodies*, is similar in tone and technique to *Decline and Fall*, although it intensifies the earlier novel's mood: it is faster, more crowded and more openly disturbed, revolving on the chaotic images of motor-racing, parties and movies. Events occur in a rapid fragmentation in which everything is at once ordinary and alarming; deaths, suicides and the fall of a government are caught up randomly in the general whirl. The society gossip-columnist Simon Balcairn is driven to suicide by the pressures of his career, but the event is too trivial to imply any indictment of the Society world: as a gesture, it has the histrionic unreality of the world it is rejecting. In the midst of this disintegration is the elusive figure of Father Rothschild, the mysteriously omniscient, inscrutably knowledgeable Jesuit. Father Rothschild is offered as a centre of spiritual value, but a centre which is necessarily suggestive rather than realised, alluding obscurely to some privileged access to significant truths and inside information. As with Paul Pennyfeather, moral value cannot be directly realised in the world; but Rothschild's worldly experience underlines the significance of his moral judgements. And since the precise nature of this worldly experience remains mysterious, we are supposed not to question his title to make judgements of this kind:

> "Don't you think," said Father Rothschild gently, "that perhaps it is all in some way historical? I don't think people ever *want* to lose their faith either in religion or in anything else. I know very few young people, but it seems to me that they are all possessed with an almost fatal hunger for permanence. I think all these divorces show that. People aren't content just to muddle along nowadays. . . . And this word 'bogus' they all use. . . . They won't make the best of a bad job nowadays. My private schoolmaster used to say, 'If a thing's worth doing at all, it's worth doing well.' . . . But these young people have got hold of another end of the stick, and for all we know it may be the right one. They say, 'If a thing's not worth doing well, it's not worth doing at all.' "

The collapse is "historical," in the same sense that the fate of Mrs Grimes in *Decline and Fall* could be laid at the door of "civilisation." The whole comment is hedged with the disclaimers appropriate to most explicit moral reflections in Waugh (Father Rothschild "knows very few young people," and later admits that "it's all very difficult"), but the total effect is a masterpiece of disingenuous defence of the Bright Young Things, who gain, through this discernment of spiritual hunger in divorce statistics and Society slang, a wholly unrecognisable moral integrity. So the one respected moral spokesman of the novel, a man who significantly combines the innocent rectitude of Paul Pennyfeather with the worldly wisdom of the Beste-Chetwyndes, throws his spiritual weight behind the decaying upper-class world.

Like *Decline and Fall*, *Vile Bodies* contemplates a world which it can in no sense adequately interpret. Upper-class values are false, but the offered alternative is a vision of "ordinary" life which is equally repugnant:

> Nina looked down and saw inclined at an odd angle a horizon of straggling red suburb; arterial roads dotted with little cars; factories, some of them working, others empty and decaying; a disused canal; some distant hills sown with bungalows; wireless masts and overhead power cables; men and women were indiscernible except as tiny spots; they were marrying and shopping and making money and having children. The scene lurched and tilted again as the aeroplane struck a current of air.
>
> "I think I'm going to be sick," said Nina.

The "real" world is seen from the detachment of an aeroplane, tilted and distanced by the observer's standpoint to reduce it to an unreal "scene," a framed and contemplated cinematic image which will dissolve and be replaced by others. The sense of giddiness and sickening disturbance, which is projected on to the observed scene, is in fact a quality of the observer's own "unreal" vantage-point, suspended precariously in the spacious nothingness of air, vulnerable to shifting, random currents which distort perception and blot out reality. Nina feels sick, but the passage is significantly ambivalent about the cause: is it the scene she observes, or her own vertiginous viewpoint, which is responsible for the nausea? Is there an "objective" emptiness in the world, or is the emptiness a quality of a way of seeing the world? The answer, in Waugh's case, is both: and this passage feels towards the obscure connection between an objective point-lessness in life and the neurosis of the Bright Young Things' behaviour. Yet the connection is deceptively established. In choosing to show the mean-inglessness of a *suburban*, rather than upper-class environment, the novel implies a criticism of Society rootlessness— *they* do not marry, work, have children— while seeming at the same time to endorse this detachment by showing the "real" world to be as empty as themselves. Thus the passage satirises Nina for her absurdly inadequate response to what she sees ("I think I'm going to be sick"), but also suggests that what she sees, from this privileged and distorting height, is the substantial truth of the ordinary world.

It is worth turning at this point from Waugh's two early satires to a more "serious" novel, *A Handful of Dust*. The novel is judged serious because of its theme: it sets out to explore a contemporary mood of breakdown and futility in terms of the collapsing relationship of Tony and Brenda Last and the accompanying erosion of the country-house tradition of which Tony is representative. What is striking about *A Handful of Dust*, however, is that although the earlier satire is less in evidence, supposedly significant events and relationships are handled with the same one-dimensional externality as if the satire of *Decline and Fall* was in fact active. The novel offers an account of trivialised and insubstantial relationships; yet both qualities belong as much to its own technique as to its content. (In this respect, incidentally, the novel has more in common with *The Waste Land* than its title.) There is a sense in which the novel exploits the fact that it deals in "objectively" vacuous relationships and responses to explain away its own superficiality of treatment. We are asked to believe that Brenda Last is in love with John Beaver: yet Beaver is even less present as a character than Paul Pennyfeather. The novel hinges on a "deep" emotional crisis— the sudden death of the Lasts' son, John An-drew— yet it takes refuge in the upper-class convention of concealed emotion to ratify its own evident incapacity to handle genuine feeling at all. The tragedy of the death has to be left implied, unstated, reflected in objective consequences such as Brenda's desertion of Tony rather than in subjective response. We are meant to sense, throughout the event, a sort of significant emotional blankness: but "blankness," as a term, runs together too indiscriminately stunned trauma on the one hand and shallow indifference on the other. At the point of explicit feeling, Waugh withdraws quickly to the style of the early satires:

> She wept helplessly, turning round in the chair and pressing her forehead against its gilt back.
> Upstairs Mrs Northcote had Souki Foucauld-Esterhazy by the foot and was saying, "There are four men dominating your fate. One is loyal and tender but has not yet disclosed his love. . . ."

John Andrew's death brings home to Brenda her love for Beaver: she believes at first that it is Beaver who has been killed, and "Until [then], when I thought something had happened to you, I had no idea that I loved you." To this extent John Andrew's sudden death (he is kicked in the head by a horse) has some plot-relevance, as it has also in being responsible for the final sundering of Brenda and Tony. Yet the incident, nevertheless, seems too dramatic for its functional role within the narrative: its literal and metaphorical meanings seem curiously disjunctive. On any realistic estimate, it would hardly take the news of Beaver's supposed death to convince Brenda of a passionate love for him — although the fact that an artificial and extraordinary crisis of this kind is needed to shift the level of the relationship from casual encounter to "love" has its own significance. The whole incident is unconvincing: and in any case it imbues John Andrew's death with narrative-significance only by a very circuitous route. Again, John Andrew never seemed sufficiently important to either of his parents to prevent a divorce if it had been really wanted; so in this sense, too, the death, viewed realistically, is less than plausible. The fact is that John Andrew's death, given its seriousness, is nevertheless more than a little reminiscent of the passing of Lord Tangent and similar grotesque accidents in the earlier novels. Like those incidents it is imposed on the novel, as a random, shocking, gratuitous gesture to the brutal absurdity of life, a testimony to the impossibility of order and control. The death is a stupid accident which "just happened," which is "nobody's fault": to this extent it acts as an effective image of the upper-class world, which is similarly brutal and absurd but whose aberrations "just happen," without too-specific moral blame. The whole incident, like Flossie's dramatic death-fall from a chandelier in *Vile Bodies*, hints at an underlying, violent negativity which it is unable formally to articulate or account for; as such, it is again less a "profound" image than a symptom of helpless disturbance. One is forced to conclude from the book as a whole that Waugh does not know how serious he is intending to be, as the frequent lapses into a *Vile Bodies* brand of satirical whimsy sufficiently evidence. The whole episode of Tony's divorce-proceedings — the overnight stay in a Brighton hotel, the attendant detectives — is another case in point: the fact that the divorce merely involves Tony in going through certain ridiculous, external motions is offered as an image of the grotesque, game-like quality of life; but it is also (as the satirical indulgence of these scenes indicates) the kind of behaviour which Waugh is happiest with, the nearest he can come to significant feeling.

The latter part of *A Handful of Dust* is devoted to Tony's adventures in South America, and his fateful encounter with the sinister Mr Todd. There are, of course, certain thematic congruencies between this part of the novel and what has gone before: in both cases, Tony is the victim of predatory forces, so that the macabre ritual of reading Dickens in the jungle is intended to parallel the futile round of English upper-class life. Both are mockeries of civilised culture, set in the midst of an encroaching chaos. Despite this thematic parallel, however, the two parts of the novel really fail to cohere: and they fail primarily because the South American experience is uncertainly handled. As a total episode, the wanderings in Pie-wie country are too realistically detailed, in the close physical descriptions of landscape and event, to be of merely "symbolic" importance; yet that, finally, is their upshot, when Tony stumbles on Mr Todd at the heart of darkness. It is not difficult to see that this ambivalence results from the novel's mixed intentions, in translating Tony from his ancestral seat to the tropics. On the one hand, the South American venture is a contact with "real" experience — with hardship, sickness, physical exertion, a vividly present landscape — in contrast to the hermetic unrealities of fashionable London; but on the other hand it is the symbolic projection of Tony's hopeless search for the paradisal city of truth, and so an extention of the novel's pessimistic "waste land" thesis. The two elements, of realism and fantasy, interweave constantly in Last's feverish consciousness.

If the episode is taken as "realistic," it is too sharply disjointed from what went before and has no effective point of purchase on that English experience. This, indeed, is the dominant impression of the early descriptions of Tony's expedition, which involve an inexplicably abrupt transition from one level to another. But if it is taken as "symbolic," it fits in with the English experience rather too neatly: it goes to "prove," by the easy choice of a particular, realistically incredible metaphor, that the emptiness glimpsed at the core of a declining English culture is indeed universal and metaphysical. The whole episode, in other words, seems too realistic to justify its symbolic point, and too symbolic to justify its realism. Waugh wants to use foreign experience in two ways: as an escape from relative unreality to relative reality: and as an extended symbol of contemporary fever, chaos and futility. Yet these modes obviously conflict: and in the end the symbolic meaning predominates, to suggest that there is, after all, no escape to a reality beyond Society. The American exploration reveals the hollowness of English culture as "metaphysically" rather than socially determined, and to this extent deepens a revolted sense of its vacuity; yet the subversiveness of that insight is curtailed by the fact that experience elsewhere is, by the same token, equally corrupt. It is a "human" rather than a social condition which is flawed; and this, while it intensifies the *significance* of English social decline, also removes its precise causes beyond the social arena. The victimisation of Tony is finally the work, not just of identifiable and changeable social factors (the fickle exploitations of a decadent social class, epitomised in Brenda), but of the "human condition" itself, which appears indifferently in Brenda Last and Mr Todd.

Waugh's choice of South America as the locus of a non-English reality deserves a final comment. English experience, in the light of Tony Last's sufferings, appears cheap and devaluated; but it is interesting that the only alternative form of life is one notable for the extremity of its difference from England. There is, in other words, no way of exposing the decadence of fashionable London from within the society itself — no other range of English social value or experience to which an appeal can be made. The upper class may be corrupt, but its complacent belief that it *is* England is accepted at face-value; and then there is nowhere to go but half-way across the world. Because *that* environment is alien and sinister, wholly different from England, it can act as an index of the extremity with which England has been rejected; yet for the same reasons, it cannot act as an effective critical standpoint on the society which has been abandoned. It is simply another world, and no fruitful commerce (other than at the level of generalising metaphor) can be established between it and home. Like the white slave traffic of *Decline and Fall* (which was also, significantly, connected with Latin America), the realms of action and experience which might supply material for a criticism of England are so extreme as to be fantastically unreal. Whether, then South America is seen "realistically" or "symbolically," it can furnish no genuine point of transcendence for those Englishmen weary of their own class. Viewed realistically, it is too alien to be effective; viewed symbolically, it is merely an intensified projection (for both Tony Last and, in *Brideshead Revisited*, Charles Ryder, who also spends some time there) of the blankness discerned at home.

Brideshead Revisited seems to me superior to the other novels we have discussed; and it is interesting to see that, despite the sourness and snobbery of his special pleading for the aristocratic order (the vulgar gibes at "humane legislation" and the rest), Waugh is at his best as a writer when the anaesthetised neutrality of the earlier satire gives way to a form of fiction in which his own feelings are directly engaged. *Brideshead Revisited* is a successful novel; but it does not escape from the ambiguities we have examined already, in relation to Waugh's simultaneous criticism and defence of the upper class. In this novel, that ambiguity assumes two general forms: one concerns the conflict between "morality" and "style"; the other relates to the characterisation of Sebastian Flyte.

On a superficial reading, *Brideshead* is a puzzling novel to interpret. Its general intention, evident enough throughout the book but also explicitly announced by its author in his 1959 Preface, is to make out a defence of the social order which the Marchmains of Brideshead symbolise, in face of the vulgarity and commercialism which are undermining it. Parts of the book—in particular the Prologue, Epilogue, and much of Book 3—would seem to bear out this purpose. In the Prologue and Epilogue, the Brideshead tradition is seen as subject to external assault from a new philistinism; in Book 3, Charles Ryder and Julia Marchmain are portrayed as the shipwrecked victims of a distasteful civilisation, clinging to each other in a storm of social disintegration which they see as "a conspiracy against us." Yet it is obvious enough, elsewhere in the novel, that responsibility for the Marchmain decline lies, not with conspiring invasions from the outside, but with the Marchmains themselves. Lord Marchmain has relinquished his traditional duties in England for a life of pleasure in Europe; Sebastian squanders his life in drink; Brideshead, the elder son, devotes his time to collecting matchboxes; and Julia, like Charles Ryder, makes an unhappy marriage for unadmirably ambitious motives. Both Julia and Brideshead marry representatives of the "vulgar" middle class, and to this extent the tradition disintegrates under a combination of "internal" and "external" pressures; but both choose their partners consciously, and are in no sense passively enticed. The house of Brideshead is on the wane, as Rex Mottram crudely but correctly puts it, because of its own wasteful prodigality; the process, essentially, is one of self-destruction.

None of this is ignored by the novel; but it is surrounded by an interesting ambivalence of feeling, which relates to the conflict between "morality" and "style." The plain fact is that, with the exception of the younger daughter Cordelia and (with some qualifications to be made later) Lady Marchmain, none of the family is especially admirable from the viewpoint of the traditional moral order it is supposed to sustain. Yet it is this unpromising material which must somehow be wrought into an impassioned defence of traditional upper-class England. . . .

The conflict of style and morality in *Brideshead Revisited*, and the uncertainty which surrounds Sebastian, are aspects of a more persistent ambivalence which we have seen in other of Waugh's novels: the need to defend, at certain crucial points, an English upper-class world which is also satirised. In this respect, for all his specific differences of treatment and subject-matter, Waugh offers an important parallel to Woolf, Forster and Huxley. Upper-class values are false, devious and dangerously hermetic, in the earlier satiric novels; and a sense of their partial, fragmentary nature can move quickly into "panic and emptiness," the vertiginous nausea which Nina feels in the last scene of *Vile Bodies*. But though these values are partial and unreal, they are also, paradoxically, all there is: there can be no effective appeal beyond them to a wider social experience, for the values survive only by virtue of their exclusiveness. The break for reality, as in the Leonard Bast episodes of *Howards End*, results only in failure and frustration.

There is a relation between the quality of upper-class values in

Waugh and the literary techniques of his novels. What gives those values their taint of unreality is their distance from the pressures of social necessity: from the constrictions of a settled, permanent, complex and institutionalised social fabric, of the sort that Nina glimpses from the aeroplane. Because upper-class experience is damagingly free of these shaping restrictions, it moves easily into fantasy, and then into nightmare; because this privileged life-style is independent of necessity, the experience it generates may be permutated, manipulated and combined, without the restraining intervention of fact. Waugh's satirical novels offer a vivid kaleidoscope in which any fragment of experience can be made to merge into any other, in which any pattern may be randomly produced by a shake or tilt of the focus. They are areas of pure freedom in which anything can happen, for there are no pre-established necessities; yet that freedom is the negative liberation of fantasy, liable at any moment to disintegrate under the anxiety of its own giddy unconstraint. Because all is possible to this privileged social class and to the literary form which mirrors it, nothing is especially valuable; because no convention or definition is more than improvised, momentary, experimental, no event or identity can be given the fixed limits of substantial meaning. It is a world close to that of Huxley's early novels, in which ideas, fantasies, insights and hypotheses can be shuttled, crossed and combined in rapid, "brilliant" succession because none of them is in the least subject to the constraints of social reality. . . .

On Individual Novels

Splendors and Miseries of
Evelyn Waugh

Edmund Wilson*

The new novel by Eveyn Waugh — *Brideshead Revisited* — has been a
bitter blow to this critic. I have admired and praised Mr.
Waugh, and
when I began reading *Brideshead Revisited*, I was excited at finding that
he had broken away from the comic vein for which he is famous and
expanded into a new dimension. The new story — with its subtitle, *The
Sacred and Profane Memories of Captain Charles Ryder* — is a "serious"
novel, in the conventional sense, and the opening is invested with a poetry
and staged with a dramatic effectiveness which seem to promise much. An
English officer, bored with the Army, finds himself stationed near a great
country house which has been turned into soldiers' quarters. It is a place
that he once used to visit — his life, indeed, has been deeply involved with
the Catholic family who lived there. The story reverts to 1923, at the time
when Charles Ryder was at Oxford and first met the younger son of the
Marchmains, who became his most intimate friend. This early section is
all quite brilliant partly in the manner of the Waugh we know, partly with
a new kind of glamor that is closer to Scott Fitzgerald and Compton
Mackenzie. It is the period that these older writers celebrated, but seen
now from the bleak shrivelled forties, so that everything — the freedom,
the fun, the varied intoxications of youth — has taken on a remoteness and
pathos. The introduction of the hero to the Catholic family and the
gradual revelation of their queerness, their differences from Protestant
England, is brought off with accomplished art, and through almost the
whole of the first half of the book, the habitual reader of Waugh is likely
to tell himself that his favorite has been fledged as a first-rank straight
novelist.

But this enthusiasm is to be cruelly disappointed. What happens
when Evelyn Waugh abandons his comic convention — as fundamental to
his previous work as that of any Restoration dramatist — turns out to be
more or less disastrous. The writer, in this more normal world, no longer

*Reprinted from Edmund Wilson, *Classics and Commercials* (New York: Farrar, Straus
and Co, 1950), 298–302. Copyright 1950 by Edmund Wilson. Copyright renewed © 1977
by Elena Wilson. Reprinted by permission of Farrar, Straus & Giroux, Inc.

knows his way: his deficiency in common sense here ceases to be an asset and gets him into some embarrassing situations, and his creative imagination, accustomed in his satirical fiction to work partly in two-dimensional caricature but now called upon for passions and motives, produces mere romantic fantasy. The hero is to have an affair with the married elder daughter of the house, and this is conducted on a plane of banality—the woman is quite unreal—reminiscent of the fulldress adulteries of the period in the early nineteen-hundreds when Galsworthy and other writers were making people throb and weep over such fiction as *The Dark Flower*. And as the author's taste thus fails him, his excellent style goes to seed. The writing—which, in the early chapters, is of Evelyn Waugh's best: felicitous, unobtrusive, exact—here runs to such dispiriting clichés as "Still the clouds gathered and did not break" and "So the year wore on and the secret of the engagement spread from Julia's confidantes and so, like ripples on the water, in ever widening circles." The stock characters—the worldly nobleman, the good old nurse—which have always been a feature of Waugh's fiction and which are all right in a harlequinade, here simply become implausible and tiresome. The last scenes are extravagantly absurd, with an absurdity that would be worthy of Waugh at his best if it were not—painful to say—meant quite seriously. The worldly Lord Marchmain, when he left his wife, repudiated his Catholic faith, and on his deathbed he sends the priest packing, but when the old man has sunk lower, the priest is recalled. The family all kneel, and Charles, who is present, kneels, too. Stoutly though he has defended his Protestantism, his resistance breaks down today. He prays that this time the dying man will not reject the final sacrament, and lo, Lord Marchmain makes the sign of the cross! The peer, as he has drifted toward death, has been soliloquizing at eloquent length: "We were knights then, barons since Agincourt, the larger honors came with the Georges," etc., etc., and the reader has an uncomfortable feeling that what has caused Mr. Waugh's hero to plump on his knees is not, perhaps, the sign of the cross but the prestige, in the person of Lord Marchmain, of one of the oldest families in England.

For Waugh's snobbery, hitherto held in check by his satirical point of view, has here emerged shameless and rampant. His admiration for the qualities of the older British families, as contrasted with modern upstarts, had its value in his earlier novels, where the standards of morals and taste are kept in the background and merely implied. But here the upstarts are rather crudely overdone and the aristocrats become terribly trashy, and his cult of the high nobility is allowed to become so rapturous and solemn that it finally gives the impression of being the only real religion in the book.

Yet the novel is a Catholic tract. The Marchmain family, in their various fashions, all yield, ultimately, to the promptings of their faith and bear witness to its enduring virtue; the skeptical hero, long hostile and mocking, eventually becomes converted; the old chapel is opened up and put at the disposition of the troops, and a "surprising lot use it, too." Now, this critic may perhaps be insensible to some value the book will have for other readers, since his is unsympathetic by conviction with the point of view of the Catholic convert, but he finds it impossible to feel that the author has conveyed in all this any actual religious experience. In the earlier novels of Waugh there was always a very important element of perverse, unregenerate self-will that, giving rise, to confusion and impudence, was a great asset for a comic writer. In his new book, this theme is sounded explicitly, with an unaccustomed portentousness and rhetoric, at an early point in the story, when he speaks of "the hot spring of anarchy" that "rose from deep furnaces where was no solid earth, and burst into the sunlight—a rainbow in its cooling vapors with a power the rocks could not repress," and of course it is this hot spring of anarchy, this reckless, unredeemed humanity, that is supposed to be cooled and controlled by the discipline of the Catholic faith. But, once he has come to see this force as sin, Evelyn Waugh seems to be rather afraid of it: he does not allow it really to raise its head—boldly, outrageously, hilariously or horribly—as he has in his other books, and the result is that we feel something lacking. We have come to count on this Serpent; we are not used to seeing it handled so gingerly; and, at the same time, the religion that is invoked to subdue it seems more like an exorcistic rite than a force of regeneration.

There is, however, another subject in *Brideshead Revisited*—a subject which is incompletely developed but which has far more reality than the religious one: the situation of Charles Ryder between the Brideshead family on the one hand and his own family background on the other. This young man has no mother and his only home is with a scholarly and self-centered father, who reduces life to something so dry, so withdrawn, so devoid of affection or color that the boy is driven to look for a home in the family of his Oxford friend and to idealize their charm and grace. What are interesting to a non-Catholic reader are the origins and the evolution of the hero's beglamored snobbery, and the amusing and chilling picture of Charles's holidays at home with his father is one of the very good things in the book.

The comic parts of *Brideshead Revisited* are as funny as anything that the author has done, and the Catholic characters are sometimes good, when they are being observed as social types and get the same kind of relentless treatment as the characters in his satirical books. I do not mean to suggest, however, that Mr. Waugh should revert to his earlier vein. He has been steadily broadening his art, and when he next tries a serious novel, he may have learned how to avoid bathos.

In the meantime, I predict that *Brideshead Revisited* will prove to be the most successful, the only extremely successful, book that Evelyn Waugh has written, and that it will soon be up in the best-seller list somewhere between *The Black Rose* and *The Manatee*.

[From "The Baroque and Mr. Waugh"]

Aubrey Menen*

I

Mr. Waugh has unfortunately chosen to publish his latest novel at a time when literary criticism has fallen into disrepute. Nowadays authors do not expect to be written about, but rather to be awarded prizes, certificates and recommendations by various panels of assessors. The reason for the growth of this system, one must suppose, is that the public knows it has worked very well with dogs and cattle: and there are good grounds for believing that it will work even better with authors. They, being rational creatures, can be expected to co-operate in keeping their tails up, ears cocked and noses aloft in a manner best calculated to pick up the scent: whereas dogs must rely on the slow processes of Nature to mould them to the public taste.

Helena has won, I believe, a rosette or two, but it is not a Champion: it is not, at least, the Champion of the Year: and since it was published as long as four months ago it is probably already forgotten. Besides, who cares? The new Spring books are being led in the ring, all as spick and span as the publishers' white coats and gaiters.

Willing to be accused of sloth, I want, in these notes, to turn back and consider the fact that literary critics, still to be found in nooks and crannies of our newspapers, have disagreed about a book which is a studied work by one of our most serious craftsmen: and they have disagreed violently. One of the few good judges left us has described it as Mr. Waugh's finest work; others have suggested it is very nearly his worst. It would be useful to study the actual arguments of both sides: but unfortunately some of the best critics have been reduced, by circumstances, to making no more than ring-side ejaculations: murmurs of approbation, brief hand-clapping, low whistles or snorts.

The case of *Helena*, this *dégringolade* of criticism is particularly disappointing. There are some critics still writing who could have helped us with it; and help is needed, for Mr. Waugh's latest novel is a disconcerting book for any thoughtful person to read.

Helena, begun in the middle as it was begun in the *Month*, is a cogent, stable, comprehensible whole. The reader awaits only the beginning to decide that it is the work of a master. *Helena*, begun at the beginning, as it can now be in the book-version, is brilliant, mercurial, dexterous and exciting: the reader only awaits the culmination of the story to decide again that it is the work of a master—but the master of a

*Reprinted from *Month*, 5 (April 1951):226–37 by permission of the Journal.

different style of writing. Now if a book falls into two dissociated parts, it is a failure. As a careful reader of the novel (I have read it about seven times) I do not think that *Helena* can be easily read as a whole; but, equally, I do not think it is a failure. On the contrary, I consider it the finest example we have of the exactly contemporary novel. These notes are intended to argue that what appears to be a destructive fault in the book is in fact an extraordinary and new technical feat. It is something which is called for by the times in which Mr. Waugh writes and which few but he can do.

II

From the middle of the book onwards to the end we find a smoothed, shaped, precise, mandarin-told tale of a mature woman, who, though an Empress, found neither pleasure nor purpose in her life. She casually adopts Christianity, and turning away from its nascent theology, makes up her mind that the Cross on which its Founder died must still exist. It does exist, but in her zeal for the historical Holy Places, Helena almost buries it for ever under one of her vast new churches. She is saved from this disaster by prayers, by fasting and by a providential dream. Tired, old, sick and quite indomitable, she sets workmen to dig where her dream told her. The Cross is discovered, Helena's life has found its purpose, and so, it would seem, has the story: for Mr. Waugh has written the closing scenes with a strength of style which surpasses anything else in the book. He has even done what nobody else has succeeded in doing in English for three centuries: he has written an acceptable prayer; The Apology of the Late Comers that Helena makes on Christmas Eve is a noble piece of writing. But the prose is not all nobility and it would be intolerable if it were. It has other merits. When a reader knows that he is going to witness the unearthing of buried treasure, however sacred, he rightly wants to see the thing through spadeful by spadeful. He wants nothing hidden from him but the treasure. Of Mr. Waugh's description of the closing stages of Helena's search, it is enough to say that there must be few of its readers who could not draw a map of just where the Cross was found and just how the workmen got to it. Nothing, it would seem, could be more realistic.

Now let us begin the book at the beginning. The beginning is a short preface. We are immediately perplexed. Nothing, it would seem, was further from Mr. Waugh's thoughts than realism. This story as he has written it, he says, is a legend.

Now it is quite obvious that it is not. Nobody can write a legend. They are invented by anonymous and inspired old women; the sort that embroider the lives of saints, who weave stories round stones, who draw enchantment out of place-names, who confuse history with delectable misunderstandings, who, in a word, are in the company of those crones whom St. Bonaventura held to be more capable of loving God than any

Doctor of Theology. It is no criticism of Mr. Waugh to say that if *Helena* were really a legend of the finding of the true Cross, it would have been far finer. Persephone, Psyche, the penitent wolf of St. Francis, can only be gratefully borrowed by writers: they cannot be invented with pen and ink. Mr. Waugh's Old King Cole is delightful; but he is not King Arthur.

But it is with Old King Cole that the story begins: and although his name is spelt Coël and [he] refers to his future son-in-law, Constantius, as "A relation of the Divine What-d'you-call-him," he is still the nursery-rhyme king; it is true that he is surrounded by so much literary guile that he can call for his pipe, his bowl and his fiddlers and get them before we really grasp what he is up to: but still, he calls for them. Mr. Waugh cannot succeed in writing a legend; but, as he promised, he begins his book with a very legendary air. The heroine herself makes her entrance as an overgrown English schoolgirl; but she is King Cole's daughter and she is, every one of her excessive inches, a fairy-tale princess. In next to no time she has fallen in love with, and married, Constantius, a prince, of course, and — naturally — incognito.

I do not mean that Mr. Waugh's beginning is jejune: it is, on the contrary, sparkling fresh. It would make a brilliant beginning to several conceivable books, but it is a disconcerting start to this one. Read alone, we must enjoy it. Read with the end of the novel in mind, we are inclined to wait, smiling, for Mr. Waugh to have done with his playfulness.

Therefore, it would seem that if we hold end and beginning together in our minds we must decide that the author has written far below his best. Is this true? Does the book, by other tests, show signs of diminished power? If it does, then we may put it down regretfully and say no more about it. If it does not, then we must in fairness examine our own way of looking at the book.

It is my opinion that Mr. Waugh's writing, with this story, has sprung into maturity. For the sake of brevity I shall take only one example, but an example which I think conclusive. Let us examine the characters of the two most important persons in the book, next to Helena: Constantius and Constantine.

Constantine makes his entrance as a young man. For many years Mr. Waugh's fancy has been providing us with portraits of young men, who, at once brazen and mysterious, go about the world on errands of importance (or at least to themselves), insulting their elders, being rude but indefatigably amorous to women; being by turns, cynical and naïve, charming and boorish, hopeful and in despair, gay and malevolent: in a word, the young man we all hoped we would turn out to be when we were in our last years at school. No such young men ever existed: they were never born of flesh and blood. If they had any forebears outside Mr. Waugh's fancy, they are Boucher's impossibly wise-eyed *Amoretti* grown up and dressed by an English tailor. It is certain that they had no earthly childhood and it seemed that the author would never be able to allow them an earthly middle age. When the young Constantius enters this latest story of Mr. Waugh's, he enters it as one of these: above the rattle of his Roman armour can be heard the impertinent voice of Basil Seal. It is all very well carried off. To hold that one young man is, for all time, very like another, and that they are all the young men of one's early books, is an outrageous, but also a delightful, fancy.

The technique has its dangers and these are always most present when Mr. Waugh turns his fancy upon women. The young Helena for instance is presented as having the pet daydream of being a horse; and as a horse, she takes a two-page imaginary gallop through the British country-side. This is, of course, a difficult thing to describe, and Mr. Waugh tackles the task with spirit. However, we remain unconvinced. A horse, we feel, is a creature of many moods; Helena always remains a perfect lady. But when the scene leads up to a meeting with her short-spoken lover, Constantius-Seal, in the stables, all is well again. We are once more provided with a very amusing love scene in the half-articulate fashion that Mr. Waugh has made his own.

Then, suddenly, Mr. Waugh gives us a picture of Constantius grown up. Historical fact (and I think only historical fact) demands that Constantius-Seal should have become his son, Constantine. Constantius himself dies in a single phrase: "I remember that my late husband once said . . ." remarks Helena at the beginning of a chapter, and, in the manner of a magic lantern, the portrait of the father fades and blends into the portrait of a man who is very much his father's son; Constantius-Seal gives way to Constantine-Seal. Constantine becomes Emperor. But what is much more important is that he also becomes gross, absurd, muddled, pig-headed, hysterical and mercilessly middle-aged. He still has the Seal charm, or a little of it; he is still abrupt and brazen, or so he would be called if he were not King. But the fancies that were so deftly braided together to produce Mr. Waugh's young men now sit on him as grotesquely as his green wig. Underneath it is the ripe and rotten fruit of a generation of which Mr. Waugh celebrated the blossoming. Constantine-Seal, at last, rules the world, as he always felt he was fit to do; and the world he rules suits him, with a vengeance. Caprice takes the place of law, melodramatic murder the place of justice, and, by an exquisite thrust of Mr. Waugh's wit, the first Emperor to acknowledge Christianity is made incontinently to replace it by a Seal-religion of personal vanity. Constantine was a much better man than Mr. Waugh makes out and Mr. Waugh's historical detail is sufficiently close-studied for us to be quite sure that Mr. Waugh knows he was. But the Constantine of this book is not a historical reconstruction. It is a projection of Mr. Waugh's old fancies into the more disturbing realm of true imagination. The author has *seen*; not invented. Constantine-Seal shows what he has seen and I think it amounts to nothing less than the abject failure of Mr. Waugh's own generation. He has imagined the maturity of his own characters; truly imagined them and therefore provided us with a clearer vision of them and their world than we could obtain for ourselves, or, indeed, from any of Mr. Waugh's previous books. Constantine, then, is a work of Mr. Waugh's imagination rather than the fancy which he has been hitherto content to use. For myself, this is decisive. I am an admirer of Coleridge and I have read, I think, everything he ever wrote, including the philosophical lectures which a contemporary scholar has ingeniously written for him. I hold fast to that one part of his opinions which I can safely say I understand. By this test, I find it impossible to say that Mr. Waugh is here writing below his best. We must, therefore, leave our examination of the author and turn our criticism upon ourselves. Are we looking at the book in the proper way? I think we can learn much in this matter by pausing for a moment to study the way that a good spectator looks at a certain style of sculpture.

This course needs an apology. I propose to argue by analogy from one art to another: namely from Baroque sculpture to the several-centred style of Mr. Waugh. There are no grounds in aesthetics for believing such an analogy to be logically true criticism: I can only, therefore, use it as an illustration. My excuse is that writing these notes and reading Mr. Waugh's book in Rome and Amalfi, the illustration seems inevitable. I agree that it is logically insecure, but I find it enlarges my understanding.

III

We have become accustomed in English to Baroque art being made an excuse for Baroque prose. I have therefore chosen a few sentences from Moretti's[1] recent analysis of works by Bernini and Borromini, not so much for their originality (although his analysis as a whole does not lack it) but because they are lucid. He begins: "Con Michelangelo scendono le ansie, i terrori, il senso ostile del tempo, questa malattia della maturità; . . ."

This is, in my opinion, an arresting sentence. Moretti says that when we come to Michelangelo we find that a sickness has fallen upon him; a sickness "of anxiety, of terror, of a sense of the hostility of time." It is a sickness of maturity: but the symptoms of that sickness do not spring from a sense of the hostility of the surrounding world. "With Michelangelo," Moretti goes on, "the feeling of time is a new dimension; a dimension in which he can project himself and which becomes the dominating factor in artistic expression."

We are concerned, then, not solely with the times in which he lived but with Time itself: the feeling of change, of irrecoverable loss, of no stability or rest anywhere. Perhaps the way the world has gone has something to do with it: but it is much more a sickness of the spirit. It is a disbalance in the soul which must affect everything the sick man does; above all, everything he creates.

Moretti continues: "From him, in this fashion, was born that plastic realization of temporal change which is characteristic of the Baroque. . . .

The stilling of the processes of time, or rather their supersession, is the problem of art in all periods; sometimes it is implicit, sometimes it is not. In the art of the Baroque, it becomes explicit."

From this sickness, Moretti goes on, springs the temporal nature of Baroque art. Time must be in some way suppressed, got round, tamed; it must somehow be stabilized. And if the sickness is part of our human nature, then we must go beyond that nature.

> The sharp demands of this obsession with time [he goes on] forces Baroque artists to evolve a method of working by stages (*plastica successiva*) that unfold and dissolve one into the other something after the fashion of music. The Baroque builds up complex structures that can only be understood in a temporal manner and the unity of which can only be grasped by making an intellectual synthesis which takes place in the memory and is a thing apart from the immediate perception.

The core of his theory, then, is this. Baroque art must be looked at in parts. The parts are joined together, but only by an intellectual effort on the part of the spectator. We, not the artist, produce the synthesis.

This is the main conclusion of his argument. I will now summarize his more precise findings. Baroque art, he says, essentially employs a method of composition in which there are two or more distinct and separate focal points. The spectator's eye travels from one to another: there is a logical progression, but the spectator will not find it mechanically. He can, and will, lose it, if his imagination is not constantly at work. The focal points are not formally associated, save in the final product of the spectator's imagination. They are not even properly linked for, as he says, "From one centre to another the plastic passages are not important and they can be the work of pupils and journeymen, exactly as the lyrical centres of Pindar are joined by everyday and commonplace phrases." In a word it is only the focal points which count: they, and the progression which, when we have it in due order, we shall find to be the whole object of the sculptor. . . .

V

We have gone so far in our decay that we no longer have complexes of sculpture or long poems in which to seek the expression of our times. It is proper, then, to look for it in novels, particularly in the novels of those writers, who, like Mr. Waugh, compose their works with a poet's or a sculptor's care. If our train of thought has been approximately right, we shall expect to find that Mr. Waugh's book consists of a series of episodes, each complete in itself and linked with the next by an unimportant, or "flat," passage. Provided we approach the story with the required intellectual alertness, we shall expect to find these episodes going together to indicate some form of escape from the instability and change which are implicit in them. There is no doubt in my mind that this is what we do find.

I have already shortly described the three principal episodes: the uneventful joining passages are described again and again by the author as just that: times in which nothing seemed to happen to Helena, long sojourns in remote places with barely a word from Rome. But if little changes for Helena during decades of her life, when she does at last go to the capital city she is surrounded by uncertainty as though by a nightmare. Nothing is stable, nothing is sure: people are murdered in the night and are never mentioned again, even religion is new: nobody knows what to believe until a Council has settled it and nobody believes the Council will settle anything.

Then, at last, comes the finding of the Cross, and for Helena, at least, a great peace in her heart. If we are looking for a gesture, what gesture could be more telling? The last chapters of the book rise to such levels that it is not too much to say that they illustrate the greatest of all conceptions of human existence: that in which the individual moves almost blindly through life conscious of only a deep disquiet, a yearning to fulfil a purpose which at best is barely discerned and which mostly is not discerned at all. Helena is disturbed by the problem that disturbed the vaster spirit of St. Augustine, living when the passage of time brought with it a more sickening sense of loss even than it did to Helena, or even than it does to-day:

> Ce qu'il cherche, c'est bien tel que sa possession comble tout désir et confère par conséquent la paix . . . c'est le problème de sa destinée; chercher à se connaître, pour savoir ce qu'il faut faire afin de mieux être et, si possible, afin de bien être, voilà pour lui toute la question.[2]

Helena is a saint, but not Augustine's sort of saint; and she is not a philosopher at all. She is down at our own level: and the beatitude she seeks is on our own level, too. She seeks a piece of wood, because it is holy. She finds it — a concrete symbol of the gigantic abstractions that were the aim of the greater saint; she finds it, and she is content.

But all this fine construction of the book can be missed unless we are prepared to approach it with a frame of mind quite different from that which we use to understand a book written in settled times. We must not expect classical stability: we must not expect a self-contained design that imposes itself upon us. I do not think we shall find it in any good book written in our times; and because we look for it, we do not find good books.

Helena is more than a good book: it is a model of a new sort of novel. Since Mr. Waugh's previous books, excellent as they were, never went beyond the technical discoveries of other men, then *Helena* must, in my view, be considered to be a much better book than any he has previously written, and in the context of our times, a masterpiece.

Notes

1. Luigi Moretti: "Forme Astratte Nella Scultura Barocca" in *Spazio*, No. 3 (Rome, 1950).

2. Étienne Gilson: *Introduction a l'Étude de Saint Augustin*, chapter I. [Editor's translation: He wants to find the kind of good whose possession will satisfy every desire and ensure peace. . . . He was concerned with the problem of his own destiny; he sought self-knowledge in order to discover what must be done to be better and, if possible, to be happy.]

What Was Wrong with Pinfold   J. B. Priestley*

Mr Evelyn Waugh's semi-autobiographical novel, *The Ordeal of Gilbert Pinfold*, has been both sharply attacked and enthusiastically praised. Literary criticism is not our concern here, but perhaps I ought to add that I liked the beginning of the story, was prepared to admire the general plan of it, but found the hallucination scenes aboard ship rather crude and tedious, quite without the nightmare quality I had expected to find in them. This surprised me in a writer I have long admired — and indeed I was one of the very first to shout his praises — a novelist of originality, great technical skill, and personal distinction. I came to the conclusion that in these scenes he had got himself bogged down somewhere between reality and invention: reality, because he was describing more or less what had happened to himself; invention, because he had decided, perhaps hastily at the last moment, to substitute imaginary imaginary voices for the imaginary voices he himself seemed to hear; and that this would explain why, being hasty substitutions, they seem far below his usual level of creation and invention. But all this is guesswork. And it is not Mr Waugh but Gilbert Pinfold who is the subject of this essay.

Pinfold, we are told, is a middle-aged novelist of some distinction. He is well known abroad, where foreign students write theses on his work. He lives in an old house in the country, where his wife, who is younger than he is, farms their property. He has a large young family. He no longer travels widely as he used to do, and now pays only infrequent visits to London, though he is still a member of "Bellamy's Club."

> Since the end of the war his life had been strictly private. In his own village he took very lightly the duties which he might have thought incumbent on him. He contributed adequate sums to local causes but he

*Reprinted from *New Statesman and Nation*, 31 August 1957, 244.

had no interest in sport or in local government, no ambition to lead or to command. He had never voted in a parliamentary election, maintaining an idiosyncratic toryism which was quite unrepresented in the political parties of his time. . . .

His wife is a born Catholic and he is a convert. His days, we are told, are passed in writing, reading and managing his own small affairs. He lives as he wants to live and, unlike most people nowadays, is perfectly contented with his lot.

Nevertheless, he drinks a good deal, indeed rather too much. And because he sleeps badly he finds himself taking larger and larger doses of an opiate or sedative that he keeps mixed with Creme de Menthe, a remedy, based on an old prescription. So it is a boozy and half-doped Pinfold who finds his way, not without difficulty, to the cabin he has booked for a three-week voyage to the East. It is in this cabin that he begins to hear the voices that torment him, belonging to persecutors who have no existence, who are creations of his own unconscious. For the benefit of Jungians, it may be added that both the Shadow and the Anima are busily engaged in these spectral intrigues. Poor Pinfold finds himself in a kind of waking nightmare, out of which he does not emerge until he returns home. The local doctor tells him he has been the victim of the bromide and chloral he has been swigging so heartily. We leave him, safe and cosy again in his study, ready to start work, but preferring to his unfinished novel a more urgent piece: *The Ordeal of Gilbert Pinfold*.

But if Pinfold imagines his troubles are over, he is a fool. He has been warned. Because the voices talked a lot of rubbish, making the most ridiculous accusations, he is ignoring the underlying truth uniting them all, the idea that he is not what he thinks he is, that he is busy deceiving both himself and other people. Consciously he has rejected this idea for some time; he has drowned it in alcohol, bromide and chloral; and now it can only batter its way through to him by staging a crude drama of lunatic voices. And though they are a long way from the truth in their detailed charges, they are right, these voices, when they tell him that he is a fake. It is of course Pinfold remonstrating with Pinfold; the fundamental self telling the ego not to be a mountebank. What is on trial here is the Pinfold persona. This persona is inadequate: the drink hinted at it; the dope more than suggested it; the voices proved it.

The style of life deliberately adopted by Pinfold is that of those old Catholic landed families, whose women live for the children and the home farm and whose men, except in wartime when, like Pinfold, they are ready to defend their country, detach themselves from the national life, behaving from choice as their ancestors were compelled to do from necessity, because of their religion. Everything we learn about Pinfold fits this style of life—with one supremely important exception, the fact, the obstinate fact, that he is by profession a writer, an artist. And this is the central truth about Pinfold, who could never have achieved any distinction as a novelist if he had not been essentially an artist. He is not a Catholic landed gentleman pretending to be an author. He is an author pretending to be a Catholic landed gentleman. But why, you may ask, should he not be both? Because they are not compatible. And this is not merely my opinion. It is really Pinfold's opinion too.

Though Pinfold may imagine he has achieved a style of life that suits him perfectly, his behaviour shows that he is wrong. Take the heavy drinking. Some men drink a lot because their work demands that they should appear to be easy and affable with persons they rather dislike; other men do it because they are naturally gregarious and like to lap it up with the boys; others again, like some politicians, journalists, actors, take to booze because their days and nights are a difficult mixture of boring waits and sudden crises. But Pinfold belongs to none of these groups. He is a solitary soaker, hoping to deaden his mind against reality. This explains too his reckless traffic with opiates and sedatives. Anything is better than lying awake at three in the morning, when the persona is transparent and brittle. So in the end the voices arrive. Their accusations are absurd, monstrous; he is an alien who has changed his name, a homosexual, a traitor, a would-be murderer; always they miss the mark, perhaps deliberately overshooting at it, as if there could be a deception even in these attempts to end deception; nevertheless, they are telling him he is not what he pretends to be. And if they stopped clowning and, perhaps with his consent, spoke plainly, they would say: "Pinfold, you are a professional writer, a novelist, an artist, so stop pretending you represent some obscure but arrogant landed family that never had an idea in its head."

Pinfold has to do some writing, from time to time, otherwise he could not earn a living. And when he is in the middle of a book he behaves like an artist, breaking the country gentleman pattern; but such times — "were a small part of his year. On most nights he was neither fretful nor apprehensive. He was merely bored. After even the idlest day he demanded six or seven hours of insensibility. With them behind him, with them to look forward to, he could face another idle day with something approaching jauntiness; and these his doses unfailingly provided. . . ." This is very revealing. When he is not working, Pinfold is bored because his persona is inadequate, because the role he has condemned himself to play is too sketchy and empty, because the intellectual and artist in him feel frustrated and starved. An author is not an author only when he is writing. Genuine authorship, to which Pinfold, who is no hack, is committed, is just as much a way of life as farming or soldiering. It is one of the vocations. This is why, at a time when most people are demanding more and more for their goods and services, the author can safely be offered less, for it is an open secret, no matter what he may say, that he is in love with his trade. If the worst came to the worst, he would take a clerkship at the gas-works and pay out of his savings to be printed.

What we may call *Pinfolding* — the artist elaborately pretending not to be an artist — is an old trick here in England, thanks to our aristocratic tradition and our public suspicion of intellect and the arts. Congreve was pinfolding when Voltaire visited him, only to be told that Congreve considered himself to be a gentleman of leisure, not a writer of plays; which drew from Voltaire the retort that he would not have wasted his time calling upon a gentleman, only upon the writer of plays. The English are born pinfolders. (Think of Elgar, his mind brooding over the heart-break of his Cello Concerto, doing his best to look and behave like a retired colonel with a passion for horse-racing.) It saves us from the solemn posturing we have observed among our foreign colleagues, who are more portentous about a short review than we could be about an epic creation. We avoid the *Cher Maître* touch. Yet I think the Continental attitude, for all its pomposity, extravagance, incitement to charlatanry, is saner, healthier, better for both the arts and the nation, than ours is. If authors and artists in this country are not only officially regarded without favour but even singled out for unjust treatment — as I for one believe — then the Pinfolds are partly to blame. They not only do not support their profession: they go over to the enemy. Congreve may have shrugged away his reputation as a poet and dramatist, but at least he identified himself with a class from which were drawn the chief patrons of poetry and the drama, whereas the Pinfolds are hiding themselves among fox-hunters, pheasant slaughterers, horse and cattle breeders.

Let Pinfold take warning. He will break down again, and next time may never find a way back to his study. The central self he is trying to deny, that self which grew up among books and authors and not among partridges and hunters, that self which even now desperately seeks expression in ideas and words, will crack if it is walled up again within a false style of life. Whatever Mrs Pinfold and the family and the neighbours may think and say, Pinfold must step out of his role as the Cotswold gentleman quietly regretting the Reform Bill of 1832, and if he cannot discover an accepted role as English man of letters — and I admit this is not easy — he must create one, hoping it will be recognisable. He must be at all times the man of ideas, the intellectual, the artist, even if he is asked to resign from Bellamy's Club. If not; if he settles down again to sulk and soak behind that inadequate persona, waiting for a message from Bonnie Prince Charlie; then not poppy, nor mandragora, nor all the drowsy syrups of the world, shall ever medicine him.

Anything Wrong with Priestley?   Evelyn Waugh*

In the *New Statesman* of August 31 Mr. J. B. Priestley published an article entitled "What was wrong with Pinfold?" "Pinfold," I should explain, is the name I gave to the leading character of my last book, a confessedly autobiographical novel which had already been reviewed (very civilly) in the literary columns of that curiously two-faced magazine. The contrast is notorious between the Jekyll of culture, wit and ingenious competition and the Hyde of querulous atheism and economics which prefaces it. Mr. Priestley's article appeared in Hyde's section. He is not concerned to help me with my writing, as he is so well qualified to do, but to admonish me about the state of my soul, a subject on which I cannot allow him complete mastership. With "Let Pinfold take warning," he proclaims in prophetic tones, and with the added authority of some tags from Jung, that I shall soon go permanently off my rocker. The symptoms are that I try to combine two incompatible roles, those of the artist and the Catholic country gentleman.

Which of those dangers to the artistic life, I wonder, does he regard as the more deadly. Not living in the country, surely? Unless I am misinformed Mr. Priestley was at my age a landed proprietor on a scale by which my own modest holding is a peasant's patch.

Catholicism? It is true that my Church imposes certain restrictions which Mr. Priestley might find irksome, but he must have observed that a very large number of his fellow writers profess a creed and attempt to follow a moral law which are either Roman Catholic or, from a Jungian point of view, are almost identical. Mr. T.S. Eliot, Dame Edith Sitwell, Mr. Betjeman, Mr. Graham Greene, Miss Rose Macaulay — the list is illustrious and long. Are they all heading for the bin?

No, what gets Mr. Priestley's goat (supposing he allows such a deleterious animal in his lush pastures) is my attempt to behave like a gentleman. Mr. Priestley has often hinted at a distaste for the upper classes but, having early adopted the persona of a generous-hearted, genial fellow, he has only once, I think, attempted to portray them. On that occasion, of which more later, he showed a rather remote acquaintance, like Dickens in creating Sir Mulberry Hawke. It is the strain of minding his manners that is driving poor Pinfold cuckoo. "He must," writes Mr. Priestley, "be at all times the man of ideas, the intellectual, the artist, even if he is asked to resign from Bellamy's Club" (a fictitious institution that occurs in some of my books). Mr. Priestley's clubs must be much stricter than mine. Where I belong I never heard of the committee inquiring into the members' "ideas." It is true that we are forbidden to cheat at cards or

*From *The Essays, Articles and Reviews of Evelyn Waugh*, edited by Donat Gallagher (Boston: Little, Brown, 1983), 527–29. © 1983 by The Estate of Laura Waugh. Reprinted by permission of Little, Brown and Company.

strike the servants, but for the life of me I can't see anything particularly artistic in either of those activities.

Naturally I hunger for Mr. Priestley's good opinion and would like to keep my sanity for a few more years. I am an old dog to learn new tricks but I dare say I could be taught an accent at a school of elocution. I should not find it beyond me to have behave like a cad on occasions — there are several shining examples in the literary world. My hair grows strongly still; I could wear it long. I could hire a Teddyboy suit and lark about the dance halls with a bicycle chain. But would this satisfy Mr. Priestley? Would he not be quick to detect and denounce this new persona? "There was Waugh," he would say, "a man of humane education and accustomed to polite society. Tried to pass as Redbrick. No wonder he's in the padded cell."

I do not flatter myself that Mr. Priestley's solicitude springs solely from love of me. What, I think, really troubles him is that by my manner of life I am letting down the side, all eleven of them whoever they are whom Mr. Priestley captains. "If authors and artists in this country," he writes, "are not only officially regarded without favour but even singled out for unjust treatment — as I for one believe — then the Pinfolds are partly to blame. They not only do not support their profession; they go over to the enemy."

I say, Priestley old man, are you sure you are feeling all right? Any Voices? I mean to say! No narcotics or brandy in your·case, I know, but when a chap starts talking about "the enemy" and believing, for one, that he is singled out for unjust treatment, isn't it time he consulted his Jungian about his *anima*? Who is persecuting poor Mr. Priestley? Mr. Macmillan does not ask him to breakfast as Gladstone might have done. His income, like everyone else's, is confiscated and "redistributed" in the Welfare State. Tennyson's life was made hideous by importunate admirers; Mr. Priestley can walk down Piccadilly with a poppy or a lily, but he will be unmolested by the mob who pursue television performers. Is this what Mr. Priestley means by unjust treatment? Pinfold, he says, is vainly waiting for a message from Bonnie Prince Charlie. Is it possible that Mr. Priestley is awaiting a summons to Windsor from Queen Victoria?

Mr. Priestley is an older, richer, more popular man than I, but I cannot forbear saying: "Let him take warning." He has had some sharp disappointments in the last twelve years; perhaps he would call them "traumas." The voices he hears, like Pinfold's, may be those of a wildly distorted conscience. There was, indeed, a *trahison des clercs* some twenty years back which has left the literary world much discredited. It was then that the astute foresaw the social revolution and knew who would emerge top dog. They went to great lengths to suck up to the lower classes or, as they called it, to "identify themselves with the workers." Few excelled Mr. Priestley in his zeal for social justice. It is instructive to re-read his powerful novel *Blackout in Gretley*, which was written at a very dark time in the war when national unity was of vital importance. Its simple theme is that the English upper classes were in conspiracy to keep the workers in subjection even at the cost of national defeat. The villain, Tarlington, is everything deplorable, a man of good family and of smart appearance, a Conservative, the director of an engineering works, a courageous officer in 1914 — and, of course, a German spy. *Blackout in Gretley* is like *The Hill* in reverse; all morals derive from social origin. The police are a fine body of men but the Chief Constables are Fascist beasts. Two attractive women in the same fast set are equally suspect; but one turns out to have been a disorderly waitress before her respectable marriage; she has a heart of gold. The other is the niece of Vice-Admiral Sir Johnson Fund-Tapley and, of course, a traitor. Only two workers show moral delinquency; of these one turns out to be a German officer in disguise; the other, and more wicked, is — a Roman Catholic. Even the bad food at the hotel is ascribed to the fact that it is managed by a retired officer. "This country has the choice during the next two years," a virtuous character says, "of coming fully to life and beginning all over again or of rapidly decaying and dying on the same old feet. It can only accomplish the first by taking a firm grip on about fifty thousand important, influential gentlemanly persons and telling them firmly to shut up and do nothing if they don't want to be put to doing some most unpleasant work."

Came the dawn. Mr. Priestley was disappointed. No concentration camp was made for the upper classes. Nor have the triumphant workers shown themselves generous or discerning patrons of the arts. Gratitude, perhaps, is not one of their salient virtues. When they feel the need for a little aesthetic pleasure they do not queue at the experimental theatre; they pile into charabancs and tramp round the nearest collection of heirlooms and family portraits; quite enough to inflame the naked artist with an itch of persecution mania.

A Handful of Dust:
Critique of Victorianism

Richard Wasson*

A Handful of Dust is commonly read as a satirical commentary on English society during the late twenties and early thirties. Taking as texts the epigraph from *The Waste Land* and Mr. Waugh's statement that "the novel contains all I have to say about humanism," critics have commented on the decline of the aristocracy and the fall of the innocent. The novel is seen as the last of those early works written before Mr. Waugh's Catholi-

*Reprinted from *Modern Fiction Studies* 7 (Winter 1961):327–37. © by Purdue Research Foundation, West Lafayette, Indiana 47907. Reprinted with permission.

cism began to manifest itself in his novels.[1] But the novel is more than an attack on contemporary decadence; it is a critique of the whole tradition of English religious and social life. That tradition is bankrupt, Mr. Waugh charges, because its Protestant and romantic nature had cut England away from the true source of ethical and religious behavior which lies in Roman Catholicism. The novel contains all Mr. Waugh has to say in criticism of English tradition, and, while it contains none of the frank apologetics of some of his later works, the Catholic position is central to its meaning.

The chief cultural villains of the piece are the Victorians. The picturesque medievalism of Rossetti and Tennyson and the melodrama of Dickens are as responsible for Tony's imprisonment in Todd's cottage as the faithlessness of Brenda and the pleasureless materialism of the Beavers and the Cockpurses. Tony's road to hell is paved with the literature of the Victorian era, which in its attempt to preserve the picturesque trappings and the ethical values of Christianity sacrificed the essence of the faith. Tony's imagination, committed to the Victorian values represented by his Victorian Gothic ancestral home, can find no way out of the dilemma of modern life except to go on a quest which is conceived in terms of Tennysonian romance and Dickensian melodrama and finally leads him to spiritual and physical death. The Victorians, of course, are not solely responsible, for they were really trying to patch up a tradition bequeathed them by the Renaissance that had no firm foundation or structure. Anglican England, according to Mr. Waugh, has no real tradition but has merely built anew over the destroyed edifice of the authentic Catholic tradition.

Mr. Waugh's view of the tradition is most explicitly expressed in his essay "Come Inside": "England was Catholic for nine hundred years, then Protestant for three hundred years, then agnostic for a century. The Catholic structure still lies buried beneath every phase of English life; history, topography, law, archeology everywhere reveal Catholic origins."[2] Two important changes have taken place which have served to make Catholicism a buried substructure—the Tudor period, when nine hundred years of Catholic tradition were scrapped by the reformation, and the Victorian era, when the Protestant tradition gave way before the onslaught of scientific agnosticism. In *Edmund Campion*, which appeared only a year after the publication of *A Handful of Dust*, Mr. Waugh dealt with the earlier period. The priest, arriving in England during the religious disturbances of the late 1580s, sees as he travels, the gutted Catholic churches, the ruined monasteries and the raw new buildings of the Tudor nobility.

> The scars of the Tudor revolution were still fresh and livid; the great houses of the new ruling class were building, and in sharp contrast to their magnificence stood the empty homesteads of the yeomanry . . . the village churches were empty shells, their altars torn out and their ornaments defaced. . . . The ruins were not yet *picturesque*; moss and

ivy had barely begun their work and age had not yet softened the stark lines of change. Many generations of orderly living, much gentle association, were needed before, under another queen, the State Church could assume the venerable style of Barchester Towers.[3] (italics mine)

This graphic description of architectural destruction and rebuilding is a metaphor for the development of the English tradition. The raw newness of the Elizabethan period needed hundreds of years of orderly living, gentle association, and moss and ivy before it could appear as venerable and authentic as the real tradition which it destroyed. It was the Victorian era which finally succeeded in making the tradition seem real, in covering the starkness of the Anglican establishment with the decorations of age. The key to the weakness of the disguise which the establishment wears lies in the word *picturesque*. The picturesque does not create authenticity but rather constitutes a clear and present danger to those seeking true faith, for it beguiles the imagination and leads it astray. In the story of his own conversion Mr. Waugh specifically disclaims the lure of the picturesque.

But those who do not know my country should understand that the aesthetic appeal of the Church of England is unique and peculiar to those Islands. Elsewhere a first interest in the Catholic Church is often kindled in the convert's imagination by the splendors of her worship in contrast with the bleakness and meanness of the Protestant sects. In England the pull is all the other way. The medieval cathedrals and churches, the rich ceremonies that surround the monarchy, the historic titles of Canterbury and York, the social organization of the country parishes, the traditional culture of Oxford and Cambridge, the liturgy composed in the heydey of English prose style—all these are the property of the Church of England, while Catholics meet in modern buildings, often of deplorable design, and are usually served by simple Irish missionaries.[4]

Mr. Waugh further attacks the picturesque in his book on Rossetti, in which he argues that scientific agnosticism led to the development "of two main attitudes" on the part of Victorians, "and for that matter on the part of most moderns" too. The first attitude is to doubt the reality of everything that was not scientifically validated. The second is the romantic view which "sees life as a series of glowing and unrelated systems in which the component parts are explicable and true only in terms of themselves, in which the stars are just as big and as near as they look and " 'rien n'est vrai que le pittoresque.' "[5] Finding their religious traditions under attack, the Victorians sought to defend their faith from turrets and bastions that were detached from the main fortress, the medieval tradition of Roman Catholicism.

Another Victorian error was to attempt to substitute an ethic of right and wrong for the sense of sin. Conscience became the guide, and a guilty conscience was substituted for the awareness of sin as the chief motive of reformative action. In *Brideshead Revisited* Brideshead tells his sister Julia that he will not bring his fiancé to the house because he does not want to bring her into the atmosphere of sin that dwells there as a result of the adulterous association between Julia and Charles. This shocks Julia into an awareness of her spiritual state, but the romantic, Protestant Charles cannot understand her feeling. He interprets her feeling as nothing more than an attack of prudish Victorian conscience.

> "Julia," I said later when Brideshead had gone upstairs, "have you ever seen a picture of Holman Hunt's called 'The Awakened Conscience'?"
> "No."
> I had seen a copy of *Pre-Raphaelitism* in the library some days before; I found it again and read her Ruskin's description. She laughed quite happily.[6]

But it means more to Julia and it is her view which wins out.

> " 'Living in sin,' not just doing wrong, as I did when I went to America; doing wrong, knowing it is wrong, stopping doing it, forgetting. That's not what they mean. That's not Bridey's pennyworth. He means just what it says in black and white. 'Living in sin,' with sin, by sin, for sin, every hour, every day, year in, year out. Waking up with sin in the morning, seeing the curtains drawn on sin, bathing it, dressing it, clipping diamonds to it, feeding it, showing it around, giving it a good time, putting it to sleep at night with a tablet of Dial if it's fretful."[7]

But it is not only the substitution of the picturesque for the authentically traditional, nor the substitution of the ethical conscience for the sense of sin that has led the English astray. By altering the ritual of the Mass and reducing it to a minor and occasional part of the service, Anglicans deprived worship of its efficacy. Further, the English made the Church an adjunct of the State and thus deprived it of its independent power. The result of these actions is that the Church has little or no effect on its parishioners.[8] The church service in *A Handful of Dust* is illustrative of the failure of the Church to capture the minds and hearts of the people who attend it, for "few of the things said in the Churches seemed to have any particular reference to themselves." (p. 38).[9] The Vicar's sermon is typical of the form of service which replaced the Mass. As an adjunct of the State the Church inevitably comes to support State action. Deprived of a timeless ritual, the service becomes subject to the vagaries of temporal change and the Vicar must keep pace with changing events. The Vicar at Hetton, however, has not bothered to keep up with the times and hence preaches the same sermons he used as chaplain to Her Majesty's soldiers in India: ". . . let us remember our gracious Queen Empress and pray that she may long be spared to send us at her bidding to do our duty in the uppermost parts of the earth . . ." (p. 39). This is, of course, a slash at Kiplingesque imperial religion; but the thrust goes to the heart of the English concept of the Church and the Church's service. A state church without the miracle of the Mass at the center of its service ultimately becomes meaningless. Without such a religious center a society, regardless of its attempts to preserve forms or ethical systems, is doomed to dissolution.

That Mr. Waugh's view of the tradition permeates *A Handful of Dust* is clear. One need only look at the chapter titles to see that English Gothic is under attack. The central symbol for the tradition is, of course, the ancestral seat of the Last family, the Gothic Hetton. As the architectural images of *Edmund Campion* depict the cultural and religious errors of Renaissance England, so Hetton represents the errors of the Victorian imagination. Built in 1864, it is replete with embattlements, turrets, and Arthurian friezes which represent the attempt of Tony's grandfather to establish the continuity of the English tradition. Tony is determined to preserve every encaustic title of it in the face of modernizers who would plate its walls with chromium, for he unquestionably accepts it as the embodiment of all that is true and best in the tradition. But Mr. Waugh makes it clear at the end of the novel that both Tony and his grandfather were disastrously mistaken in their judgments when he says the inheritor of the estate, Cousin Teddy, hopes "one day to restore Hetton to the glory that it had enjoyed in the days of Cousin Tony" (p. 301). Mr. Waugh has painted the glory of those days only too well, and the implication is that Tony and his grandfather were as mistaken about the nature and glory of the good old days as Teddy now is. What lies at the core of English tradition is the gutted churches and the raw Tudor houses that Edmund Campion saw, and the Gothic Hetton is only an attempt to disguise the break in the tradition. Moss, ivy, and Gothic imitations can make the English tradition seem venerable but they are only decorative paint on a picturesque mask. The Victorian error is akin to that with which Mr. Waugh has recently charged Cecil Beaton: "Ancient buildings existed for him merely as a picturesque setting, not as monuments to the living past."[10] The Victorians and Tony Last differ in that they mistook picturesque settings for monuments of the living past. Tony, who accepts the mask and can draw sustenance only from Hetton and what it represents, has no forces to pit against the mechanical and materialistic faithlessness of modern society except those transmitted to him by the Victorian imagination. Betrayed by his time, he goes on a quest for salvation, but so conditioned is he by Victorian Gothic forms that his imagination can conceive only of a romantic quest, not a truly religious one. "The City" he seeks is not the Holy City, the City of God, but rather a transfigured Hetton. His journey is to Camelot, not Rome.

Mr. Waugh patterns the city Tony searches for closely upon the city in Tennyson's "The Holy Grail." "Hetton transfigured" combines the features of Camelot with the features of the city that Percivale sees in his vision of the Grail:

> It was Gothic in character, all vanes and pinnacles, gargoyles, battle-
> ments, groining and tracery, pavillions and terraces, a transfigured

Hetton, pennons and banners floating on the sweet breeze, everything luminous and translucent; a coral citadel crowning a green hilltop sewn with daisies, among groves and streams; a tapestry landscape filled with heraldic and fabulous animals and symmetrical, disproportionate blossom. (p. 222)

> . . . the sacred mount of Camelot,
> And all the dim rich city, roof by roof,
> Tower after tower, spire beyond spire,
> By grove, and garden-lawn and rushing brook. . . .
>
> Rich galleries, lady-laden, weighed the necks
> Of dragons clinging to the crazy walls,
> Thicker than drops from thunder, showers of flowers
> Fell as we passed; and men and boys astride
> On wyvern, lion, dragon, griffin, swan . . .
>
> I saw the spiritual city and all her spires
> . . . and from this star there shot
> A rose-red sparkle to the city. . . .
>
> And I rode on and found a mighty hill
> And on it a mighty city walled; the spires
> Pricked by incredible pinnacles into heaven.[11]

Not only are the goals of the searches alike but the circumstances of the two quests are similar. Both heroes are led by guides, Percivale by Galahad, Tony by Dr. Messinger. Dr. Messinger leads Tony up a river — which on the good doctor's map has "a mythical appearance" — just as Percivale is led by Galahad. Both are finally deserted by their guides. Percivale finds himself "alone and in a land of sand and thorn" (l. 376), while Mr. Waugh notes that, "There was a dense growth of thorn here, overhanging the river bank" (p. 274). Mr. Todd lives in "one of those little patches of sand and grass that crop up occasionally" (p. 284) in the area. Tony is forced to pick "his way through the surrounding thorn scrub" (p. 282) in order to get to the savannah on which Mr. Todd lives. On the journey Tony is "consumed with thirst and drank mug after mug of river water" (p. 268); Percivale is "thirsty even unto death" (l. 375) and drinks from a nearby brook. Both become ill and suffer from delusions. In one of these dreams Percivale is confronted by a woman who offers him rest.

> ". . . but when I touched her, lo! she too
> Fell into dust and nothing and the house
> Became no better than a broken shed,
> And in it a dead babe; and also this
> Fell into dust, and I was left alone."
> (ll. 396–400)

This passage reads like a capsule summary of Tony's experience, for Hetton, with its chromium-plated room, is now little better than a broken shed. Brenda, her true nature revealed when she demands that Tony sell Hetton, has turned to dust and the dead babe is, of course, John Andrew. The line "fell into dust, and I was left alone" becomes a refrain that runs through several stanzas in the *Idyll* and it is surely not far-fetched to assume that Mr. Waugh had them in mind.[12]

At the conclusion of each quest is the vision of The City.

> . . . the sound of music rose from the glittering walls; some procession or pageant was passing along them. He lurched into tree-trunks and became caught up in roots and hanging tendrils of bush vine. . . . At last he came into the open. The gates were open before him and trumpets were sounding along the walls saluting his arrival; from bastion to bastion the message ran to the four points of the compass; petals of almond and apple blossom were in the air; they carpeted the way as after a summer storm, they lay in the orchards at Hetton. Gilded cupolas and spires of alabaster shone in the sunlight. (p. 283)

> And I rode on and found a mighty hill
> And on it a mighty city walled; the spires
> Pricked by incredible pinnacles into heaven.
> And by the gateway stood a crowd; and these
> Cried to me climbing, "Welcome Percivale,
> Thou mightiest and purest of men."
> (ll. 421–426)

Both get a noisy welcome from the shining city.

Mr. Waugh uses these parallels to show that Tennyson's conception of the quest is a false and misleading conception. That this is so is proved by an examination of the quest theme in Mr. Waugh's forthrightly Catholic novel, *Helena*. Helena, the saint who is reputed to have found the true cross, also goes in search of "The City," but she knows that such cities are seldom architectural transfigurations which house only pure-souled men. Such cities are "not so very different from anywhere else."[13] Helena's search is not a search for some picturesque place, but a "Timeless search for God,"[14] as Mr. DeVitis has so aptly put it. Hers is "the Augustinian search for the city before men, the Church, whose builder and maker is God."[15]

There are several episodes in Tony's quest, which, when compared with Percivale's story, show that Mr. Waugh, through describing Tony's foolishness, is describing the folly he sees in Tennyson's version of the quest. One need only compare the description of Galahad's disappearance with Dr. Messinger's drowning to see that Mr. Waugh thinks that Messinger's fate should have been Galahad's. A more significant parallel is in the Thérése de Vitré episode. Daughter of a family which has one of the best houses in Trinidad, she meets Tony aboard the ship which takes her home from her convent school in France to marry one of seven suitors, none of whom she knows well. Tony has a brief shipboard romance with her, but is warned by Dr. Messinger that women lead questors astray.

Percivale in his journey "chanced on a goodly town, with one great dwelling in the middle of it" (ll. 571–572), where he meets his lady love. "All this land and wealth were hers" (l. 568). Like Tony's Thérése, the woman kisses him and offers him her wealth, but, like a good questor, Percivale remembers Arthur's warning "that most of us would follow wandering fires" (l. 598). Though the same elements are in each episode, it is clear that the meanings are opposed. In Tennyson's work the questor behaves properly; in Mr. Waugh's work he behaves wrongly because Tony's rejection of Thérése is, as her name implies, a rejection of life. It is no coincidence that Tony rejects the Catholic Thérése in favor of his vision of a transfigured Hetton for dreams fostered by a romantic and Protestant tradition. That Tony has embraced a spiritual death in his rejection of her is symbolized by the stuffed fish which they bought while "in good spirits" in Barbadoes. Later when Thérése learns that Tony is married and has no intention of changing his status, she writes him off. Upon their return to the ship they find that the fish has been lost. The fish, of course, is a Christian symbol associated with the rebirth of life and when purchased had something to do with good spirits. When Tony refuses to have anything to do with Thérése, he in effect rejects the promise of new life, and the meaning of the fish changes. It now becomes an emblem of Tony, who is truly a stuffed and dead thing. The irony is that in Tennyson it is the woman who turns to dust, while in Mr. Waugh's book it is Tony. In Tennyson the questor is praised; in Mr. Waugh, damned.

While Mr. Waugh is primarily concerned with Tennyson in the "Search For The City," the section is not without its melodramatic overtones that lead in the "Du Côte dé Chez Todd" chapter to a close parallel with Dickens. I have already pointed out that Dr. Messinger is Galahad's counterpart, but he is a more ambitious creation than that. His literary genealogy includes the family of explorer-adventurers, men whose brave deeds in exotic lands give them an aura of authority that they may or may not deserve. He comes into the novel breathing the hot breath of melodramatic adventure onto pages that have previously been brightly satiric. He is a parody of melodrama, just as he is a parody of Galahad. Mr. Waugh seems to be saying that the melodramatic hero is as inadequate as the romantic one and it is here that Dickens rather than Tennyson becomes his game. In the last part of the novel he apes a typically Dickensian situation. Like Oliver Twist, Tony is kept prisoner in the house of a villain who first appears to the hero as a saviour, but turns out to be the very image of evil. Like Oliver, Tony wonders if his friends will come to rescue him and makes feeble efforts at escape which are easily thwarted by his grinning captors. But Tony is not saved and his captor easily outwits those who come to find him.

Tony's failure as questor and as melodramatic hero is symbolic of the failure of the Victorian imagination to come to grips with the problems of good and evil. Instead of seeing the problem in terms of sin and salvation, they see it in terms of ethical right and wrong. The whole concern of the *Idylls* is with the purity of the motives and acts of the questor. Galahad is the knight most likely to succeed because his behavior and heart are pure. Lancelot is successful because of his manful struggle to purify himself of the lust that led him to his affair with Guinevere. The whole moral of Tennyson's quest is "that the highest life consists in the conscientious discharge of plain and manifest duty. . . ."[16] The emphasis of the grail story is not on the search for God or faith or Church but on purity of spirit and behavior—it is the awakened conscience that Julia and Charles reject that is the motive of the quest. Dickens, too, is ethical rather than religious. The drama of Dickens centers around the conflict of the purely good with the purely evil. Oliver Twist, for example, is saved by his good-hearted friends from the clutches of the purely evil Fagin. The bright goodness of their hearts seems force enough to dispel the dark forces that shroud the evil Monks and his mob. In Dickens good hearts are inherently stronger than bad ones.

The weakness in both the Tennysonian and Dickensian views is that they fail to take into consideration the fact of original sin, which in Mr. Waugh's novel is represented by Mr. Todd. Todd, living in the jungle, seems at first to represent a kind of Rousseauistic natural man, but turns out to be a murderous enslaver of men. Inherent goodness and conscientious attention to duty are not powerful enough to overcome the primitive evil of the race, which is represented by Todd. The only force powerful enough to triumph over original sin is faith in the redeeming Christ and His Church. It is precisely this faith that the hero of romance, or the hero of melodrama does not have. Purity of spirit, such as displayed by Galahad and Oliver, is not enough to triumph over evil. When Tony, the captive of the Victorian imagination, comes face to face with the inherent evil of the race, he is powerless against it. The search for Camelot, the quest for the ethical, can only lead to such an end.

This view of the novel helps to explain certain facts about its structure that, though they have given critics of it a certain uneasiness, have never been adequately treated. The first four chapters chart the evils of the morally vacuous gentry in London and at Hetton. Tony seeks to maintain the Victorian standards represented by Hetton, but is unable to stem the flow of those eroding forces which threaten to wash Hetton before them. Suddenly he revolts and rises "to the vigorous heights of personal responsibility"[17] by turning Brenda's demands down cold. Stirred into action, he turns his back on London, on England, and sets out on what appears to be a heroic quest for the promised land of a transfigured Hetton. The whole tone of the novel, as was earlier pointed out, shifts from steely city satire to the comic melodrama of a jungle adventure. This alteration can be explained by the facts of publication. Mr. Waugh wrote in *Life* in 1946 that the germ of the novel came from a short story "about a man trapped in a jungle, ending his days reading Dickens aloud."[18] The novel grew from speculation about how the man came to such a plight. Yet when Mr. Waugh came to publish the novel in serialized form, the publisher demanded a revision of the ending. In *Mr. Loveday's Little Outing,* a collection of shorter works published in 1936, two years after the novel appeared, Mr. Waugh printed "An alternative ending to *A Handful of Dust,*" which "takes the place of chapters V, VI and VII of the book. The entire Brazilian episode is thus omitted. Tony Last leaves London on the breakdown of his wife's arrangements and goes on a prolonged and leisurely cruise."[19]

In the serialized version of the ending Tony returns from his voyage (which is not described) to find Brenda waiting for him in the car at the dock. As they return to Hetton, she tells him that she has been living in the flat since Beaver deserted her for Mrs. Rattery, whom he has married. The spurt of moral vigor that enabled Tony to turn down Reggie's offer has spent itself, for instead of dealing straightforwardly with the problem that now confronts him, he falls asleep and the crisis with Brenda is avoided. He soon slips back into the old life with "all the old faces around him." When Brenda gets him to go around to Mrs. Beaver and break the lease on the apartment, he decides to keep it under an assumed name so that he may have an affair of his own.

There are four important differences to be noted between the two endings. First, the cultural pattern which was the basis of the analysis given above is simply not in the serialized ending, for there is no heir to Hetton. Secondly, the tone of the novel is much more consistently observed in that ending. The tone and scene remain constant. Thirdly, Tony is no tragi-comic questor whose heart is betrayed by the images which guide its quest. He is merely a weak victim of the society in which he lives in the serialized ending, but he is almost heroic in his blindness in the book version of the novel. His blindness is the blindness of his cultural tradition, rather than the age in which he lives. Fourthly, Mr. Waugh has, though distorting certain elements of the novel's polished surface, given the novel a more coherent depth. Without the ending's indictment of the Victorian heritage and legacy, the full meaning of Hetton and its peculiar Gothic qualities would never be explored. The Arthurian rooms would remain jests at Victorian taste, but would never become emblems of the imagination of an age. In the final version Mr. Waugh has exploited to the full the cultural criticism that is only suggested in the serialized version of the novel.

Notes

1. Edmund Wilson, *Classics and Commercials* (New York, 1950), p. 146 ff. Anthony DeVitis, *Roman Holiday* (New York, 1956), p. 25 ff. Frederick J. Stopp, *Evelyn Waugh, Portrait of an Artist* (Boston, 1956), p. 90 ff.

2. *The Road to Damascus*, ed. John O'Brien (Garden City, N.Y., 1949), p. 20.

3. London, 1947, p. 127.

4. "Come Inside," p. 18.

5. *Rossetti* (London, 1928), p. 52.

6. (Boston, 1945), p. 290.

7. *Brideshead Revisited*, p. 28.

8. *Edmund Campion*, pp. 22, 27.

9. Page references in the text are to the undated New Directions edition of *A Handful of Dust*.

10. "Footlights and Chandeliers," *Spectator*, No. 6943 (July 21, 1961), p. 96.

11. "The Holy Grail," *Idylls of the King*, William J. Rolfe, ed. (Boston, 1896), pp. 46–74, ll. 227–230, 346–350, 526–530, 424–426. Further references to lines in this edition will be included in parentheses after quotations of lines.

12. Variations on the phrase "a handful of dust" also appear in "The Lotus Eaters," and in the first madness stanza of *Maud*.

13. (Boston, 1951), pp. 93–94.

14. DeVitis, p. 63.

15. Martin E. Marty, *A Short History of Christianity* (New York, 1959), p. 103. It should be noted that Charles Ryder too is granted a vision of the grail in the form of a lamp on the Brideshead chapel door. No picturesque vision this, it is described as being of "deplorable design," the same phrase Waugh used to describe modern English Catholic church buildings in his essay "Come Inside."

16. Henry Elsdale, *Studies in the Idylls* (London, 1878), pp. 57–58.

17. Stopp, p. 94.

18. "Fanfare," *Life* 20 (April 8, 1946), p. 56.

19. (London, 1936), p. 36.

All Gentlemen Are Now Very Old   James F. Carens[*]

Kingsley Amis, in attempting to explain new tendencies in the English novel of the 1950s, argued that pre-war satiric modes had been explicitly rejected. Nevertheless, when Amis described the attempt of certain recent English novelists to combine "the violent and the absurd, the grotesque and the romantic, the farcical and the horrific," he revealed that the influence of the early Huxley, Waugh, and Powell was still felt. Indeed, in *Men at Arms*, *Officers and Gentlemen*, and *Unconditional Surrender*, Evelyn Waugh revealed that he was as ready and able as ever to modulate effectively from one key to another.

Although since the time of *Brideshead* Waugh's manner has been modified by the attempt to adjust his satirical vision to a more conventional and realistic novel form, he has never, as Amis has suggested,

*Reprinted from *The Satiric Art of Evelyn Waugh* (Seattle and London: University of Washington Press, 1966), pp. 157–73, by permission of University of Washington Press. © 1966 by University of Washington Press.

abandoned satire.[1] The two principal satirical modes of the Guy Crouchback novels are burlesque and a particularly low-keyed ironic realism. The
satirist's command of these two modes, exercised by means of a masterfully
handled "counterpoint" technique, permits him successfully to achieve a
satire with both positive and negative poles. In the three Guy Crouchback
novels, Waugh does not permit waves of sentiment to dilute his satirical
energy as he had in *Brideshead*; nor does his desire to express a positive
value superior to the objects of his satire lead him into didacticism and
satirical apology, as in *Helena*. In the Crouchback novels Evelyn Waugh
successfully adjusts his conservative satirical vision to the conventions of
the novel. These three novels are his most satisfying attempt to expose fully
while creating meaningful positive values as well.

A number of strands in the complex web of these novels reveal how,
despite their extraordinary pessimism, they affirm in a way that the early
nihilistic works never could. Allusions to the great feast days, to the
sacraments, and to the services of the Church are reminders, in all three,
of a supernatural order that contrasts with the disintegrating forces of the
war. These allusions are in no sense obtrusive; they form an inevitable part
of the pattern of Guy Crouchback's existence. Guy's elderly father, who is
often associated with these observances and rituals, embodies Waugh's
social and religious ideals. This serene innocent has his comic side; he has,
for example, acknowledged no English monarch since James II. Nevertheless, the chastity of his mind, the dignity of his bearing, and the essential
decency of his spirit, all revealed to us from time to time in contrapuntal
passages, function, as Waugh intended them, "to keep audible a steady
undertone of the decencies and true purposes of life behind the chaos of
events and fantastic characters."[2] Even the gentleness of Mr. Crouchback's
"offstage" death, contrasting as it does with the violence of other deaths in
Unconditional Surrender, serves to emphasize the importance of his role.

Then, too, Guy Crouchback himself, differing, as we have seen
[elsewhere], from the antiheroes and victims of Waugh's earlier novels,
helps to establish values. Inarticulate, frequently foolish, an easy dupe of
illusion, limited by his social bias (though much less a snob than Charles
Ryder), Guy Crouchback is, still, a man of honor and courage. In him,
Catholicism and an aristocratic code of duty merge to offer a striking
contrast to the vulgarity, cynicism, and amorality which are both cause
and consequence of the war.

The symbolic figure of Roger of Waybrooke, a Christian knight of the
Middle Ages, is constantly in Guy's consciousness. In Sir Roger, who
appears throughout the trilogy as a standard of measurement, Waugh has
again fused his conservative political commitment to an aristocratic
tradition and his religious devotion to Roman Catholicism. Roger of
Waybrooke, we learn at the opening of *Men at Arms*, was an English
knight who set out for the Second Crusade. Sailing for Genoa, he was
shipwrecked on the coast of Santa Dulcina. "There he enlisted under the

local Count, who promised to take him to the Holy Land but led him first against a neighbor, on the walls of whose castle he fell at the moment of victory." As was Mr. Crouchback, Sir Roger, "a man with a great journey still all before him and a great vow unfulfilled," is delicately touched by Waugh's irony. Yet Sir Roger's quixotic idealism has had its own reward, for he is canonized in Santa Dulcina, where the people have taken him to their hearts. As Guy Crouchback sets off on his own quixotic crusade against the "Modern Age," an undertaking prompted by the Nazi-Soviet pact, he visits the tomb of Sir Roger to run his hand, as do the fishermen of Santa Dulcina, along the knight's sword. "Sir Roger, pray for me," he says, "and for our endangered kingdom."

An incident at Guy's club, soon after his return to England, indicates that others do not approach the war with the same high purpose, devotion to moral cause, and disdain for the modern age in arms. It also reveals the central object of the conservative satire in both novels. When Guy indignantly criticizes the Russian invasion of Poland, for example, he finds no sympathy among the old soldiers who fill the club:

> "My dear fellow, we've quite enough on our hands as it is. We can't go to war with the whole world."
> "Then why go to war at all? If all we want is prosperity, the hardest bargain Hitler made would be preferable to victory. If we are concerned with justice the Russians are as guilty as the Germans."
> "Justice?" said the old soldiers. "Justice?"

Although the plot of *Men at Arms* deals with Guy's training and with his first experience of action in North Africa, a recurring leitmotif of ironic details carries the theme of national irresponsibility and dislocation of value that is to emerge in full force in *Officers and Gentlemen*. There are, for instance, Ian Kilbannock's air marshal ("the most awful shit"), for whom the war is an opportunity for gaining entrance to Bellamy's and for social climbing; Trimmer, another, though not deliberate, climber, "a slightly refined Cockney" type who is really more interested in trucking about the radio in a jazzy little dance than in becoming an officer in the Halberdiers; young Leonard, whose selfish wife nags him until, at the moment of the Brigade's departure for North Africa, he reluctantly applies for transfer, subsequently to die in a German bombing raid on London; and Halberdier Shanks, who applies for leave at the moment of the evacuation of Dunkirk so that he and his girl can perform the slow valse in a competition. Was this, Guy asks himself, the "spirit of Dunkirk"?

Officers and Gentlemen closes with England's bitter defeat on Crete and the development of the Russian alliance, which Guy regards as a betrayal of his crusade. In this book Waugh pushes to the fore the theme of the dissolution of moral, political, and social standards. Book One recounts the confused and disorderly period following Dunkirk and Guy's haphazard training with the commandos; Book Two is an account of the

Cretan disaster, which Guy witnesses as an intelligence officer. The chaos that reigns on Crete is a more violent expression of the moral anarchy satirized in *Men at Arms* and in Book One of *Officers and Gentlemen*.

Mr. Crouchback's travails as a resident of the Cuthbert's seaside hotel are only one ironic revelation of the decay of social values which the conservative Waugh regrets. When Mr. Crouchback's hosts enter into a conspiracy with the quartering officer to evict the aristocratic *ingénu*, he remains serenely unaware of their actual purpose. These shabby people — who would like to make a clean sweep of their guests, take people by the week, and so profit from the sufferings of those whose homes have been blitzed — simply cannot understand old Crouchback. When the old gentleman has been spared eviction by pure chance and patriotically surrenders his sitting room to another, Mr. Cuthbert suspects some duplicity: "He's a deep one and no mistake. I never understood him, not properly. Somehow his mind seems to work different than yours and mine." In effect, Mr. Crouchback — like the Dedjasmach Matafara of *Waugh in Abyssinia* and the Greek general who appears in Book Two, gracious amidst the chaos on Crete — is the survivor of an older and passing order. It may be said of Mr. Crouchback, as the cynical Corporal Ludovic says of General Miltiades, *"All gentlemen are now very old."*

In addition to this ironic realism in the account of Mr. Crouchback and the Cuthberts, burlesque is found throughout the novel, sustaining the pessimistic-conservative, satirical view of things. As the book opens, Ian Kilbannock's air marshal, frightened by an air raid, is discovered on all fours lurking under the pool table at Bellamy's. From this point on, a low burlesque metaphor of animalism mocks not only the inconsequence, confusion of purpose, and lack of principle marking the war effort, but also Guy's sense of mission as he sets out "on the second stage of his pilgrimage, which had begun at the tomb of Sir Roger." Gazing into a mirror after he has placed a gas mask over his face, still "full of hope and purpose," Guy sees a gross snout. An officer sulkily complaining to him of the short rations in the mess insists that, "We practically live . . . like wild beasts." When at last Guy sentimentally tracks his late friend Apthorpe's heir, Chatty Corner, to his "lair" on Mugg Island, where Guy is to be trained, he is greeted by a serving woman's "bark" and then by the shaggy, ape-like Chatty. Ivor Claire, who is to disillusion Guy, is first seen plucking the eyebrows of his Pekingese. Trimmer, who, after leaving the Halberdiers, assumed a false identity and re-enlisted, now emerges as McTavish, a kilted officer in a Scottish regiment. He is observed as he seeks amatory adventure in a Glasgow hotel; passing into the hotel's restaurant "with all the panache of a mongrel among the dust-bins, tail waving, ears cocked, nose a-quiver," Trimmer locates his prey when he meets Guy's former wife, Virginia, with whom he spends the week end. The triumph of sexual immorality reflects a social anarchy that would now seem to be complete.

This doggy burlesque reaches its apogee, however, in Book Two's counterpointing of the catastrophe on Crete with Trimmer's triumph on the home front. "Scottie," as Virginia's fashionable friends call him, continues in his "nosy and knowing" way to avoid actual combat. However, by ironic chance he is the only man available to lead Operation "Popgun," an aptly named expedition against a totally unimportant Channel island. The episode is a parody of warfare and an ironic inversion of what is happening on Crete. Purely by accident, Trimmer and his men, accompanied by a drunken Ian Kilbannock (now doing propaganda work), are landed on the Continent. When Trimmer discovers the error, he flees in terror to the waiting boat and, tripping over a railroad tie, receives a slight injury. His men blow up the railroad track. "We shall light such a candle by God's grace in England," Kilbannock proclaims in a drunken parody of Thomas Cranmer's words and in mock heroic apostrophe to Trimmer's exploit, "as I trust shall never be put out." In his drunkenness Kilbannock has spoken more truly than he knows, for Timmer's exploit is taken up by the press, particularly (and appropriately) by the *Beast*, and he is puffed up into a national hero.

When it is discovered that Trimmer not only has "sex-appeal" but that his lower-class origins are a definite feature of his popularity, he is sent, as was that other modern man Miles Plastic, on a tour of English factories to boost morale and production. Since the "poor beast" is now in love with Virginia Troy, she is compelled, reluctantly, to accompany him.

Simultaneously, through the counterpoint, Waugh concentrates his satire on Major Hound, Guy's superior, a staff officer with no stomach for battle and no sense of honor, who is forced to take command of Hookforce when Tommy Blackhouse is injured. In the nether world of Crete, Hound, efficiency itself at headquarters, goes to pieces; his debasement typifies the entire Cretan episode and the loss of national honor. Soon Hound suggests that Guy call him by his nickname, "Fido." As his terror and confusion mount, he is more and more dehumanized and doggy. His "tail" is "right down"; he begins to scratch and snuffle. After a particularly harrowing German bombardment, he sights a culvert; Fido has found his "kennel." He creeps in, happily; "He found the curve of the drain comfortable . . . like a hunted fox, like an air marshal under a billiard table, he crouched in torpor." Finally, having deserted his command in the midst of the confused withdrawal, "Fido" is led by "delicious, doggy perceptions" to the scent of food, and to whatever unpleasant fate Corporal Ludovic, also a deserter, administers to him.

Officers and Gentlemen is not solely an aristocracy-worshiper's description of the collapse of values in the lower and middle classes during warfare, for Evelyn Waugh reveals, as burlesque turns into bitter irony, that even his aristocrats have failed him. Throughout the novel Guy has idealized Ivor Claire, whom he has regarded as the quintessential aristocrat, one of England's finest flowers, and the kind of man upon whom success in the war really depended. When Ivor is ordered to remain behind on Crete with the men who will face German prison camps, however, this fine flower of the aristocracy reasons that "honour" is "a thing that changes." He deserts his post, thinking of Freda, his Pekingese; and he has himself transferred to India, where he can stay out the war with his horses. As Guy recovers from the Cretan defeat and from the effects of his harrowing escape from the island in a small, open boat, he has to face another defeat: knowledge of Ivor's desertion. "After less than two years' pilgrimage in a Holy Land of illusion," Guy finds himself in a world where "gallant friends proved traitors and his country was led blundering into dishonour."

Yet this is not the most bitter irony of the novel. Before the final withdrawal from Crete, Guy finds the body of an English youth in a deserted village: "This soldier lay like an effigy on a tomb—like Sir Roger in his shadowy shrine at Santa Dulcina." The youth's identification disk indicates that he is a Roman Catholic; Guy, following regulations, carries it with him to Egypt. But Guy does not learn of the frivolous action which completes the betrayal of Sir Roger. When he turns over, for mailing to headquarters, an envelope containing the identification disk of the English soldier to Julia Stritch, the dazzling aristocrat of *Scoop*, she fears that Guy has given her evidence that might incriminate Ivor. Amoral to the core, Julia no longer appears as a delightful example of aristocratic indifference to convention. "Her eyes . . . one immense sea full of flying galleys," this pagan, this Cleopatra, drops the envelope into a wastebasket. In truth, the value Evelyn Waugh opposes to the chaos he burlesques or exposes through irony in *Officers and Gentlemen* cannot be identified with any class or group in contemporary England. The quixotic, aristocratic principle of devotion to honor and to God, which the symbolic figure of Sir Roger embodies, remains untarnished; but *Officers and Gentlemen* reveals not only the collapse of the class system, but of those who Waugh, for many years, has believed should embody Sir Roger's ideals.

Unconditional Surrender, which appeared six years after *Officers and Gentlemen*, offers no relief from the social and historical pessimism of that book. It opens with a prologue that foreshortens the dreary experience of "two blank years," during which Guy is attached to a newly formed brigade of Halberdiers, only to be left behind to yet more dreary duties as a headquarters liaison officer when the Second Brigade leaves for action. "But it was not for this that he had dedicated himself on the sword of Roger of Waybrooke that hopeful morning four years back." In addition, Book One further intensifies Waugh's depiction of the betrayal of national honor; for the sword, which is "exposed for adoration" to the drab queues shuffling through Westminster Abbey, is a symbol, not of the nation's heroic past or present valor, but of the public's sentimental regard for its Russian ally. "It had been made at the King's command as a gift to 'the steel-hearted people of Stalingrad.' " The dandiacal Sir Ralph Brompton, an aging homosexual diplomat and a Communist, emerges as a typical figure of the period. More fatuous than sinister, Sir Ralph has connections everywhere, and he moves behind the scenes throughout, advancing his causes (political and sexual) and influencing the course of events. Indeed, absurdly enough, it is Sir Ralph who eventually releases Guy from the tedium of liaison work and selects him for posting to Yugoslavia.

No doubt Waugh's hostility to the Russian alliance and his detestation of the Yugoslav Partisans produces a kind of historical astigmatism in him. In *Unconditional Surrender* his protagonist simply refuses to consider the historical and political necessities which led to the Anglo-American alliance with Russia and to the triumph of Tito and his Partisans. And yet, if the work constantly tends to overstate Communist influence on Anglo-American policy, I think the comic exaggeration of the role played by such figures as Sir Ralph and the ironic handling of the favor shown the Yugoslav Communists by Guy's superiors is no misrepresentation of the political and moral confusion prevalent during the closing months of the European war.

The novel reveals, at a deeper level of implication, Waugh's imaginative and moral grasp of the impulses released in the Second World War. Before the appearance of *Unconditional Surrender* and with the totally disenchanted conservatism of the first two volumes as evidence, it was doubtful whether in developing his announced theme — Guy's "realization that no good comes from public causes; only from private causes of the soul" — Evelyn Waugh would be able to suggest that the private cause of the soul need not isolate Crouchback from the rest of mankind, need not sever him from others. It was uncertain whether Waugh, having freed himself from romanticized devotion to a class, could attain some degree of that wide and generous sympathy which he had previously lacked. That Waugh does so without in the least compromising the profundity of his pessimism is a measure of the success of the final novel, and of the entire work.

In *Officers and Gentlemen* Corporal Ludovic, with his customary asperity, noted in his journal that Major Hound seemed "strangely lacking in the Death-Wish." The death wish dominates the final novel, just as a series of deaths punctuates the action. This is the force that moves in Virginia, when, after the birth of Trimmer's child, she cannot bear "its" presence; and it is the force that operates when she and Guy's Uncle Peregrine are killed by a doodle bomb. It is the title and pervasive mood of Ludovic's gaudy novel, a sick product of "disordered memory and imagination," composed by a Ludovic fleeing from memories of the reality of Crete. It moves Ben Ritchie-Hook to throw his life away in a fake Partisan attack during a mission to Yugoslavia. And it is the besetting sin to which Guy admits when he makes an act of confession. For in the last of these excellent novels Guy comes to understand not only that he was wrong in imagining that he might restore his own personal honor through acts of warfare, but that he, in common with all of Europe, has given himself not to life but to death.

Sensing that his commitment to a public cause has only frustrated the impulse behind it, Guy finally learns that charity is far more important than honor. When he decides to legitimatize Trimmer's child by remarrying Virginia, Kerstie Kilbannock attempts to dissuade him: " 'You poor bloody fool,' said Kerstie, anger and pity and something near love in her voice, 'you're being *chivalrous* – about *Virginia*. Can't you understand men aren't chivalrous anymore . . . ?" Though he looks ridiculous, once again "playing the knight errant," Guy is no longer paying tribute to Sir Roger through violence. Understanding that he has never in his life performed a "single positively unselfish action," he sees his rescue of the distressed Virginia as a single small action, not sought after but thrust upon him, by which he may relieve the burden of human misery.

The third book of the novel contains the most moving passage Evelyn Waugh has written. Stationed at Bari, Guy is offered another chance "in a world of hate and waste" to perform "a single small act to redeem the times." Once again he does not seek the responsibility; instead, a group of Jewish "displaced persons" – refugees and survivors of concentration camps, victims first of Italian and German terrors and now of Partisan hostility – appeal to him for aid. Working through UNRRA, Guy attempts to evacuate them to Italy. Every effort he makes is thwarted, however, by the suspicion, stupidity, and anti-Semitism of the Partisans. Ironically the "displaced persons" escape the Yugoslav camp where they have been interred only after the British mission has been removed from Bari. Guy sees them once again, in Italy. They are as pathetic as ever, "back behind barbed wire in a stony valley near Lecce."

It is the least fortunate of these refugees, Madame Kanyi, a woman of superior intellect and perception, who enunciates the central insight to which the Crouchback novels lead. Madame Kanyi's husband runs the local power plant, and she is consequently a virtual prisoner of the Yugoslavs. After she leads the deputation of refugees who appeal to Guy for assistance, even her chance subsequent meetings with him are kept under surveillance by the hateful spy, Bakic. At a final, entirely innocent interview, when Guy carries a load of brushwood to her hut, Madame Kanyi sees the lurking form of a spy in the leafless shrubbery, and she asks: "Is there any place that is free from evil?" Her melancholy wisdom, the product of suffering and persecution, leads her then to suggest that it was not only the Nazis who wanted the war. The Communists wanted it too – to come to power; many of her own people wanted it – "to be revenged on the Germans, to hasten the creation of the national state." Indeed, she says, "there was a will to war, a death wish, everywhere. Even good men thought their private honor would be satisfied by war. They could assert their manhood by killing and being killed." And Guy responds in a moment of self-recognition: "God forgive me, . . . I was one of them."

Guy Crouchback's most shattering discovery of the ambiguity of human action and of the inevitability with which warfare corrupts comes later, when he learns from the odious and cowardly Gilpin (a Communist who has been attached to the British Mission by Sir Ralph Brompton) that his own last meeting with Madame Kanyi and even the stack of magazines he left behind for her have played a role in her terrible fate. She was, says Gilpin, "the mistress of the British Liaison Officer"; in her hut was found "a heap of American counter-revolutionary propaganda." The Kanyis, he boasts, were "tried by a People's Court. You may be sure justice was done." Tempted to strike a fellow officer, Guy drops his fist, overwhelmed by a sense of futility.[3]

Unconditional Surrender should not be read, as the two preceding volumes so easily can be, as a self-contained work. I do not mean to suggest that it is an imperfect work, for not only is the ordonnance of the books as satisfyingly proportioned and the prose as fine as in the earlier volumes, but its very quality of rounding off the first two novels is admirable. *Unconditional Surrender* completes the action of the trilogy most obviously in the way it traces Guy, his friends, and associates to the end of the war. We learn of the fates and lots of many individuals—the deaths of Mr. Crouchback, Uncle Peregrine, Virginia, and Ben Ritchie-Hook; the disappearance of Trimmer, the literary triumph of Ludovic; and finally the fruitful second marriage of Guy, who resides, as his father had hoped, in a small house on the family estate.

The book resolves the thematic conflict of the trilogy, for the happy ending reserved for Guy Crouchback is much more than a tidying up of plot and characters. It signifies Guy's return to life after disillusionment, descent into hell, and discovery of self. One of Waugh's funniest (and most profound) ironies is his counterpointing of the careers of Guy and Ludovic. For as Guy approaches a tragic awareness of his own limitations and reaches some understanding of the terrible ambiguity involved in any action, he emerges from the sterile isolation of his life as it was at the opening of *Men at Arms*. And, while Ludovic retreats ever deeper into fantasy (to escape from his Cretan memories and from his unfounded fear of Guy's knowledge), he absurdly assumes and grotesquely parodies Guy's earlier obsessions. He purchases a Pekingese and clownishly devotes himself to it, in a vain attempt to identify himself with Ivor Claire; in his overblown novel, he gives expression to the romanticism and aristocracy-worship that deluded Guy in the past. And finally, he purchases from Guy the Castello to which the latter had retreated when he isolated himself from others before the war.

As the enthusiastic reviewer for the *Times Literary Supplement* suggested, the Waugh of the Crouchback trilogy is very different from the author of the early novels; he has grown and extended the range not only of his expression but also of his sympathies.[4] Even in the most lighthearted scenes of the Crouchback novels we find overtones that simply did not exist in the more brittle early or middle works. For instance, when Guy's erring former wife dines with his prissy Uncle Peregrine, the following scene takes place:

> "Peregrine, have you never been to bed with a woman?"
> "Yes," said Uncle Peregine smugly, "twice. It is not a thing I normally talk about."
> "Do tell."
> "Once when I was twenty and once when I was forty-five. I didn't particularly enjoy it."
> "Tell me about them."
> "It was the same woman."
> Virginia's spontaneous laughter had seldom been heard in recent years; it had once been one of her chief charms. She sat back in her chair and gave full, free tongue; clear, unrestrained, entirely joyous, without a shadow of ridicule, her mirth rang through the quiet little restaurant. Sympathetic and envious faces turned towards her. She stretched across the table cloth and caught his hand, held it convulsively, unable to speak, laughed until she was breathless and mute, still gripping his bony fingers. And Uncle Peregrine smirked. He had never before struck success. . . . He did not now quite know what it was that had won this prize, but he was highly gratified.
> "Oh, Peregrine," said Virginia at last with radiant sincerity, "I love you."

Virginia belongs, of course, in the line of Margot Maltravers and Brenda Last; but she has a genuineness and warmth never glimpsed in her predecessors. Waugh can now go beneath the impudence and the irresponsible charm of the type to discern Virginia's pathos, trapped as she is and beyond her youth. In a partly self-spoofing passage, he allows the pretentious editor Everard Spruce to relate the dead Virginia to a literary tradition: "Virginia Troy was the last of twenty years' succession of heroines. . . . The ghosts of romance who walked between the two wars." Her original, Spruce correctly senses, was Aldous Huxley's Mrs. Viveash; Michael Arlen's Iris Storm and Ernest Hemingway's Brett, a "coarsened" image, were her sisters. Virginia, Spruce announces in his extravagant rhetoric, "was the last of them—the exquisite, the doomed and the damning, with expiring voices—a whole generation younger. We shall never see any one like her again in literature or in life." Much as I admire the outrageous effects of *Vile Bodies* and *Black Mischief* and the brilliant, uncommitted irony of *A Handful of Dust*, I cannot regret that Evelyn Waugh came to a stage in his career when he could not only see Virginia, quite engagingly, in the perspective of literary history but also, without sentimentalism, make us feel her mortality.

Evelyn Waugh has not, indeed, been content to repeat himself.[5] Nor has he been willing for the Crouchback novels to be regarded as "separate and independent" works. In his preface to *Sword of Honour*, Waugh implies that the appearance of the novels "at intervals throughout a decade" may have tended to obscure their essential unity of conception, and he asserts that he has always intended his account of Guy Crouchback's experiences in the war "to be read as a single story." To that end, when he prepared his "recension" of the three works, he effaced the original structural divisions and divided the work into eleven chapters. He also excised a few passages and some minor details. (Regrettably, readers of the recension will find no reference to either Captain Truslove or General Miltiades.) The recension is, however, substantially the same as the original volumes; and some who feel that it was possible to read *Men at Arms* and *Officers and Gentlemen*, in particular, as autonomous works may be conscious of the original structural rhythms of the three volumes in the recension. Yet if Waugh, in his preface, seems to ignore the underlying tripartite structure of *Sword of Honour*, he has every right to insist that we see the wholeness of his work.

The imaginative unity of this major work of Waugh's later career is fundamental. The "Garibaldi" restaurant episode in *Men at Arms* and the mad Scottish Nationalist episode in *Officers and Gentlemen*, seemingly unrelated but actually linked, are but one token of Waugh's command of his material. In the first of these episodes, a restaurant proprietor who is also a part-time spy overhears Guy's conversation, absurdly misunderstands, and sends a confused report to his superiors. In the second, the lunatic grandniece of the laird of the Isle of Mugg deposits bundles of pro-German propaganda in an automobile Guy has used. Oddly distorted versions of both events find their way, eventually, to a top-secret file, establishing a record of pro-Fascist activity on the part of Captain Crouchback.

In themselves the incidents are crazily amusing, and they help to build up Waugh's picture of the sheer futility of much of the war effort. But they are also part of Waugh's total irony, for in *Unconditional Surrender*, despite the secret file, Guy is selected as a respectable front man in the Yugoslav mission that Sir Ralph Brompton has packed with Communists. And one of the Communists has the effrontery to report to Guy another false rumor, circulated by the Yugoslavs, that Madame Kanyi was a counter-revolutionary and the mistress of a British liaison officer!

Whether Waugh's narrative of Guy Crouchback's pilgrimage is read as a trilogy of closely related volumes or, in the omnibus edition, "as one story," there is no denying its artistic unity. The distancing critical power of time has established *A Handful of Dust*, I believe, as one of the most distinguished novels of its time. The very least that can be said of *Sword of Honour* is that it reveals an intense satiric vision of the social and moral consequences of the Second World War, that it constitutes the triumph of Evelyn Waugh's later manner, and that it represents a mature artist's highly individual commitment to life. The very qualification Waugh imposes on that commitment, his sense of the awful ambiguity of even the best of man's actions, serves to intensify it. Evelyn Waugh has made no surrender, unconditional *or* conditional, to the modern age. But when Guy Crouchback accepted Trimmer's child as his own and went to the aid of the displaced persons, his creator, undiminished in satiric power, revealed that pity too was within his range.

Notes

1. Kingsley Amis, "Laugher's to Be Taken Seriously," *New York Times Book Review* (July 7, 1957), p. 1.
2. Quoted in Frederic J. Stopp, *Evelyn Waugh: Portrait of an Artist* (London, 1958), p. 168.
3. Apparently this episode of Madame Kanyi and the displaced persons has haunted Waugh's imagination, for he treated it once before in the short story "Compassion" (1949). As developed in *Unconditional Surrender*, it has even deeper resonances.
4. "The New Waugh," London *Times Literary Supplement* (Oct. 27, 1961), p. 770.
5. The thinness of the recent short story, "Basil Seal Rides Again," which Waugh describes in the dedication to the handsome limited edition as a "senile attempt to recapture the manner of my youth," reveals that he should not, indeed, try to return to that manner.

Evelyn Waugh: The Height of His Powers

L. E. Sissman*

Nineteen seventy-two marks the thirtieth anniversary of the publication of a novel that nobody seems to read these days, a novel of breathtaking symmetry, grace, craft, and discipline, a novel from which many of our younger writers of self-indulgent, sprawling, amorphous fiction could learn the structure of their art.

It is generally and uncritically accepted these days that *A Handful of Dust* (1934) was the greatest of Evelyn Waugh's novels, fulfilling the early promise of *Decline and Fall* (1928), and that his career as a writer gradually ran downhill from there. There is some truth to this, but it falsifies the value of a writer whose creative life, unlike that of so many twentieth-century writers, possessed not only a first act but a second and third as well. The first act, whose theme was a dazzling, sardonic irreverence toward the crumbling Empire between the wars, came to an end in 1942; the second, more dourly preoccupied with the Second War and its fatal consequences for the English upper class—with the striking, farcical exception of *The Loved One* (1948) ended with the completion of

*Reprinted from *Innocent Bystander, the Scene from the 70s* by L. E. Sissman (New York: Vanguard Press, 1975), 111–15, by permission of Peter Davison, Literary Executor of the Estate of L. E. Sissman; appeared earlier in *Atlantic Monthly* 229 (March 1973):24, 26.

the *Sword of Honour* trilogy in 1962; the third, short and glorious, overlapped the second, including the brilliant *Ordeal of Gilbert Pinfold* (1957) and the unfinished autobiography, *A Little Learning* (1964).

Speaking for myself, I would rank *Decline and Fall* and *Pinfold*, for their very different but equally genuine qualities as art, with *A Handful of Dust*, placing *Vile Bodies* (1930) and *The Loved One* somewhat lower in the scale. The *Sword of Honour* books would seem to come next, followed by *Scoop* (1938), and such dilute and repetitious work as *Black Mischief* (1932) and the embarrassingly wishfulfilling (though often beautifully written) *Brideshead Revisited* (1945) at the bottom of the list.

If you haven't as yet recalled the title of the 1942 novel this column is about, perhaps my point about its undeserved obscurity has been made. In any case, not to temporize longer, its title is *Put Out More Flags* (available in paperback), and it is the best record I have read of England in the first year of the Second War. In it, at the very height of his powers, Waugh somehow fuses the savage, deadly comedy of his earlier books with the ominous seriousness of his later ones. The abrupt and arbitrary rises and falls in his earlier characters' fortunes recur in *Put Out More Flags*, but here they are seen not as the operation of the author's whim but as a logical — or illogical — consequence of the war, itself a consequence of Waugh's upper-class characters' failure to deal effectively with Hitler in the thirties. In other words, this is the first of Waugh's novels to relate his people directly to history, to the worldwide consequences of their actions and omissions. It may also be the last; the *Sword of Honour* sequence, for all its sedulous following of the course of the war, is really the subjective, even paranoid, history of a single individual, Guy Crouchback, who feels increasingly disillusioned and betrayed by the alliance with Russia and the triumph, with Western assistance, of what can only be called "godless Communism." Because of this bias, Waugh loses his own objectivity in the later trilogy, turning characters who should have been rounded and alive into flat saints (Mr. Crouchback) and villains (Frank de Souza).

But *Put Out More Flags* is not like that. It rejoices in its author's skill at developing living characters, understanding them, sympathizing with them, however repellent they might have been to the later Waugh. Character after character from his earlier books deepens and broadens when faced with the reality of war. Alastair Digby-Vaine-Trumpington, who appears in *Decline and Fall* as the sort of feckless student who might have inspired Sir John Betjeman's "Varsity Students' Rag" — "And then we smash'd up ev'rything, and what was the funniest part / We smashed some rotten old pictures which were priceless works of art" — has by now matured into a serious, uxorious, quietly heroic young man who volunteers for the army as a private and refuses officers' training. Likewise, Peter Pastmaster, the son of the scandalous Margot Metroland, shows a new sense of responsibility, marrying thoughtfully — more about his intended later — and volunteering for hazardous duty with the Commandos.

It is a measure of Waugh's art that we accept these metamorphoses of stock figures into real people without demur. But the greatest proof of his skill lies in another group of characters upon whom the larger part of the action turns: Ambrose Silk, Basil Seal, his sister, Barbara, and his mistress, Angela Lyne.

In Ambrose Silk, Waugh does something quite astonishing for him: he creates a detailed, sympathetic, understanding picture of what would, in his earlier (and perhaps his later) books, have been merely a figure of fun — a homosexual, half-Jewish intellectual who hangs out with the odds and sods of London bohemianism. But there is nothing merely funny about Waugh's portrait of Silk, who is immediately established as a first-rate writer and the unhappy victim of his sexual conflicts:

> A Pansy. An old queen. A habit of dress, a tone of voice, an elegant, humorous deportment that had been admired and imitated, a swift, epicene felicity of wit, the art of dazzling and confusing those he despised — these had been his; and now they were the current exchange of comedians; there were only a few restaurants, now, which he could frequent without fear of ridicule, and there he was surrounded, as though by distorting mirrors, with gross reflections and caricatures of himself.

Nor is there anything merely funny about Basil Seal, the black sheep and remittance man of *Black Mischief*, who reappears here in deeper, more sinister colors as a man who "rejoiced, always, in the spectacle of women at a disadvantage: thus he would watch, in the asparagus season, a dribble of melted butter on a woman's chin, marring her beauty and making her ridiculous, while she would still talk and smile and turn her head, not knowing how she appeared to him," as, in his own words, "one of those people one heard about in 1919: the hard-faced men who did well out of the war."

Basil does well out of the war, up to a point: he unhesitatingly takes advantage of his sister's latently incestuous attraction for him — the scenes in which this attraction surfaces, played out in chilling nursery talk between Basil and Barbara, are among the best expositions of sibling love I've ever encountered — makes money and finds a temporary mistress out of a scheme in which he must find a country billet for three appallingly uncouth *évacué* children, and earns himself a reputation as a spy-catcher for the War Office by turning in poor Ambrose, now the editor of a literary magazine, as a crypto-fascist.

But out of this apparent continuation of his old self-serving career grows a new character: suddenly confronted with the imminent ruin of Angela Lyne, his former mistress, who is drinking herself to death out of loneliness, he does the first real volte-face of his life by returning to her, cajoling her back to health, marrying her, and himself joining the Commandos. This change of spots is made entirely plausible by the grainy, palpable reality of the two women in Basil's life: Barbara, spellbound now as twenty years before by her brother's sexual power over her; Angela, rich, fashionable, withdrawn, despairing, preoccupied with death, an embodiment of the woman in *The Waste Land* who says, "My nerves are bad to-night."

Very few male novelists can draw women well; Waugh is a towering exception. His Angela personifies all the vain (in both senses) smartness of the years between the wars; the waste of her life symbolized the waste of the old values of upper-class England; her words when Basil tells her, in proposing, that he will be a terrible husband forecast the future of that class and place: "Yes, darling, don't I know it? But you see one can't expect anything to be perfect now. In the old days if there was one thing wrong it spoiled everything; from now on for all our lives, if there's one thing right the day is made."

But the joys of *Put Out More Flags* do not reside entirely in its major characters, male and female, drawn at full length; for each of these, there are a dozen vignettes of people and places, sketched, it would seem, in a second with an artist's almost contemptuous skill. Thus one of the most enchanting women in fiction, the young Lady Molly Meadowes, who marries Peter Pastmaster, materializes, doughty and adorable, before the reader's eyes in a mere four and a half pages. Thus the fusty, echoing, obfuscatory aura of the great bureaucratic ministries of wartime London is caught forever in a line or two, in a single dizzying stroke of observation. And thus a mosaic is built, a great mural embracing all London, all England, on the brink of the dissolution forever of its old order.

I hope you will give yourself the pleasure of reading — in between the often promising but unfulfilling novels being published now — this triumphant, ordered, perhaps triumphant *because* ordered, exemplar of the art of fiction. If I'm not mistaken, *Put Out More Flags* is the greatest of Evelyn Waugh's great novels. As such, it deserves to be revived and reread as long as we read English.

[From "The Magnum Opus: Sword of Honour"]

Robert Murray Davis*

In 1964, probably in midyear,[1] Waugh began the process of converting the war trilogy into the "magnum opus" — the singular must be emphasized — he had planned from the beginning. His principles in revising were clearly stated: In the process of publishing three separate

*Reprinted from *Evelyn Waugh, Writer* (Norman, Okla.: Pilgrim Books, 1981), 326–32, by permission of the author. © 1981 by Robert Murray Davis.

volumes in ten years, he had introduced various "Repetitions and discrepancies . . . which, I hope, are here excised. I have also removed passages
which, on rereading, appeared tedious."[2] In making the revision, he used
the cheapest and most expedient means. Penguin editions of the three
novels were used for copy text; corrections, deletions, and a few additions
were made in red ink.[3]

Waugh's motives for local revisions, as for most of his structural
revisions, are fairly obvious. Many deletions make the narrative more
direct, paring away extraneous material like Tony Box-Bender's appraisal
of chemical warfare as "the end" and Guy's memory of initiation customs
in regiments other than the Halberdiers (*Men at Arms*, pp. 30, 44). Also
cut were anticipations of later, historical events irrelevant to the novel,
such as the authorial comment on the introduction of army psychiatrists
too late to detect Apthorpe's mania (p. 183) and Guy's subsequent reading
of *The Heart of the Matter* and reflection that he might have gone, though
in fact he did not go, to confession to Father Rank (p. 232). Perhaps on the
theory that the one-volume version would have more than a Russian
plethora of proper names, Waugh disburdened the text of minor characters in the Cretan debacle by canceling the names of Roots, Slimbridge,
and Smiley and identifying them solely by their military functions
(*Officers and Gentlemen*, pp. 170ff.) and by removing altogether B
Commando and its fanatical Colonel Prentice and the fruity-voiced officer
whom Guy suspects of being a German spy (pp. 117, 157, 172–73). In the
Bari episode he deleted Sir Almeric Griffiths and General Cape's nurse
(*Unconditional Surrender*, pp. 156, 169–70). Other characters had, on
reconsideration, exfoliated beyond necessary limits, and thus Waugh
deleted most of the description of Sergeant Soames, preserving only his
likeness to Trimmer (*Men at Arms*, p. 172), and some of the details about
Uncle Peregrine's war work and his activities at Christmas (*Unconditional
Surrender*, pp. 125, 143–45).

Incidents as well as characters were cut, notably Air Marshal Beech's
embarrassing rhyme about Elinor Glyn, Ritchie-Hook's extended game of
housey-housey, the false alarm in which Guy suspects the Loamshires of
being German agents (*Men at Arms*, pp. 125, 138–40, 209–13), and the
summarized war of nerves between the Commandos and the Navy,
including the Brigadier's nickname, "The widow Twankey" (*Officers and
Gentlemen*, pp. 108ff.), though a holograph insertion restored the phrase
characterizing the captain as "the booby on the roof." Personal references
are also deleted: Everard Spruce's inherited clothes (*Unconditional Surrender*, p. 40) do not survive, nor does the reference to Winston Churchill
as "a master of sham-Augustan prose" (*Men at Arms*, p. 176). The
elaborate description of the Rising of '45 over which Waugh had labored so
hard in writing *Men at Arms* was suppressed; so was the recurrent
reference to Captain Truslove, foe of the Pathan, whose activities in a boy's
book are compared to Guy's (pp. 165–66 and elsewhere), perhaps because

Guy's renewed adolescence is clear enough without it, perhaps because Waugh wished to make him less ridiculous. Later Waugh cut much of the description of Ludovic's *The Death Wish*, including the judgment that "The dialogue could never have issued from human lips, the scenes of passion were capable of bringing a blush to readers of either sex and every age" and the characterization of Lady Marmaduke Transept (and her last name) with its sudden drop from "splendidly caparisoned" to "bitch" (*Unconditional Surrender*, pp. 187, 188).

Most of these revisions affect plot and theme very little. Others seem to represent Waugh's clarification or change of intention. For example, he changed Ian Kilbannock from a "sporting journalist" to a "gossip columnist" (*Men at Arms*, p. 25; *Officers and Gentlemen*, p. 9; *Unconditional Surrender*, p. 185) to place him even lower in the journalistic scale, and besides deleting de Souza's Military Cross he gave him two of Trimmer's more sensible lines (*Men at Arms*, pp. 88, 89), as well as the disastrous reply to Ritchie-Hook about biffing (p. 115), perhaps to make de Souza seem less omnicompetent. Waugh also inserted the sentence "The great explosion which killed Mugg and his niece was attributed to enemy action" at the end of the Isle of Mugg episode (*Officers and Gentlemen*, p. 104; *Sword of Honour*, p. 380) to clarify an allusion several pages later. Most important, however, is the passage that resolves the fragmentary plot concerning the activities of Colonel Grace-Groundling-Marchpole:

> Colonel Grace-Groundling-Marchpole, like General Whale and Mr. Churchill and many other zealous fellow countrymen, was at that time becoming a smaller and smaller bug. But he had no sense of failure; rather of triumph. Everything was turning out as he had long ago expected. Every day he closed a file. The pieces of the jig-saw were fitting together and the whole was taking shape.
> Crouchback, Box-Bender, Mugg, Cattermole — fascist, nazi, scottish nationalist, communist — all were part of a single, intelligent whole.
> That morning he had resigned the Crouchback file to the cellars.
> [p. 762]

Elsewhere, in a series of cancellations, Waugh removed sympathetic comments about the Yugoslav partisans, including Joe Cattermole's explanation of their hostility on the grounds of country and race (*Unconditional Surrender*, pp. 163–64), General Cape's admission that they have good reason to be suspicious (p. 166), their solicitude for the public gardens (p. 178), the partisans' anxiety "to do what was right" in offering to let the village priest conduct a funeral service for the dead Englishmen (p. 224), the singing of the *Te Deum* (p. 228), and the comment that the people making trouble for the Jews have "no coats and boots" (p. 229).

Undoubtedly aware of the charges of snobbery frequently made against his postwar novels, Waugh deleted some material that critics might have used to support their charges. Mr. Goodall's speech about Guy's connections dispersed under "the usurper George" (*Men at Arms*, p. 110) was deleted, as was the description of Mr. Crouchback as member of a class of "Jobs" brought low by the modern age (p. 34). The potentially more inflammatory paragraph ending with, "Regular soldiers were survivals of a happy civilization where differences of rank were exactly defined and frankly accepted" (*Officers and Gentlemen*, pp. 70–71) was deleted, and later all references to General Miltiades were expunged, so that Ludovic's journal entry about Guy's desire to believe that gentlemen are fighting the war was rendered irrelevant (p. 186) and cut.

Several important deletions affect the reader's response to Guy. In writing *Men at Arms*, Waugh had revised and elaborated the paragraph on the justice of the allied cause in morality and in the conventions of romance (p. 174), emphasizing Guy's mixed motives. Perhaps because he wished to make Guy less self-righteous, he deleted the passage for *Sword of Honour*. Also removed was the much later summary of Guy's activities that includes references to "il santo inglese," to his brother Gervase's medal, which he now wears (in an insertion for *Sword of Honour*, probably in proof, Waugh has Guy note its disappearance [p. 526]), and to his brother Ivo's despair, which Guy now begins to feel (*Unconditional Surrender*, pp. 168–69). In the single volume Waugh must have felt that the summary was needless, and in any case the references to limbo and to Guy's passive wish for death are not related to despair. One other deletion removes an error. In *Officers and Gentlemen*, Waugh wrote of the day of Guy's escape from Crete: "He had no clear apprehension that this was a fatal morning, that he was that day to resign an immeasurable piece of his manhood" (p. 221). Besides being melodramatic, the passage seems to be untrue. Nothing in the context bears out the judgment: unlike Ivor Claire, Guy has not been ordered to surrender; he displays almost uncharacteristic enterprise in boarding the boat; and there is nothing dishonorable about seeking to evade capture in order to fight again. Whatever his purpose in writing the passage, Waugh decided not to include it in the final version.

These local revisions have a subtle cumulative effect; the structural revisions are more obvious, as the outline indicates:

Men at Arms	Sword of Honour
Prologue "Sword of Honour"	Chapter 1 (title the same)
Book 1 "Apthorpe Gloriosus"	Chapter 2 (title the same)
Book 2 "Apthorpe Furibundus"	Chapter 3 (title the same)
Book 3 "Apthorpe Immolatus"	Chapter 4 (title the same)
	Officers and Gentlemen
Book 1 "Happy Warriors"	Chapter 5 "Apthorpe Placatus" (sections 1–7 of Book 1 of *Officers and Gentlemen*)

Interlude	Chapter 6 "Happy Warriors" (sections 8–10 of Book 1 as sections 1–3 of Chapter 6; Interlude as section 4)
Book 2 "In the Picture"	Chapter 7 "Officers and Gentlemen"
Epilogue	Chapter 8 "State Sword" (part of Epilogue is used)
Unconditional Surrender	
(Synopsis of Preceding Volumes)	Omitted
Prologue "Locust Years"	Chapter 8, sections 2–3 (part)
Book 1 "State Sword"	Chapter (9) / 8 /, sections 3–6
Book 2 "Fin de Ligne"	Chapter (10) / 9 / (title the same)
Book 3 "The Death Wish"	Chapter (11) / 10 / "The Last Battle"
Epilogue "Festival of Britain"	Chapter 11 "Unconditional Surrender"

The renumbering in the first half of what had been *Officers and Gentlemen* is explained by Waugh's admission after he had finished the trilogy: "Originally I had intended . . . *Officers and Gentlemen* to be two volumes. Then I decided to lump them together and finish them off. There's a very bad transitional passage on board the troop ship."[4] *Sword of Honour* deals with the problem by using as a structural principle an idea first stated on the dust-jacket flap of *Officers and Gentlemen*, which, Waugh said, "begins with the placation of [Apthorpe's] spirit, a ritual preparation for the descent into the nether world of Crete." Thus Book 1 of *Officers and Gentlemen* is divided for the final version. The first seven sections resolve the Apthorpe bequest, introduce the characters who are to dominate Chapters 6 and 7, and seal the friendship between Guy and Tommy Blackhouse. The new Chapter 6 includes the serious training and embarkation of the Commando and the enclosed minor action of the affair between Trimmer and Virginia.

The transition between the second and third volumes required a bit more ingenuity. As the discussion of *Unconditional Surrender* indicated, Waugh was quite aware of the difficulties he posed for his reader. He had ended *Officers and Gentlemen* with Guy's return to England in order to impose temporary and artificial two-volume unity: the first book ending in illusion, the second in disillusion. To emphasize the structural pattern of the magnum opus, he combined in Chapter 8 of *Sword of Honour* the Epilogue of *Officers and Gentlemen*, the Prologue, its beginning revised, of *Unconditional Surrender*, and, after some hesitation, Book 1 of that novel. Waugh's first impulse, to preserve "State Sword" as a separate chapter, may have been purely mechanical. On reflection—judging from the Penguin copy's substitution of "10" for "Epilogue" and subsequent shift to "Eleven," as in the proof copy of *Sword of Honour*, that reflection came before proof stage—he must have decided that all of the material preceding "Fin de Ligne" was transitional.

In hindsight, his decision clarified the structure of the resulting volume. Chapters 1 and 11, containing the exposition and resolution, form, without using the terms, prologue and epilogue. The nine remaining chapters form a triad. At the end of each, Guy prepares to return to England, having experienced the death or disgrace of a character who embodied an illusion that blocked his progress toward grace and truth. In Chapter 4, that character is Apthorpe, the "brother-uncle" whose efforts to become the good soldier parody Guy's. In Chapter 7, it is Ivor Claire, the symbol of "quintessential England," the gentleman-soldier whom Guy admires and rather pallidly imitates. In Chapter 10, three deaths—Virginia's, Ritchie-Hook's, and Mme. Kanyi's—deliver Guy from sexual and military versions of romantic illusion and from the illusion that a just cause necessarily prevails in the secular world.

The other obvious revision came in the titling of the chapters, a matter that Waugh always considered an aspect of structure. The change of "In the Picture" to "Officers and Gentlemen" deletes the rather facile irony of the second volume's title for Book 2 and preserves and emphasizes the deeper irony involved in the behavior of Trimmer, Hound, Claire, and others. Waugh's motives for altering "The Death Wish" and "Festival of Britain" are more difficult to account for. Waugh may have felt that he had leaned too heavily on the formula from psychology, a field he professed to despise, and therefore decided to let the characters' desire for death carry the theme without comment. In positive terms, "The Last Battle"—a variant of the third volume's American title, *The End of the Battle*—emphasizes not capitulation but honorable striving, and there may be a connection between the title and Waugh's deletion of Sir Almeric Griffiths, whose only obvious purpose in *Unconditional Surrender* was to label Guy as possessing "the death wish." Though Guy's confession that he wishes to die is preserved in *Sword of Honour*, its appearance in isolation emphasizes that he and perhaps he alone may have "a very good disposition" (p. 718) toward death. The title of the next chapter, "Unconditional Surrender," preserving like Chapter 7 the title of a book in which it originally appeared, is still more difficult to explain. As the title of a book its confession of defeat is largely vitiated by the time the reader arrives at the resolution of the action, in which "things have turned out very conveniently for Guy." As the title of the final chapter, the words seem to emphasize more firmly the capitulation to the modern world and its standards. One could argue that the title contains an even deeper and more palatable irony: Guy, in giving up his crusade and accepting the consequences of his charity toward Virginia and her child, including the passing of Broome to Trimmer's offspring, is able at last to live happily in the world, his imagination free of the false romanticism that immures Ludovic in Castello Crouchback.

With the final adjustments made to *Sword of Honour*, Waugh's career as a writer essentially came to an end. In the time remaining to him, Waugh the private man became increasingly embittered by changes in the liturgy of the mass and the statements of ecumenicists to the point that, in his final diary entry, he prayed that he would not apostasize and concluded, "I shall not live to see things righted."[5] But Waugh the novelist had solved a major structural problem in what he regarded as his major work. A few years earlier, when asked, "Are there any books which you would like to have written and found impossible?" he pronounced what as writer and self-critic could serve as his literary epitaph: "I have done all I could. I have done my best."[6]

Notes

1. Waugh used the back of two typescript pages of his broadcast-article on Alfred Duggan for the manuscript of the Dedication and the transitional passage into what had been *Unconditional Surrender*. The piece was broadcast on July 2; it was then published as "Alfred Duggan," *Spectator* 213 (July 10, 1964): 38–39.

2. Evelyn Waugh, *Sword of Honour* (London: Chapman and Hall, 1965), p. 9.

3. The three copies, stripped of covers, front matter, and irrelevant material like the synopsis preceding *Unconditional Surrender*, are in the Waugh collection at the Humanities Research Center, University of Texas – Austin. Page references in the text are to the Penguin editions of the three novels.

4. Julian Jebb, "The Art of Fiction XXX: Evelyn Waugh," *Paris Review*, no. 30 (Summer–Fall, 1963):83.

5. Easter, 1965. See Sykes, *Evelyn Waugh*, Chap. 26, for a fuller account of Waugh's last years.

6. Jebb, "The Art of Fiction XXX: Evelyn Waugh," p. 85.

[From "The War Trilogy: Introduction"]

Jeffrey Heath*

. . . The War Trilogy constitutes Waugh's final return to a number of his favourite themes: Fortune, Providence, vocation, withdrawal, the family, and it dramatizes his final attempt to be "a man of the world."

The voices of three distinct aspects of Waugh contribute to the War Trilogy's curious harmonics. There is the voice of Waugh's persona Guy

*Reprinted from *The Picturesque Prison: Evelyn Waugh and His Writing* by Jeffrey Heath (Kingston and Montreal: McGill-Queen's University Press, 1982), 212–16, by permission of the author and the publisher. © 1982 McGill-Queen's University Press.

Crouchback, the voice of the narrator, who sometimes pretends to share Guy's naiveté, and, unassimilated into the latter, occasional undertones from the real-life Waugh. In the early sections of *Men at Arms* Guy Crouchback unaffectedly loves the military life, but an undercurrent of irony shows that the narrator no longer wholly shares Crouchback's affection. The narrator prefers the private life, yet without advocating complete withdrawal. But behind it all there is the felt presence of the Waugh who has turned his back on the world. There are thus three attitudes, not always sufficiently separate, perhaps, to the important new theme of *caritas*. Persona and narrator eventually agree that a limited form of private charity is the best way to work for good in the world, but there is the sense throughout that Waugh himself was never fully able to achieve the ideal he enshrined in his narrative voice.

Some readers find it hard to reconcile the comic cruelty of Waugh's early satires with the theme of charity in the trilogy. Others remark, in his repeated acts of rudeness and intolerance, a lack of *caritas* so profound that it contradicts the essence of his professed faith. Waugh had, there can be no doubt, more faith than he had hope or charity. Compassion did not come easily to him, and it is certain that his chronic lack of charity was his cardinal fault. He admitted that he found it "impossible . . . to love mankind in general,"[1] but he tried very hard to behave charitably towards individuals. He believed that real charity should be personal: "organized charity, in the form of a welfare state," was "a pure fraud."[2] True charity, he said, was "the job of private associations among people, primarily of religious bodies," and the A. D. Peters files show that he contributed extensively to such bodies.[3] He gave the serial rights of *Scott-King* to Father D'Arcy and the Jesuits, along with the profits from the de luxe edition of *The Loved One*. A handsome chunk of Waugh's profits from the MGM *Brideshead* fiasco went to the Church; the proceeds from his *Life* essay on Forest Lawn went to the Convents' Aid Society, and he signed over his French bank balance to a convent in Grasse; after 1948 he gave the proceeds from all translations of his books to Catholic charities in the countries concerned. There are many other examples of Waugh's charity, but the strange thing about them is the way they coexist with demands for "more dollars," "fine big retaining fees," and "whacking advances." Present also are blunt instructions about lawsuits for late payment and failure to "cough-up," and demands that Peters should "investigate and castigate" with "the utmost rigour of the law" unhappy persons suspected of "plagiarism" and "get the hand-cuffs on" them. Giving to charity — especially in the post-*Brideshead* years — made good business sense. As Waugh wrote to Peters on one remarkable occasion in 1949, "I can't afford to earn like this. . . . This is getting desperate. We must get rid of the whole of the cinema rights of *Scoop* on the Jesuits if the deal goes through." Waugh often gave to charity, but it is not easy to maintain that he was often charitable in the fullest sense of the word.

When after the war Waugh turned away for the last time from the life of action, he tried to maintain a link with the world by acting upon it through religious bodies and the family. Indeed, the War Trilogy is a celebration of the family which, being at once private and communal, provides Guy Crouchback with a mature form of solitude denied to Waugh's earlier protagonists. But one may doubt whether even the restricted charity Guy achieves was ever more than an ideal for Waugh himself.

In general outline, the trilogy depicts the course of Guy's slow realization that his father's maxim is right: "Quantitative judgments don't apply."[4] As Waugh said, "I shall deal with Crouchback's realization that no good comes from public causes, only private causes of the soul."[5] Waugh wrote to Cyril Connolly, "The theme . . . is the humanizing of Guy."[6] Despite the fact that Waugh had a general plan for the trilogy before he began (the theme of "private causes" and the images of the swords of Sir Roger and Stalingrad were "there from the beginning"),[7] the history of its composition is long and irregular. The trilogy "appeared at intervals throughout a decade"[8] and Waugh plainly found his task a difficult one. It was a far more enterprising work than any he had undertaken before and, as *Scott-King* and *Love Among the Ruins* show, his creative powers were beginning to fail. The first volume, *Men at Arms* (entitled "Honour" in manuscript), appeared in 1952 with the announcement that the author "hopes to complete a trilogy of novels, each complete in itself, recounting the phases of a long love affair, full of vicissitudes, between a civilian and the army."[9] But by 1955 Waugh appeared to have abandoned the idea of a trilogy. *Officers and Gentlemen* (or "Happy Warriors," as Waugh at first called it), would be the final volume: "*Officers and Gentlemen* completes *Men at Arms*. I thought at first the story would run into three volumes. I find now that two will do the trick," Waugh wrote.[10] "It is short and funny & completes the story I began in *Men at Arms* which threatened to drag out to the grave."[11] *Unconditional Surrender* (entitled "Conventional Weapons" in its early stages) did not appear until six years later. Waugh wrote: "I knew that a third volume was needed. I did not then feel confident that I was able to produce it. Here it is." (Waugh had not felt able to produce the third volume because of the difficulties so vividly described in *Pinfold*.) When an interviewer inquired whether he had carried out a plan which he had "made at the start" of the trilogy, Waugh replied, "It changed a lot in the writing. Originally I had intended the second volume, *Officers and Gentlemen*, to be two volumes. Then I decided to lump them together and finish it off. There's a very bad transitional passage on board the troop ship. The third volume really arose from the fact that Ludovic needed explaining. As it turned out each volume had a common form because there was an irrelevant ludicrous figure in each to make the running."[12] Initially the Crouchback saga was to have been "four or five"[13] novels long, and "all the subsidiary characters, like 'Trimmer' & 'Chatty Corner' & 'de Souza' [were] each [to] have a book to himself."[14] A volume dealing with Dunkirk was to have followed *Men at Arms*. Waugh interviewed a veteran of that battle in order to get his impressions, but although the veteran was cooperative, the Dunkirk volume was never written. "It was useless," Waugh said. "I should have realized that one cannot live other people's experiences."[15] Finally, in 1965 there appeared a "recension" under the title of *Sword of Honour*. In his preface Waugh admitted that he had been "less than candid" in assuring his public that each novel was "to be regarded as a separate, independent work. . . . The product is intended . . . to be read as a single story. I sought to give a description of the Second World War as it was seen and experienced by a single, uncharacteristic Englishman, and to show its effect on him."

In the new Uniform Edition Waugh adds very little (he tells us, for example, that Mugg and his niece blow themselves up) but removes "repetitions," "discrepancies," and "tedious" passages, mainly from *Men at Arms* (a novel which he privately described as "unreadable and endless," "slogging, inelegant," and "interminable").[16] He removes extraneous characters, like Prentice, Roots, Slimbridge, and Smiley, reduces confusingly detailed summary (especially from the weak "Interlude" section of *Officers and Gentlemen*) and smoothes the flow of the narrative by reorganizing the chapter divisions and in some cases giving them new titles. Waugh reduces Trimmer's early importance by attributing a number of his speeches to Frank de Souza, and he changes Kilbannock's occupation from racing columnist to gossip columnist. In the revised version Ritchie-Hook is given less attention, and the scene in which Guy returns Chatty's possessions is abbreviated, as are the parachute-school episode and the airplane crash in Croatia. Gilpin becomes slightly less odious.

Some of the changes make certain characters and situations less ambiguous. Throughout, Waugh omits details about saintly Mr. Crouchback's fortune and possessions which might be unfavourably construed. Uncle Peregrine is no longer parsimonious, and no longer responds with displeasure when Virginia announces her intention to become a Catholic. Guy himself is presented as slightly less naive through the omission of some of his more romantic reflections on the justice of the war and the certainty of victory. There is less insistence on his poverty, and one important passage which could be construed as critical of Guy's escape from Crete is omitted. Even the old tenor is made more sympathetic by the removal of any suggestion that he is an alcoholic.

In one kind of change which Waugh does not mention, he eliminates several passages which could be interpreted as insulting to religion. Cuts of this sort include the apathetic Catholic chaplain's unenthusiastic sermon; the "not over scrupulous" Catholic, Hemp; and even the alleged abuses of the confessional at Staplehurst. Throughout, Waugh confers capital letters on Church rites and activiites while reducing secular titles to lower case.

Many readers will regret the more important deletions as serious aesthetic losses. As a result of the cuts there is no trace of the symbolic painting at Kut-al-Imara House; Ambrose Goodall's fascination with Guy's ancestry; Air Marshal Beech's song about Elinor Glyn; the officers' bingo game; the over-technicoloured film of Bonnie Prince Charlie; Captain Truslove, Congreve, and the Pathans; the Loamshire officers' episode; the soldier with the hot-potato voice on Crete; General Miltiades and his obsolete courtesy; the English composer who announces that Guy has "the death-wish"; the description of Ludovic's book which links it with *Brideshead Revisited.*

The most important change comes at the end, where Waugh wisely decides not to let Guy and Domenica have any "children of their own." By making little Trimmer their sole heir, Waugh places unambiguous emphasis on the pre-eminence of spiritual ties over mere family ties, and on the importance of new blood-lines in carrying on old institutions. There can be no doubt that this is a change for the better, and it is hard to imagine how Waugh missed it in the first place. Indeed, he did catch it very early, making the revision (which he then revised again in 1965) in the 1961 Chapman and Hall second edition of *Unconditional Surrender.*[17] With the notable exception of the new conclusion, Waugh's changes are rarely improvements; indeed, the trilogy loses far more than it gains through the omissions noted above. After weighing the alternatives, I have decided to accept the original text of the trilogy as aesthetically superior and biographically more revealing, but also to accept the second edition ending as logically right and theologically more satisfying.

Notes

1. *Diaries*, p. 550.

2. "Frankly Speaking," BBC radio, 16 November 1953.

3. At the Humanities Research Center Library, Austin, Texas.

4. Evelyn Waugh, *Unconditional Surrender* (London: Chapman and Hall, 1961), p. 10.

5. Frederick J. Stopp, *Evelyn Waugh: Portrait of an Artist* (London: Chapman and Hall, 1958), p. 46.

6. *Letters*, p. 383.

7. Julian Jebb, "The Art of Fiction xxx: Evelyn Waugh," *Paris Review* 8 (Summer–Fall, 1963): 83.

8. Evelyn Waugh, Preface, *Sword of Honour* (London: Chapman and Hall, 1965), p. 9.

9. *Men at Arms*, dustjacket.

10. Bernard Bergonzi, "Evelyn Waugh's The *Sword of Honour*," *Listener*, February 1964, p. 306.

11. *Letters*, p. 433.

12. "The Art of Fiction xxx: Evelyn Waugh," p. 83.

13. *Letters*, p. 363.

14. Ibid., p. 383.

15. David Malbert, "Civil Waugh," *Evening Standard* (London), 19 September 1976, p. 19.

16. *Letters*, pp. 354, 363, 353.

17. See Winnifred M. Bogaards, "The Conclusion of Waugh's Trilogy: Three Variants," *Evelyn Waugh Newsletter* 4 (Autumn 1970): 6–7. See *Letters*, p. 599: "No nippers for Guy and Domenica" (1961).

[From "Nostalgia"]   Ian Littlewood*

To justify the word "corrosive" we need only compare Waugh's nostalgia with that of his father. It was apparently a feeling they shared: "My father always assumed," Waugh tells us in *A Little Learning*, "(as I do now) that anything new was likely to be nasty" [*LL* 115]. And yet if one reads Arthur Waugh's account of his university days at Oxford in *One Man's Road*, the impression of similarity fades. The father's memories are uncorrupted by selfconsciousness. He chronicles the student's round of work and sport and high jinks with an adolescent relish that bespeaks a spirit still open to the same enthusiasms. In his undiminished loyalty to New College he proffers catalogues of long-forgotten contemporaries with a naive confidence that for his readers too he is tendering household names.

The words of his son have no such warmth. "Hertford was a respectable but rather dreary little college," [*LL* 158] he begins. Waugh makes it clear that Oxford was a golden period, "a Kingdom of Cokayne," but his nostalgia is sourer than his father's, more disabused. In all the details of happiness there is a melancholy consciousness of the gap that divides past from present; the nostalgia is sharpened and made sad by a pervasive sense of the decline that has marked both himself and his university. Forty years ago the writer was a young man. He makes no attempt to recreate the happiness of this time; he merely, with consummate elegance, records it. When it comes to the catalogue of friendships, he resists the temptation to which his father had eagerly yielded. He presents instead a necrology; one by one his friends are summarized in brief, elegaic phrases: "their names and the names of those still alive who have drifted apart, might stir wistful memories in fifty or more elderly men; no more."

It is a nostalgia quite different in tone from that of *One Man's Road*— or for that matter from the reminiscences of Waugh's brother Alec. Both

*Reprinted from Ian Littlewood, *The Writings of Evelyn Waugh* (Totowa, NJ: Barnes & Noble, 1983), pp. 129–36, by permission of the author. © 1983 by Ian Littlewood.

Arthur and Alec Waugh can enjoy the memory of past happiness without conceding it any lasting power to add to the bitterness of the present; they do not repine. The result is a paradox: though their memoirs place them in an earlier, more innocent world than that of Evelyn, they were able to adjust to the demands of a changing society far more readily than he. Whatever their misgivings, they retained an openness to the conditions of the present. And yet of the three of them it is Evelyn who is our contemporary. The ironic tone of self-consciousness in *A Little Learning* sets its author apart. His was a modern sensibility in a way that theirs was not. But also, one should add, a religious sensibility. He writes from the knowledge of a fallen, sinful world, and his nostalgia is infected with that knowledge. It is corrosive because it affirms with grim consistency that the celebration of the past entails a repudiation of the present.

It is not just in the final trilogy that Waugh begins to recognize something unhealthy in this attitude. As early as *A Handful of Dust* we are invited to look critically at a character's obsession with an unreal past; behind the dreams of Arthurian romance are the relics of childhood that decorate Tony's bedroom. Later, in *Scoop*, William Boot returns gratefully to the childhood security of Boot Magna; but it is a security that can be threatened by sharper realities than the surrounding decay. For his latest contribution to *Lush Places* William draws a conventionally idyllic picture: ". . . *the wagons lumber in the lane under their golden glory of harvested sheaves*, he wrote; *maternal rodents pilot their furry brood through the stubble . . .*" [*S* 222]. Easy enough to let it stand as good-humoured parody, but Waugh insists on a final addition to the moonlit scene of Boot Magna: "Outside the owls hunted maternal rodents and their furry brood." At the end of a comfortable book it leaves a splinter of doubt in the mind.

In *Put Out More Flags* doubts are closer to the surface. The ambiguities of Basil's relationship with his sister have already been noted [elsewhere]. Waugh is indulgent but not unreservedly so: "Poor Basil," reflects Ambrose, "it's sad enough for him to be an *enfant terrible* at the age of thirty-six; but to be regarded by the younger generation as a kind of dilapidated Bulldog Drummond . . ." [*PF* 34]. In a book that tends on the whole to support the reversion of the middle-aged to adolescence this is not more than a pin-prick, but it does express a reservation — and one that is taken up with considerably more emphasis in *Brideshead Revisited*.

This, the most nostalgic of Waugh's novels, is also the one that subjects nostalgia to the closest scrutiny. Relationships of the kind between Charles and Sebastian are not commended by Cara without qualification; "I think they are very good," she explains, "if they do not go on too long," [*BR* 98]. The condition sounds a note of warning. It has already been heard, in another key, from Anthony Blanche, whose role in the novel is a brilliant concession to the possibility that an indefinitely extended child-hood might sometimes be other than charming — even more important, that charm itself might sometimes be other than admirable. Sebastian's preoccupation with Nanny Hawkins and Aloysius is part of this charm; the trappings of childhood are the credentials he brings with him from Paradise. In warning Ryder against them, Blanche effectively forestalls the sort of criticisms that might be forming in the reader's mind; his astringency is there to prevent Sebastian's sweetness from cloying. It may well succeed in this, but his reservations, once made, cannot be ignored. There *is* a sort of charm in the whimsical attachment to childhood, but it can also be a danger—specifically, Blanche warns, a danger to the artist. Later we find that Ryder has turned his art to the service of another sort of nostalgia: "The financial slump of the period, which left many painters without employment, served to enhance my success, which was, indeed, itself a symptom of the decline. When the water-holes were dry people sought to drink at the mirage" [*BR* 216]. The image of a mirage at an empty water-hole subtly endorses Blanche's subsequent judgement, which Ryder himself accepts, that his art has been vitiated by charm.

For a writer as committed to nostalgia as Waugh, who is in the process of writing a book as nostalgic as *Brideshead Revisited*, this is a penetrating admission. To some extent it anticipates the later and more devastating criticism implied in the account he gives of Ludovic's novel, *The Death Wish*. It is described as one of those books by half a dozen English authors which were turning "from the drab alleys of the thirties into the odorous gardens of a recent past transformed and illuminated by disordered memory and imagination" [*US* 188], turning, that is, in exactly the same direction as *Brideshead Revisited*. The Death Wish? To talk of something "unhealthy" in this nostalgia was perhaps an understatement. "Sleep innocently," says Blanche, after his first, unheeded warning against charm. Words to a child. Near the end of the book he is still talking of charm, but to a man no longer innocent: "It spots and kills anything it touches. It kills love; it kills art; I greatly fear, my dear Charles, it has killed *you*" [*BR* 260]. And with this contribution Blanche disappears from the novel.

In the face of this sort of evidence it seems perverse of such critics as Terry Eagleton and D. S. Savage to suggest that the ambiguity of feeling in the novel was a self-contradiction which somehow crept in against the novelist's will. Savage catches the characteristically patronizing tone in a general comment on Waugh's writing: "Yet beneath the mask there is, somewhere in Waugh, a confused and well-meaning man—who, one feels, would speak truthfully if only he knew how—striving in a sort of anguished perplexity for self-expression." It is with the air of announcing a personal *trouvaille* that he tells us of *Brideshead Revisited* that "the real theme is, once more, that of bondage to childhood and the impossibility of growth to adult maturity." But this theme has not been wrested from jealous obscurity by the critic, it is one that the novelist himself quite deliberately makes manifest.

Cara's warning about such relationships as that between Charles and Sebastian is approved by more than the words of Anthony Blanche. Even at the moment when Ryder is most conscious of his loss, the imagery keeps a note of reservation clearly in the reader's mind:

> A door had shut, the low door in the wall I had sought and found in Oxford; open it now and I should find no enchanted garden.
> I had come to the surface, into the light of common day and the fresh sea-air, after long captivity in the sunless coral palaces and waving forests of the ocean bed. . . .
> "I have left behind illusion," I said to myself. "Henceforth I live in a world of three dimensions — with the aid of my five senses."
> [*BR* 163-4]

Once again we catch an echo of Wordsworth's Immortality Ode as the clouds of glory fade into the light of common day, but the enchantment that Ryder leaves behind is not an unqualified vision of delight: the exotic lure of coral palaces and waving forests has to be set against the force of the words "captivity" and "sunless"; the decline into the light of common day is also a rise into the fresh sea-air. Ryder may, as he later claims, be wrong in imagining that there is ever a real world "of three dimensions" in which one can live, but when he asserts that he has "left behind illusion," he firmly associates the experience of the enchanted garden with the unreal City of Tony Last's romanticism and the equally unreal "Holy Land of illusion" in which Guy Crouchback takes up arms at the beginning of the Second World War. In one sense, perhaps, these illusions are part of that "vagabond-language" of which Ryder speaks in *Brideshead Revisited*; they are the loves which, shadow-like, prefigure an ultimate reality. But they are not themselves that reality, and to continue in them — or to encourage others to continue in them — is to foster a state of mind that is infected.

The warnings sounded in *Brideshead* are not isolated caveats, thrown in by the author merely to add sinew to what might otherwise be a rather flabby production; they are part of a continuing and increasingly critical examination of a number of the elements of nostalgia that have been the subject of this chapter. There is, for example, in the years between Ryder's worthless exhibition and Ludovic's *Death Wish*, the tormented figure of Gilbert Pinfold — another artist whose penchant for romantic and nostalgic images threatens to contribute to his destruction. In *The Loved One* the playfully perverse relationships by which characters have in the past evaded the claims of adulthood come to a grisly climax in the romance between Aimée and Mr. Joyboy, honey-baby and poppa. Julia Stitch, so irresistible in *Scoop*, returns in *Officers and Gentlemen*, doubly seductive in virtue of the memories she brings with her from a happier time, but glimpsed now, just occasionally, in a more sinister light. Her social charm can be unprincipled and narcotic. The adolescent enthusiasms of *Put Out*

More Flags persist into the war trilogy, but by the end of it they are being treated with weary disillusionment; the activities of Hazardous Offensive Operations, we are told, include researches into "fortifying drugs, invisible maps, noiseless explosives, and other projects near to the heart of the healthy schoolboy" [*US* 26].

The tone is no longer indulgent; it is past time to grow out of these things. As we have seen, the limitations of extended childhood were already becoming apparent in *Brideshead*. Sebastian's idyll is fatally liable to intrusion, and since he "counted among the intruders his own conscience and all claims of human affection, his days in Arcadia were numbered" [*BR* 123]. In time, "like a fetish, hidden first from the missionary and at length forgotten, the toy bear, Aloysius, sat unregarded on the chest-of-drawers in Sebastian's bedroom" [*BR* 102]. Earlier, Ryder had referred to it as a "teddybear"; "toy bear" was Anthony Blanche's term. The change of phrase registers, on Ryder's part, the faintest shade of adult disdain. But more important, the image suggests what it is that finally displaces the preoccupation with childhood. The affair between Ryder and Julia founders because she sees it as an attempt to set up a rival good to God's; here, in this image of Aloysius as a heathen fetish, it is implied that the security of childhood, the nursery world that is to be found at Brideshead, might also constitute a rival good to God's.

As the Epilogue makes clear, Waugh's ultimate concern in this novel is not to indulge nostalgia but to transcend it. And he underlines his point with the emphasis of a heavy paradox. Brideshead has been vandalized and defiled; surveying the desolation, Ryder lingers in memory over the graceful world that has been destroyed; gloomily he goes off about the army's business. And then, as he enters Brigade's ante-room, the conclusion: " 'You're looking unusually cheerful today,' said the second-in-command" [*BR* 331]. It is a deliberately challenging note on which to end. In this last page Waugh has attempted a massive shift in his hero's perspective. For an explanation we must look to the art nouveau chapel which Ryder had visited a few moments earlier.

Inside, the lamp is burning again before the altar. Without reflecting on its significance, Ryder stays to say a prayer and then returns towards the camp. Everything seems to justify the unyielding bitterness of his story: "the place was desolate and the work all brought to nothing; *Quomodo sedet sola civitas.* Vanity of vanities, all is vanity." In the mood of the preacher he looks back with regret to what is gone. But then abruptly there intrudes a thought which reduces all this desolation to a matter of insignificance. The lament from Ecclesiastes is not the last word,

it is not even an apt word; it is a dead word from ten years back.
Something quite remote from anything the builders intended has come out of their work, and out of the fierce little human tragedy in which I played; something none of us thought about at the time; a small red flame—a beaten-copper lamp of deplorable design relit before the

beaten-copper doors of a tabernacle; the flame which the old knights saw from their tombs, which they saw put out; that flame burns again for other soldiers, far from home, farther, in heart, than Acre or Jerusalem. It could not have been lit but for the builders and the tragedians, and there I found it this morning, burning anew among the old stones. [*BR* 331]

Whether or not we take this rhetoric to be successful, the point it makes is clear: *sub specie aeternitatis* the decline of Brideshead is of slight importance; to exaggerate its loss is to range human values against divine. What matters is that the lamp — even a lamp of deplorable design — still burns in the chapel.

Aspects of the Life and Works

[From "Fantasy and Myth"]   Frederick J. Stopp*

One thing satire, as a form, is incapable of doing: it cannot provide the plot for a novel. Traditionally, satire has always borrowed its ground-plan, parasitically and by ironic inversion, from other forms of ordered exposition in art or in life: misericords bear parodies of the liturgy, ironical encomia are laudatory speeches in reverse. *Punch* prints annually a satirical almanac for the events of the coming year. So a comic entertainment can have, of itself, no mounting plot, no catharsis, no terminal goal. The link binding together the elements of comedy of manners, farce, and satire, must be borrowed from some simple setting of the mythical imagination. Mr. Waugh has for many years rung the changes on a simple plot combining two elements: one, the loss of innocence and expulsion from a haven of refuge, the other, the hero going forth to win a kingdom. The association of these two, basically disparate elements, the one pessimist, the other optimist, provides him with that striking consistent line of poetic fantasy which, in Part Two [elsewhere], has been seen to run through all his plots; his private world is one of constantly changing light and shade, but of stable outlines. Even the more serious novels do not abandon the pattern.

The innocent hero is, as was seen, the mainspring of the action. In the setting of satire the Innocent is a Candide, but in the setting of myth he is something more: a visionary. The Innocent has a capacity for shocked surprise which admirably serves the purpose of the satirical observer of life. But he has his limitations. He cannot as much as enter the scene of his adventures except by the merest accident; he cannot properly animate the scene, or supply the mainspring of the action; he can neither develop, nor achieve the fruition of his desires, since he has none. The wide-eyed savage is brought into Society, comments with wonder and, perhaps, growing cynicism on what he sees, loses his innocence and is withdrawn.

In *Decline and Fall* and *Vile Bodies* the speed and intensity of the

*Reprinted from *Evelyn Waugh: Portrait of An Artist* by Frederick J. Stopp (Boston: Little, Brown and Company, 1958), 201–7, by permission of the publisher. © 1958 by Frederick J. Stopp.

175

action relieves the hero of much of the onus of providing the initial impetus. He is precipitated into the world of chaos by the simplest fall from grace: the imputation of indecent behaviour. Perhaps Paul Penny-feather tempted fortune by reading "a rather daring paper" on drunken-ness to the Thomas More Society; Adam Fenwick-Symes, perhaps, by writing his autobiography, a dangerous proceeding. The erotic theme is not used again till *Work Suspended*, and again much later, when it has its apotheosis in *Helena*. But from *A Handful of Dust* onwards, all Mr. Waugh's heroes are visionaries. From Tony Last to Guy Crouchback their mind's eye is turned inwards, though their steps are directed outwards. Their inward vision takes always one of two forms: a fantasy of adventure, or one of allegiance, a desire for action (Seal, Boot, Crouchback), or a desire for a home, a City, a club, a *civitas* (Last, Plant, Scott-King, Helena). In all cases, fortune takes the hero by the word of his unuttered wishes, and the arm of coincidence reaches out to offer him the substance of his desires: Last a home, Plant, the expert in fictional murder, a real death, a birth, and the chance of himself being reborn, Scott-King an experience of Mediterranean realities, Crouchback a cause. In two cases, the especial remoteness of the fantasy is underlined by its being given a "last-minute" quality: Boot, with his Bengal Lancers, Crouchback, with his Truslove and other fantasies. Helena's fantasy, also, has a last-minute quality, in that consummation is delayed till the end of her recorded life; she is, as a "late comer," a type of several Waugh heroes. In one case, that of Miles Plastic, the vision, when it appears, is totally regressive: incendia-rism and the bearded lady are the extent of his revealed secret desires, a fairground craving rather than a visionary revelation. But then his name is *Plastic*, he is the creature of a new age.

It is the quality of the hero's fantasy and of its relation to the outside world which predisposes him to develop from the innocent to the cad or to the victim. Basil Seal's visions relate to the extent to which he can precipitate disorder and profit from it, as the eater of women, the lone agent, the hard-faced war profiteer. He is a creature of chaos rather than of order; so, like his later half-brother Dennis Barlow, he finds little difficulty in achieving the fruition of his desires, as long as a disintegrating society is the setting. But in the earlier novels and the later entertainments, the answer is normally a dusty one, and the hero — Adam, Seth, Tony, or Scott-King — is delivered back to his limbo, having understood in varying degrees the nature of his experience, or is utterly dispersed. After the fall from grace, the loss of innocence, there is, in the earlier setting, no way back. Only William Boot both retains his innocence and makes the grade. Boot's two desires, fused in the figure of the great-crested grebe, are to wander among lush places, and to fly. This, the typical twofold urge of the romantic soul, is the staple of magical desires throughout the ages; the myth of Alexander and the legend of Dr Faust both take their respective magical adepts up into the sky and down to the deepest regions. His wish, therefore, being almost without realistic content, can the more easily be gratified, and for him stones become gold — another Romantic theme — and he returns with the scoop.

But from 1939, Mr Waugh began to develop a new style of writing; henceforth, it was clear, the mixed elements of farce and tragedy were to be but a subordinate ingredient in the mixture. The earlier works, as satire, had involved no statement of the norm by which the social scene had been judged and found wanting; as myth they had provided the innocent with no way forward from loss of innocence, no way back from dispersion. The disintegration of *A Handful of Dust* had to be answered by some process of reintegration, whether by flux and transformation in the hero's own character, or by the transfiguration of a world of chaos into a vision of order.

Work Suspended was to have been the first essay in the new mode. Instead of a haven to be succeeded by chaos, the hero was given a false haven, a pension in Fez, bearing in it already the pattern of a new life to which he was to be called by the incursion of the irrational. Death passed over the head of John Plant, and took the father, and the agent of death — Dr Messinger translated in Arthur Atwater — provided the first clear double in Mr Waugh's novels, in conflict with whom the transformation of the hero's character became possible. Not that fantasy was to give place to an unrelieved realism, still less to introspective analysis of mental contents. The hero's progress was still — and will always be — projected into outer figures and situations. But the discordant elements of farce and tragedy were to be fused into a uniform thread of poetic symbolism. . . . It is, however, by his straight writing in three major works of the post-war period, *Brideshead, Helena*, and the war novels, *Men at Arms* and *Officers and Gentlemen*, that Mr Waugh's work is now commonly judged. It is here that a consideration of the progress of the visionary hero will reveal the resources which he has been able to summon up to replace those forces which are now called on only for occasional service, in the entertainments. His achievement leads through *Brideshead* to a peak in *Helena*, followed by a — perhaps temporary — decline in the novels of Army life. . . . *Helena* is the first-fruit of Mr Waugh's liberation from an imagined union implicit in the term "household of the faith," from a desire to realize a world of the spirit in allegiance to a great home. Helena scoops her prize for the simple reason that the initial fantasy — erotic and civic, Helen of Troy and the carved bed — is projected back, by way of poetic analogy, from its preordained end; submission to the Cross is the final consummation of both parts of the fantasy. The forerunner theme (Constantius leading to Christ) is taken over from *Brideshead* and becomes one of the numerous antinomies, reflecting the transition from vision to reality, on which the work is based: failure becomes success, the poetry of Troy is revealed as the fact of Golgotha, the private myth merges into the mystical vision. The pattern of dispersion and concentration, attempted in earlier works from *Work Suspended*, is finely achieved. As in *Brideshead*, the process by which the action is refocussed on to the spiritual plane is twofold. Helena leaves her British castle for palaces in Nish, Dalmatia, and Rome, and ends by penetrating into the underground structure of the cistern to find the balks of timber of the True Cross. In this final uniting, in the symbol of the spiritual marriage, of the marital chamber and the tomb, the regressive symbols of the caves and grottoes last met in *Put Out More Flags* are transcended: physical restriction becomes spiritual liberation. At the same time, however, Colchester and Rome are seen as progressively more inadequate symbols of allegiance to a universal Church, the ideal of a *civitas* that should burst out beyond the *limes*.

Consider how *Helena* so completely provides the answer to the most resounding and grim failure of the Innocent in the earlier work, *A Handful of Dust*. Both central figures seek in marriage some new and better allegiance to a home: Hetton Abbey, the City of Rome; both are betrayed. Each then continues the quest for the City in another mode, Tony in his despairing archaeological expedition to the jungles of Brazil, Helena in the pursuance of her first-expressed desire to excavate the City of Troy. Tony is the "Last" to try to find Avalon in an English county, Helena the first to find "Troy" in the Holy Land. Both are sought out by a messenger, Tony by Dr Messinger, Helena by the Wandering Jew. The one is taken to a living death in a grotesque parody of the Eden from which he has been expelled. The other finds the True Cross in a cistern on Good Friday. Mr Waugh's sacred and profane memories are so consistent and interwoven that the profane imaginative pattern is succeeded, after fifteen years, by its sacred counterpart in the way in which type answers to antitype in the Christian, typological view of the continuity of history. Tony Last's expulsion from Hetton and his end in Brazil is the fall of the old Adam — *o felix culpa!* — redeemed, in time, by the action of Helena. The early novel shows the greatest possible dissonance between the romanticism of English Gothic and the social novel of present-day manners; the later one the happiest association of poetic symbol and Christian legend.

For the general public, and the critics, Mr Waugh is still the author of *Brideshead*, a work in which the forced and one-sided extraversion of the war years caused a rank luxuriation of fantasy images. But *Helena*, where poetic fantasy was disciplined by a more astringent technique to the requirements of a perfectly appreciated theme, and which continues his greatest earlier work, represents much more clearly his present-day full-dress manner of writing. But to achieve this success, he had to go to a legendary, Christian past. The war novels show the difficulty of applying the new mode to the de-Christianized present.

Crouchback, like Helena, is a visionary; he and the secular world around him are not more at odds than were Helena and pagan Rome. But while Helena's was a heroic and Homeric fantasy, embraced with epic gusto, Crouchback's contact with the sources of vitality have wasted away till they are represented by echoes from childhood adventure stories (Captain Truslove) and the popular, naive religion of his Italian home (Sir Roger de Waybroke). Neither can provide the gateway to a larger life. Both Helena and Crouchback explore their fantasies. But while Helena's love affair is expansive in its object, Crouchback's flirtation with Army life throws up substitute figures which elbow him, paralysed, to the wings. Each one is eliminated late, and with difficulty, and the last is the worst illusion of all. The fantasies to which they, in turn, give rise in his mind, are increasingly remote; the images associated with Ivor Claire (an Eastern Prince, a man withdrawn in prayer), are as decorative and undynamic as anything in *Brideshead*. The withdrawal of the life force from these figures leads to no visible enrichment or rise in stature in the hero himself; his vision is progressively restricted, from a Crusade to an operation, then to drill on the barracks square. Chesterton's words about Mr Pickwick are relevant here: "Pickwick goes through life with that god-like gullibility which is the key to all adventures. The greenhorn is the ultimate victor in everything; it is he who gets most out of life. . . . The whole is unerringly expressed in one fortunate phrase—he will always be 'taken in.' To be taken in everywhere is to see the inside of everything. It is the hospitality of circumstances. With torches and trumpets, like a guest, the greenhorn is taken in by Life. And the sceptic is cast out by it." But the greenhorn must be taken in, not in a moment of weakness, but in an impulse of generosity, which compels the hospitality of circumstance. So the pattern sketched by Chesterton fits happily the picaresque mood of Dickens, the fairy-tale tone of *Scoop*, the legendary and poetic style of *Helena*. But Crouchback, in whom generosity was not lacking, but impulsiveness was, is cast out. It is not his religion which isolates him, it is himself.

Presumably, the two volumes now written contain only the stage of dispersion, to be followed by that of re-orientation and of concentration. The Crouchback saga has arrived at the stage when Helena was old, lonely, and forgotten in Dalmatia. The mantle of the Innocent is shared here between the two Crouchbacks, the son and the father. It is Crouchback senior who is "taken in" by life, and for whom life produces its Mr Baldwins—Major Tickeridge, Colonel Trotter, Major Grimshawe. While his father's presence is effective, Guy's progress is assured. "Somehow his mind seems to work different than yours and mine," comments the grasping Mrs Cuthbert, ungrammatically but with perception. Perhaps the continuation will bring the *aristeia* of the father; the spirit of Broome will succeed the illusion of the crusade. . . .

Waugh Begins   Anthony Burgess*

We need no cybernetic word-count to demonstrate how frequently the verb "repine," in its negative conjugation, occurs in the works of Mr. Evelyn Waugh. None of his later heroes—Scott-King, Gilbert Pinfold, Guy Crouchback, the author himself—ever repines, in spite of the march of barbarism, the failure of the vintage, and the decay of classical syntax. The pose is robed and stoic. In the last imperial outpost the doomed values of language and chivalry are upheld, though always with a certain discreet self-mockery. Indeed, Scott-King takes a definite masochistic pleasure (not uncommon here, we are told, though unknown to the New World) in the rise of horrible Modern Europe. The red-eyed scavenger is creeping in. Mr. Waugh goes so far as to open the gates of Hampstead to him, cooing about its peace: "Oh, but I have done an unselfish thing in telling him this! For I know he will yearn to be about the business of Balbus, and, as likely as not, he will plant himself upon the meadow with the willows, that looks so spring-like from my book-room door today. Nevertheless one must not repine. My work in this line is done. Balbus has built his wall." The style, and the slippered epoch it so well expresses, will tell the reader which Mr. Waugh this is—not the comic-stoic mock-Augustan novelist but the whimsical man-of-letters, managing director of Chapman & Hall, friend of the great fraud Gosse. But the "one must not repine" is a significant link, a shared nose or villainous trick of the eye. The father, despite all the differences in the world, prepared us for the son.

And, of course, in reading this first volume of Mr. Waugh's autobiography, we are most interested in the genesis of a vocation, a temperament, and a style. We can ignore the remoter heredity, though Mr. Waugh makes it very entertaining; what we cannot ignore is the father, with his continual "flamboyant declamation to imaginary audiences," his despondent waltz-song ("*Nobody cares for me in the least. Everyone thinks I'm a horrible beast*"), his mercuriality and his dramatic asthma, but, most of all, the limitations of his literary taste. "Mr. Rupert Brooke," he wrote, "has the itch to say a thing in such an arresting fashion as to shock the literary purist into attention even against his will." The art of D.H. Lawrence needs "a shower bath of vital ideas." T.S. Eliot is the drunken slave who, in the classic custom, was exhibited at the height of a feast to the sons of the household, "to the end that they, being ashamed at the ignominious folly of his gesticulations, might determine never to be tempted into such a pitiable condition themselves." Well, the son's best novel takes its title from *The Waste Land*, but, with some inevitable advancing of the frontier of taste, the limitations have been passed on.

*Reprinted from *Encounter* 23 (December 1964):64, 66, 68, by permission of the journal.

Does not Mr. Pinfold abhor jazz and Picasso? Did not his creator affirm on television that James Joyce went mad to please the Americans? The Gibbonian classicism of *A Little Learning* is a great joy, but it is an act, a posture, and it derives from the father's more Dickensian histrionics as much as the fictional gift itself. It is no more a "natural" style than the Elianism of Mr. Waugh's father's bookish contemporaries, though it evokes an England of firmer tastes and more powerful convictions than were known to E.V. Lucas (whom Mr. Waugh cites as his father's peer), Jack Squire, or W.W. Jacobs. The perfect mastery of the exact conceptual locution, often implying—as in Gibbon's own *Autobiography*—a moral judgment that is not really there, is the source of all of Mr. Waugh's humour and irony, as well as his carefully outmoded elegance. But when he falls from his own high standards—as when he uses the ghastly neologism "undergraduette" in the Oxford part of the book—we are shocked as we are shocked by no other author. In Mr. Waugh style is a kind of morality, and a solecism strikes with the force of an act of delinquency. But such lapses are very rare. Stylistically this is a consummate achievement, yet (and this is no paradox) the beauty of the writing draws away our concern with the subject-matter as recorded *fact*. Was Mr. Waugh's Oxford, for instance, really as he describes it? It reads, with the Arcadia of *Brideshead Revisited*, like some world of idyll far older than anything Mr. Waugh could have known. Still, we do not care much, and though Mr. Waugh's three delightful maiden aunts undoubtedly have historical referents, he is as welcome as is Apthorpe to invent them so long as we continue to be beguiled by the wonder of form and language. The professional fiction writer seeks the suspension of our disbelief when he writes a novel; it is hard to break the habit of credulity when we read his autobiography. Credulity, though, is a different condition from the ineluctable need to accept fact as fact.

The youth who emerges from this book is neither forward nor, as Mr. Waugh himself is only too ready to admit, particularly likeable. At Lancing he and his cronies christened a boy, for no good reason, "Dungy." "Once this large, desperate youth approached me in the cloisters and said: 'If you'll stop calling me "Dungy" I'll do anything you like. I'll publicly kick *anyone* in another House.' I replied: 'Oh, go and kick yourself, Dungy.' " Along with the "malice and calculation" went a gulosity that was to reappear in *Brideshead Revisited*, though later (and I believe wrongly) expunged: "[We] began with crumpets, eight or more a head, dripping with butter. From there we swiftly passed to cake, pastry and, in season, strawberries and cream, until at six we tottered into chapel taut and stupefied with eating. . . . Little pots of *foie gras* and caviar occasionally came from London and we were as nice in the brewing of tea as a circle of maiden ladies." And so on. Lust is the only deadly sin not to appear, and Mr. Waugh's youth, after a phase of mutual exhibition with a little girl, is innocent of sexuality. Indeed, the only sexual revelation in the entire book comes at the end, and the prototype of Captain Grimes—Mr. Waugh's colleague at a school not much like Llanabba—makes it. There had been a vast outing in honour of the headmaster's birthday:

> When it was all over and the boys in bed we sat in the common-room deploring the miseries of the day. Grimes alone sat with the complacent smile of an Etruscan funerary effigy.
> "I confess *I* enjoyed myself greatly," he said as we groused.
> We regarded him incredulously. "*Enjoyed* yourself, Grimes? What did you find to enjoy?"
> "Knox minor," he said with radiant simplicity. "I felt the games a little too boisterous, so I took Knox minor away behind some rocks. I removed his boots and stockings, opened my trousers, put his dear little foot there and experienced a most satisfying emission."

There are pederasts of more distinction in the book, but no other podorasts.

As for the young artist, we are reminded that Mr. Waugh, though he bloomed as a novelist early, started with the ambition to be a calligrapher and illustrator—an ambition as modest as that of the father in the field destined for the son. We have met Mr. Waugh's illustrations to his own novels and, with the indulgence appropriate to the *violon d'Ingres*, admired. There are other examples of his first and secondary art here and the technique is, I should think, faultless. The aim is cognate with that of the prose stylist—to achieve ironic effects (I am thinking particularly of "The Tragical Death of Mr. Will. Huskisson") through a severely classical, almost sculptural, line, but the flavour is of a mere hobby—like the flavour of the essays of Lucas and the senior Waugh. And, even in the author's attitude to the art that became his profession, there is something amateur and hobbyish: we need the discipline of Latin and Greek in order to write good English prose: "the old-fashioned test of an English sentence—will it translate?—still stands after we have lost the trick of translation." That excludes a great deal of modern English literature, much of it valuable, and it fixes the writer at an immovable frontier, administering the laws of a dead empire. But Mr. Waugh is probably disingenuous here, as he is in his very opening sentence: "Only when one has lost all curiosity about the future has one reached the age to write an autobiography." It is that charming television act again—the old man in a dry month. Mr. Waugh is writing for the future.

The reader will be surprised at the lack of any literary passion in this first phase of Mr. Waugh's development—no books set him on fire, unless they are about the pre-Raphaelites. The young man who reads History and leaves Oxford with a bad third betrays no concern with scholarship. Mr. Waugh, an ironic statue in a toga, practitioner of perfect prose, has always tended to frighten us as Gibbon or Johnson or Junius frighten us—

with the hint of a formidable library, much of it in his brain. We need not be frightened any more, nor need we cringe, with an underdog whine, in the presence of the accents of aristocracy. Mr. Waugh's father worked in an office, worried about money, and went to Lord's or the cinema before going home to Hampstead. At Oxford the contacts with the ruling class begin, and there is a sufficiency of name-dropping. The *Brideshead Revisited* postures are a legitimate indulgence for a novelist unrid of his father's romanticism, but the dream of a great Catholic aristocracy has a faint whiff of the sentimental about it. That there is no sentimentality in the harking back to Augustan solidity — temperamentally, if not historically, cognate — is a tribute to Mr. Waugh's perfect artistry, though artistry itself is all poses.

Mr. Waugh's conversion to Catholicism will appear, one presumes, in the next volume. A cradle-Catholic myself, and hence one of a long line of underdogs, I tend both to despise (always unjustly) and envy (sometimes justly) a man like Mr. Waugh who, with calm 18th-century logic, can sail into the Church after the sort of *echt* English upbringing presented in *A Little Learning.* It is the best of both worlds. Mr. Waugh gives us what he calls "A Brief History of My Religious Opinions," and the cradle-Catholic is aware of the great social, as well as theological, gulf fixed. In an earlier chapter we look in wonder on St. Jude's, Hampstead Garden Suburb, and its eccentric incumbent:

> Mr. Bourchier was a totally preposterous parson. When he felt festal he declared a feast, whatever the season or occasion marked on the calendar. He dressed up, he paraded about, lights and incense were carried before him. When the mood took him he improvised his own peculiar ceremonies. Once he presented himself on the chancel steps, vested in a cope and bearing from his own breakfast table a large silver salt-cellar. "My people," he announced, "you are the salt of the earth," and scattered a spoonful on the carpet before us. . . . Despite all Mr. Bourchier's extravagant display I had some glimpse of higher mysteries.

Well, this was the England of Mr. Waugh's boyhood and it is perhaps no more difficult for the Old Catholic to understand than the world of the minor public school with its "good Church traditions." The curious reader will take delight in pincering out from the brew the gobbets and slivers of genuine influence — the medieval illuminations, the comedy of bourgeois life, the individualists of Oxford and above all, the paternal devotion to tradition.

The first volume, like Mr. Waugh's first novel, records a decline and fall. An academic failure, indecisive in his choice of vocation, inclined, like St. Augustine himself, to debauchery, in need of a greater solidity than Anglican Hampstead could provide, young Evelyn Waugh looked at the successes of his friends and tried to escape from his loneliness and dejection. Less resilient than Paul Pennyfeather, his wounds unpalliated by the large confidence of "Grimes," he sought a semptiernal quietus in the waters of the North Wales coast. The jellyfish stung him and sent him back to the future; the sea proved lustral, not lethal. Naturally, we rejoice. We look forward to reading about the larger learning, a lifetime's lessons on how not to repine.

Waugh Revisited   John Gross*

English novelists seldom produce first-rate autobiographies, and even when they do the results tend to be pretty unrevealing. Perhaps they feel that they have already given away more than enough in their fiction. At any rate, the first volume of Evelyn Waugh's memoirs keeps well within the reticent tradition of Trollope in his *Autobiography* or Kipling in *Something of Myself*. Waugh's manner has always been that of a man ready to set the dogs on trespassers; and if the mood of *A Little Learning* is surprisingly mellow, at no point can it be said to take us very far into the author's confidence. It is a book which lives down to its title: for the most part it deals with Waugh's schooldays and his undergraduate years at Oxford, but it contains little about education, either literary or sentimental, while the "brief history of my religious opinions" is brief indeed (three pages). The tone throughout is relaxed and bantering. Some memorable characters wander across the stage, but they are invariably seen through the wrong end of the telescope: while it is all of a piece that the darkest moment in the book should quickly be turned into farce. While teaching at a prep school in North Wales, the young Waugh fell prey to suicidal gloom. One night he could bear it no more: he went down to the beach and started swimming out to sea, leaving behind his clothes and a scrap of paper on which he had copied a line from Euripides (in Greek), about the ocean washing away all human sorrows. After a few yards, however, he was forced to turn back. He had been stung by a jelly-fish.

Waugh punctuates *A Little Learning* with some splendid tomfoolery, along with lines of *Vice Versa* and *The Diary of a Nobody*, two of his father's favorite books which were read aloud to him as a child. He displays a positively Pooterish readiness to record his own discomfitures, particularly while school-mastering: "One of my major defeats was when I cried wrathfully to a moonfaced, vacuous creature: 'Are you deaf, boy?,' to which all his fellows replied: 'Yes, sir, he is.' And he was." But far more than clowning it is the style which smacks of the past: resolutely old-

*Reprinted with permission from *The New York Review of Books*, 3 December 1964, 4–5. © 1964 Nyrev, Inc.

fashioned, full of elaborate mock-courtesy and resounding clichés. Commenting on a similar vein of long-winded levity in Saki (another of Waugh's masters), V.S. Pritchett once said that "the cinema, if nothing else, has burned this educated shrubbery out of our comic prose." But it is still possible for Waugh, with tongue only just in cheek, to reveal that "I was promiscuous in my choice of familiars," or to record that "It was a beautiful night of a gibbous moon." He is dangerously fond of words like "plethora" and "corpulent"; and he must be the last surviving English author able to talk about a "Hindoo," as though he were being employed (like his forebears) by the East India Company.

Such verbal bowings and scrapings soon grow tiresome, and by comparison with Waugh's novels the writing in A *Little Learning* is often disconcertingly slack. But even so, his mastery of the language is apparent on every page: just when he threatens to turn verbose, he saves himself with a flash of fantasy, an unexpected image, a curt but beautifully apt definition. Apart from the padding, his style is vivid, elegant, and concise: but it is no more a genuinely classical style than Brideshead was a genuine country-house. The pose of the man of quality, born a couple of hundred years too late and turning his back on a shoddy twentieth century, has been cultivated as assiduously as the aristocratic dream; but behind it Waugh remains unmistakably a modern, as well-informed as a gossip columnist about the world which he affects to despise. Gilbert Pinfold, in the ordeal of that name, "abhorred plastics, Picasso, sunbathing, and jazz — everything in fact that had happened in his own lifetime." But in the course of the same paragraph we are told that whenever he came across something which displeased him — a bad bottle of wine, a fault in syntax — his mind "like a cinema camera trucked furiously forward to confront the offending object close-up with glaring lens." By their imagery shall ye know them. A trivial example, perhaps: but anyone who doubts the paradox of Waugh the contemporary-in-spite-of-himself should look up the Guy Crouchback *Men at Arms* series (still generally underrated, in my view). This trilogy contrives to be at one and the same time a bizarre private myth, almost Yeatsian in its arrogance, and an outstanding piece of fiction (probably the best from an English writer so far) about World War II, often deadly accurate in detail.

Now, in his autobiography, Waugh keeps up the illusion of traveling backwards, though none too solemnly. The Modern World makes a brief official appearance, in the person of Barbara, his elder brother's fiancée: a mildly bohemian, mildly left-wing, mildly agnostic student (1917 vintage) who took young Evelyn round the galleries during the school holidays, converting him to Picasso and all that he was later to abhor. At the age of fourteen he published an article entitled "The Defense of Cubism"; but before long he was following his natural inclinations again, trying to counterfeit thirteenth-century manuscripts and to draw like Aubrey

Beardsley. The Middle Ages resumed their sway (the fancy-dress Victorian version of the Middle Ages, that is); and Waugh's first book was to be a Life of Dante Gabriel Rossetti. It is characteristic that among the illustrations to *A Little Learning* there should be portraits of four of Waugh's great-great-grandfathers, but no picture of his parents, and that he should spend an entire chapter establishing his pedigree. The Waughs themselves were by origin one of those tough Lowland Scottish families who started moving south in the late eighteenth century, and whose contribution to the English professional classes has been out of all proportion to their numbers. Alexander Waugh, D.D., the first of them to settle in London, was a dissenting minister (with nearly 8,000 sermons to his credit) whose home became a well-known port of call for fellow-expatriates, among them the young Carlyle. His son joined the Church of England, and spent most of his life as a parson in Dorset; his grandson was a physician practising just outside Bath. Long before Evelyn Waugh himself was born the family had become thoroughly anglicized.

It would be hard, indeed, to imagine a more English figure than his father. Arthur Waugh was a bookman in the old carpet-slippers and *belles lettres* tradition. He lived in a golden haze of Eng. Lit., with the emphasis at least as much on Eng. as on Lit. (He once told a young man aspiring to a literary career, that "with a thorough knowledge of the Bible, Shakespeare and Wisden you cannot go far wrong" — Wisden being the standard reference-book for everything connected with cricket.) His general outlook is perhaps best indicated by some of the authors who dedicated books to him (there were many others): E.V. Lucas, Austin Dobson, J.C. Squire. Like them, he has long since been relegated to the footnotes of literary history; for many readers his only claim to fame must be that he once described T.S. Eliot as a drunken helot, and Eliot bothered to put the fact on record. But in his day he was a figure of some repute, both as an influential literary journalist and the chairman of an old established publishing house. (His son who was christened Arthur Evelyn St. John, says that he has always disliked the name Evelyn, which was a maternal caprice; but presumably he liked the idea of having to avoid confusion by appearing as Arthur Waugh Jr. even less.)

Waugh's portrait of his father is the best thing in the book. (His mother, as is so often the case with autobiographies, remains in the shadows.) It is an affectionate portrait, and an admiring one: with good reason, since Waugh senior in many ways was an admirable man. "His whole bent was towards amiability"; he was genial and impulsive, full of boyish enthusiasm and with almost none of the literary man's occupational malice.

The devotion with which Waugh sketches his character suggests that he is trying to make amends for past ingratitude. If this is the case, he succeeds; his praise carries complete conviction, and though we occasionally catch a glimpse of Arthur Waugh's faults — obstinacy, cosiness, self-indulgence — we are not encouraged to dwell on them. Whether his son would always have shown such filial piety is certainly open to question. There is a brilliant description in *Brideshead Revisited*, for instance, of the war of nerves between the hero, down for the vacation from Oxford after having run through his allowance, and his unsympathetic aged parent, wonderfully evasive and determined not to let him have a penny. (But I take due note of the author's warning at the beginning of that book: "I am not I; thou art not he or she; they are not they.") At any rate, there is a real sense in which Evelyn Waugh the novelist is his father's son, Arthur Waugh, Jr. The nostalgia which runs through his work is not, all said and done, for the Middle Ages; but for the warm glow of an Edwardian childhood spent in a comfortable literary home, and dominated by a man who was himself incurably romantic about the past. (But then it is always especially easy to be nostalgic about those who feel nostalgia themselves.) The only work by Arthur Waugh which I have looked at is a guide to Tennyson dating from the 1890s, deferential to the point of obsequiousness in tone and never more so than when dealing with the *Idylls of the King*. It is Tennysonian chivalry which provides the moral touchstone in his son's masterpiece, *A Handful of Dust*. (Curious to recall, incidentally, that according to his epigraph Waugh took the title from a line in that piece of drunken helotry, *The Waste Land* — "I will show you fear in a handful of dust" — when he might have found it in "Maud": "Dead, long dead, long dead! And my heart is a handful of dust.") Tony Last, the hero of *A Handful of Dust*, is a rather stuffy but completely honorable man — the last of the true Lasts — who is destroyed by his wife's infidelity with a young parasite-about-town. He ends up held captive in the jungle and presumed dead, while his dreadful cousins — the pseudo-Lasts — take over the home which he had adored: a country house (rebuilt 1864) where each of the bedrooms, with its frieze of Gothic text, is named after a character in Malory. Innocence has been overwhelmed — the innocence of Waugh's nursery, which he particularly remembers for its "pictorial wallpaper representing figures in medieval costume."

The clown with a broken heart? This kind of diagnosis can come suspiciously pat to a critic's purpose; but in Waugh's case it surely applies. It is impossible not to make out behind the satirist a wounded romantic (or a bruised sentimentalist). If he wasn't so incredibly funny, the chief impression his work would leave would be one of resentment and baffled rage. The sources of his comic fury are not to be found in *A Little Learning*, however. His story is of a happy childhood; beyond the family circle he was able to explore the pleasures of growing up in Hampstead, at that time little more than an overgrown village on the outskirts of London, subsequently much eroded by suburban development (though not entirely obliterated, as he implies). There is a Betjemanesque vein of feeling in most well-to-do Englishmen of Waugh's age; they are the last generation old enough to remember the complete self-confidence which never quite returned to their class after 1914. Many of them have tried to evoke the golden age before now, some with greater success than Waugh; to take a recent example, there is the cartoonist Osbert Lancaster's exquisitely detailed childhood memoir, *All Done from Memory*. By comparison Waugh's recollections of Hampstead are nothing much out of the ordinary. But they are attractive enough, a pleasant set, of water-colors.

One reason for his happy memories is that he was spared the rigors of going to a prep school as a boarder: anyone who has read Orwell's "Such, Such were the Joys" will know what that might have entailed. Instead, he went to a local establishment run by a hearty old soul called Mr. Granville Grenfell (like all true novelists, from an early age he had the knack of surrounding himself with characters whose names might have come straight out of his own books). He cherished the privacy of life at home, and followed his own tastes in drawing and reading: by the time he was twelve he had rejected routine adventure stories in favor of *Sinister Street* and *Morte d'Arthur*. But shades of the public school around the growing boy. He had been destined for his father's old school, Sherborne, but this became impossible after his elder brother Alec had published his semi-autobiographical novel *The Loom of Youth*, so instead he was sent to Lancing.

The "frankness" of *The Loom of Youth* provoked a scandal in 1917; one paper called it "the *Uncle Tom's Cabin* of the Public School system." Today it is not only difficult to see what all the fuss was about but almost impossible not to take the book in the opposite sense, as a deeply loyal and full-throated tribute to the dear old *alma mater*. It is measure of how times have changed that Evelyn's casual reminiscences shouldn't raise a murmur, although they are much more damning than Alec's exposé. Not that he hated Lancing; on the contrary, he accepted the system, if not the men who were running it, and ended up a prefect. But the full traditional squalor is there, all the same: ragging, fagging, flogging, the communal bath after football in tepid mud, the food which "would have provoked a mutiny in a mid-Victorian poor-house." Two character-sketches enliven the bleak record, the portraits of "two mentors": Francis Crease, a fastidious, lonely bachelor who fostered Waugh's interest in the art of the illuminated manuscript, and J.F. Roxburgh, an ambitious, dandified assistant master — "everything about J.F. was calculated to impress" — who taught literature at Lancing (and made a Fowler-like fetish of correct usage) until he left to take up a plum headmastership elsewhere. Of the two sketches, that of Crease, alternately peevish and extravagant, is the more striking; but taken together they illustrate very neatly the variety of homosexual temperaments which the English educational system manages to accommodate at its upper levels.

The unvoiced objection to Lancing is that it wasn't smart enough, wasn't Eton. And at Oxford Waugh never quite got over finding himself in an unfashionable college, Hertford: he is defensive about it even now, in a *Vile Bodies* tone of voice ("a respectable but rather dreary little college"). One can't exactly say that he is disingenuous about his time at Oxford, since he is unsparing on the subject of his own initial callowness. Yet something seems to have been left out. At one moment he is a conventional freshman, buying his cigarette-box carved with the college arms, learning how to smoke a pipe, planning a career in undergraduate debating and journalism; at the next he is in with a fast and fashionable set, a regular swell. The transition is unconvincingly smooth; his social climb must have involved some exertion on his own part, although no doubt he was taken up mainly on account of his gifts (in those days he was still better known for his drawings and woodcuts than as a potential author). He was as intoxicated as Scott Fitzgerald by the gilded youth of his day; and if most of the gilt has worn off by now, it must be admitted that there were some debonair figures among his contemporaries: Harold Acton, Robert Byron, Cyril Connolly (the young Cyril Connolly); and a dozen others. The account of this group is spiced with some moderately juicy gossip, and one or two good anecdotes: I cherish the Hysteron-Proteron club, whose members used to live through the day in reverse, "getting up in evening dress, drinking whisky, smoking cigars and playing cards, then at ten o'clock dining backwards starting with savouries and ending with soup." But Waugh doesn't manage to cast the same spell as he did in the first half of *Brideshead* and the silly-clever snobbery soon palls — although we're still in the cocktail-party Twenties, still all very young, and it isn't so offensive as it is going to be later on.

After Oxford, a brief spell at art school, and then off to the rigors of teaching small boys in North Wales. Waugh longed to escape, and almost managed to get a post as private secretary to Scott-Moncrieff, the translator. But the job fell through; fate had a more important literary contact in store for him. He was joined on the staff of his prep-school by a dapper little ex-army man with highly specialized sexual tastes, who was to serve as the basis for one of his most memorable characters, Captain Grimes. *Decline and Fall* is already on the way.

The final impression left by *A Little Learning* is of a man who doesn't understand himself particularly well. But it is sloppy middlebrow piety to assume that a novelist must always have exceptional insight into human nature, or specialize in diagnosing human relationships, as though he were a social worker-cum-marriage counselor. For many writers — and Waugh is one of them — it would be damaging to understand too much: the integrity and intensity of a novelist's peculiar vision may well be diluted rather than strengthened by fair-mindedness and introspection. At the beginning of one of his most remarkable books, *The Ordeal of Gilbert Pinfold*, Waugh comes close to portraying himself. The voices which subsequently afflict Pinfold turn out to be the result of taking the wrong medicine: they don't lead to a reappraisal of his character as presented at the beginning. A wiser man might have insisted on the connection, enquired more deeply; but I doubt whether he could have written *The Ordeal of Gilbert Pinfold*. "Be yourself" often makes a better motto for a writer than "Know thyself"; a little learning may not be such a dangerous thing after all.

Evelyn Waugh's Travel Books   Richard J. Voorhees*

The publication of Evelyn Waugh's diaries was awaited with almost unseemly eagerness and greeted with a great to-do. The value of the diaries as a mine for scandal-mongers is obvious; their value as documents for scholars and critics is a matter into which I do not wish to venture here. But the extraordinary attention paid to them emphasizes the neglect of a number of documents which have been available for a long time: Waugh's travel books.

Commentary on the travel books amounts to a very small part of a sizable body of the scholarship and criticism that Waugh's work has begotten. And Waugh himself furnished a warrant to anybody who chooses to disregard a half dozen of his books. Christopher Sykes, in his recent biography, calls the first of them a minor work, and Waugh, in a copy inscribed for Sykes, calls the last of them a potboiler. Furthermore, Waugh writes in the Preface to *When the Going Was Good* (1947): "The following pages comprise all that I wish to reprint of the four travel books that I wrote between 1929 and 1935. . . . These books have been out of print for some time and will not be reissued. . . . There was a fifth book, about Mexico, which I am content to leave in oblivion, for it dealt little with travel and much with political questions." (The sixth travel book is *Tourist in Africa*, published in 1960).

I should say, however, that Waugh's attitude is unfair to himself and unfortunate for his readers. His novels are available in a wide variety of editions, but his travel books are likely to be found only in the libraries of large universities. It would be silly to deny that these books are uneven (are not the novels, like anyone else's, also uneven?), but they are all valuable. First, they are entertaining. They would be worth reading if someone other than Waugh had written them or if Waugh had written nothing else. Second, they are informative about Waugh's principles and convictions. Third, they have significant links with his fiction.

In the decade before World War II, Waugh traveled extensively. His first wife accompanied him on the Mediterranean cruise which he recounts in *Labels* (1930), though she became ill and had to be hospitalized on the ship and in port. By the time he wrote *Labels*, their marriage

*Reprinted from *Dalhousie Review* 58 (Summer 1978):240–48, by permission of the journal.

had failed. With a novelist's license, he transformed himself into a single man (the American edition of *Labels* is plausibly called *A Bachelor Abroad*) and her into "Juliet," the wife of "Geoffrey." But, as Christopher Sykes has noted, the made-up Geoffrey, worrying about his wife's illness, also represents an aspect of Waugh. Most of Waugh's later travels were solitary. He disliked literary cliques and collaborations, and Frederick J. Stopp is no doubt right in saying that during the travel years his dislike increased. Parsnip and Pimpernell (Auden and Isherwood?) who together, Waugh says, almost add up to one writer, move absurdly in and out of Waugh's novels, and their doings are reported in his last short story, "Basil Seal Rides Again," published in 1963. One has become a professor at the "University of Minneapolis," and the other a professor at the "University of St. Paul."

As Stopp has observed, Waugh invented a new version of an old literary form and a new kind of traveler. In *Labels* Waugh describes the kind that Hilaire Belloc invented earlier: The pilgrim on his way to Rome wears shabby clothes and carries a big walking stick. In his haversack are sausages, wine, a map, a sketch book. He talks with poor people in roadside inns and sees in their very diversities the unity of the Roman Empire. He knows something of military history and strategy. But he traveled, Waugh concludes, at a time when few men had marched with an army. Since that time there has been a world war.

The persona of Waugh's travel books, especially the first of them, is less romantic than anti-romantic and less likely to travel to Rome than to some outlandish, even savage place. But instead of adopting G. K. Chesterton's axiom and regarding inconveniences as adventures, he regards adventures as inconveniences. He is not the kind of traveler who, after walking twenty miles through elephant grass, delights in drinking cocoa from a tobacco tin and eating moldy biscuits, and he can imagine nothing more nauseating than a stew of newly killed game. He could do very well without the dangers of exotic diseases and predatory animals. He is aware, not of unity, but of contrast: of civilization opposed to the jungle, of borders and collisions of culture. The social intercourse of the jungle (sitting in a dark hut, drinking strange drinks, swapping compliments through an interpreter) is exhausting.

Nevertheless, Waugh does not remove all romance from his travels and does not wish to. Indeed, he is fascinated by "distant and barbarous places." When, in 1930, he went to Addis Ababa for the Coronation of Haile Selassie, he also traveled to the interior of Abyssinia, Kenya, the Belgian Congo, Zanzibar, and Aden. Before he left England, friends and old reference books told him fantastic tales about Abyssinia: The Abyssinian Church consecrated bishops by spitting on their heads, and it had canonized Pontius Pilate. The Royal Family traced its descent from Solomon and the Queen of Sheba. The proper heir to the throne was hidden in the mountains and bound in chains of solid gold.

Waugh was gratified to learn that the reality was quite as bizarre as the rumors. Addis Ababa, he thought, resembled the Israel of Saul and the Scotland of Macbeth, but more than anything else it resembled the world of Lewis Carroll, where rabbits carry watches in their waistcoat pockets and royalty walks around croquet lawns with executioners. Abyssinian men wore daggers and bandoliers. Behind them walked slave boys carrying their rifles. The bullets in the bandoliers might not fit the rifles, but no matter, for they were a medium of exchange and a symbol of status. At the monastery of Debra Lebanos the Mass itself seemed hardly a Christian ceremony, for it was said mostly behind closed doors. The resident aliens were as extraordinary as the natives. In Harar an Armenian hotel keeper called Bergebedgian sold a liquor labeled "very Olde Scotts Whiskey," "Fine Champayne," or "Hollands Gin," depending upon the preference of the customer. At parties and bazaars Mr. Bergebedgian made himself completely at home, pulling things out of drawers, removing food from ovens to taste it, pinching young girls, giving half-piasters to young children. Waugh happily transferred this sort of thing to *Black Mischief* (1932).

But Waugh also discovers that civilized men are not so different from savages as they would like to think. Droll and ironic and farcical, the resemblances between the two accumulate. Like the English, the primitives of British Guiana are solitary and require a lot of drink to become sociable, are not ambitious or demonstrative, are fond of pets and of hunting and fishing. The fashionable night club in "a rowdy cellar" to which Waugh goes upon his return from Africa is "hotter than Zanzibar, noisier than the market at Harar, more reckless of the decencies of hospitality than the taverns of Kabola or Tabora." The journalists who cover the Italian-Abyssinian War are, in their way, more barbaric than the barbarians. They stage combat scenes and complain that in the Chinese wars an entire army corps could be hired by the day and, for extra pay, actually be shot at. As intrigued by gadgets as any savage, they have equipped themselves, at their newspapers' expense, with rifles, telescopes, ant-proof trunks, medicine chests, pack saddles, gas masks. The language of their cables, designed for economy, is a kind of primitive jargon. When a nurse is reported killed in a bombing raid, New York and London "Require earliest name life story photograph American nurse upblown Adowa." No nurse has died at Adowa, and the journalists cable back, "Nurse unupblown.'"

In his fiction Waugh fires, with a double-barreled hilarity, at both the savage and the civilized. In *Black Mischief* the attempts of the Emperor Seth to modernize Azania are ludicrous, but the modernism to which he aspires is even more ludicrous. In *Scoop* (1938) the journalists acquire enough gear to outfit expeditions to all points of the compass. (The running joke about Apthorpe's gear in the World War II trilogy also owes something to the Abyssinian experience.) They have names like Shumble,

Whelper, and Pigg, and their professional attitude is summed up by one Corker: " Ring people up at any hour . . . make them answer a string of damn fool questions when they want to do something else — they like it." In *A Handful of Dust* (1934) the savagery of London is more appalling than that of the jungle, and its effects are tragic as well as comic.

Waugh the traveler is as brave as Waugh the soldier will be. In British Guiana and Brazil he tramps through country for which there are no maps, into which no policeman or government officer has gone. The streams all seem to run the wrong way, as they do in *A Handful of Dust*. Once, lost and hungry, he stumbles upon a house and a human being, food and directions, in the face of odds against which, he calculates, only a miracle could have prevailed. He smokes, eats, and drinks all sorts of dreadful stuff. At Port Said he buys a cheap hubble-bubble from a vendor who keeps several going by drawing on each in turn and, though warned by a doctor that he will catch some abominable disease, he smokes without ill effect. In Brazil he is introduced to a drink called cassiri. From the description of cassiri in *A Handful of Dust* the reader may suppose that Waugh invented it to make Tony Last's ordeal more hideous, but Waugh has already described it in *Ninety-Two Days* (1934): "It is made from sweet cassava roots, chewed up . . . and spat into a bowl. The saliva starts fermentation. . . ." Waugh is at first understandably reluctant to sample it, but he later finds it refreshing and drinks it by the pint.

Tough though he is, and alone by preference, Waugh suffers occasionally from tedium and depression. Waiting four days between Harar and Aden, he wonders whether anybody has compiled "an anthology of bored verse." It might have for frontispiece Sickert's "Ennui" and include an appendix of suicide letters selected from the newspapers: "I am fed up and resolved to end it all. . . . Yesterday the clock broke, and there is four shillings for the milk. Give Aunt Loo my love. . . . If the milkman says it's more, it's only four shillings."

But there are circumstances and states of mind which cannot be converted into jokes. In Antigua, at Christmas, Waugh reflects upon the melancholy of Christmas holidays in the Tropics. Returning to England, he wakes to hear the ship's foghorn, dismal and perhaps premonitory, for "Fortune is the least capricious of deities, and arranges things on the just and rigid system that no one shall be very happy for very long." As the ship passes through the Dardanelles, an American lady asks him, "Can't you just see the quin-que-remes? From distant Ophir, with a cargo of ivory, sandal-wood, cedar-wood, and sweet white wine?" No, but he thinks that he might, with more imagination, see troopships of Australians going to their deaths in the Great War. All of this is twenty years before the ennui and melancholy of Gilbert Pinfold, before the preoccupation with death in the World War II trilogy.

Politically, the Waugh of the travel books is, as one would suppose, a conservative, but some reviewers thought him much worse than that and called his second book on Abyssinia and his book on Mexico pieces of Fascist propaganda. The truth is that in *Robbery Under Law: The Mexican Object Lesson* (1939), he writes on behalf of capitalism, not Fascism. He protests the expropriation of British oil wells. But it is also the truth that he sees a case for the Italians in Abyssinia, and it is the case that he sees for the British in other countries. Abyssinia is obviously in a fine old mess, but Aden and Kenya, under the British, are in good, civilized shape. (He goes so far as to argue that the very fact of British domination has kept Malta Maltese and Mediterranean and prevented it from being turned into a tourist trap or a bogus charm spot.) The Italians, in turn, will bring civilization to Abyssinia. The fighting is not over, but already they are building roads. (One may think of Pontius Pilate in a story by Anatole France called "The Procurator of Judaea": "What? Refuse an aqueduct? What madness!")

Yet Waugh, like the later Jacobites, is less acquisitive and practical than he is romantic and nostalgic. He is not altogether proud of the whole British Empire and, though patriotic, he is not chauvinistic. Indeed, what he loves most in his own time seems "barely represented" in his own country, and what he loves most in his own country seems to be only the survival of an earlier age. He admires the English settlers in Kenya, not because they are growing rich (he says they are struggling), but because they are re-creating the life of the English squirearchy. (In the war trilogy Guy and Virginia Crouchback talk of their happy times in Kenya, and Waugh sums up their recollections: "the whole Restoration scene re-enacted by farmers, eight thousand feet above the steaming seaboard.")

Waugh's conservatism draws lines of class but not lines of colour. In Algeria he notes approvingly that Moorish landowners sit next to French army and navy officers in cafes, and that white porters and street sweepers trade cigarette ends with coloured ones. Why, he wonders, are the British and the native people of their Empire not equally fraternal? In Abyssinia he visits a noble old chief beside whom Haile Selassie is an upstart, but who represents a tradition that is doomed. He is both regretful and grateful, for he feels that he has traveled across the centuries to "the court of Prester John."

It is in his esthetics that Waugh shows himself not only conservative but also parochial and prejudiced. At an exhibition in Paris he discovers "the very apotheosis of bogosity." It is a head of white wire, "so insignificant . . . so drab and . . . inadequate that it suggested the skeleton of a phrenologist's bust. . . . It was called Tête: dessin dans l'espace, by M. Jean Cocteau; near it stood a magnificent sculpture by Maillol." In a museum at Cairo, looking at certain works of Arab art which are contemporary with masterpieces in the Musée Cluny, he is suddenly brushed by the Crusader's emotions: zeal for the Cross and contempt for the Crescent. Scholarship at the University of Elazhar is so miserable that it makes that of every school in the West look vigorous, and Agia Sophia is "a majestic shell filled with vile Turkish fripperies."

Like other conservatives, Waugh is pessimistic about the possibilities of human nature: Man will never be self-sufficient this side of the grave; political and economic conditions can do little to augment either his virtue or his happiness; inequalities of wealth are inevitable. A class system is necessary to hold a country together, and the anarchistic impulse in society is so strong that keeping the peace is virtually a full-time task of government. Such attitudes may partly explain something in Waugh which goes back farther than his interest in religion: his interest in the nursery. In the nursery one has order and that figure of affection which is also a figure of authority, the nanny. Syke's biography makes clear that Waugh loved his nurse Lucy as he loved very few other people, and in *Scoop* William Boot refuses to go to a grand banquet in his honor because he fears that in the eyes of his old nurse he will look ridiculous. The literary work to which Waugh refers most often, in the travel books as in the novels, is a children's book, *The Wind in the Willows*, by Kenneth Grahame. "Boviander," he says, in *Ninety-Two Days*, "is the name given to the people . . . who live . . . along the lower waters of the great river . . . they fish, and spend most of their time, like the water rat in *The Wind in the Willows*, 'messing about in boats.' " In *Remote People* Mr. Bergebedgian, making ready for a party one night, arms himself with an automatic pistol and deals out clubs to his servants. A French clerk takes a revolver, and Waugh himself, carrying a swordstick, thinks it is all "very much like Rat's preparation for the attack on Toad Hall." The book most often quoted and referred to after *The Wind in the Willows* is *Alice's Adventures in Wonderland*.

In spite of the value that he places on order, there is in Waugh a deep vein of anarchism. As he disembarks at Malta, the ship's medical officer tells him that he risks imprisonment if he does not carry a quarantine form with him and report every day to the Minister of Health. He loses the form and never goes near the Ministry of Health. He writes identical letters to two hotels at Malta, suggesting a free stay in exchange for favorable mention in his book. Having learned that the Great Britain is the better, he tells the Great Britain man at the dock to take his baggage. When the man from the other hotel flutters his letter at him, "A forgery," says Waugh, "I am afraid you have been deluded by a palpable forgery."

Friends assumed and Waugh declared that the remarkable Peter Rodd was the model for Waugh's raffish hero Basil Seal, but I cannot help thinking that in Basil there is a good deal of Waugh himself. On the eve of his departure for Azania (Abyssinia), where he fights for the Emperor Seth, Basil cashes a rubber check at his club (among the troubles between the young Waugh and his father was a notable one over a check that bounced). He steals his own mother's emeralds and at Port Said sells them for a fifth of their true value. He drinks and then fights with a Welsh engineer (as the diaries and other accounts indicate, Waugh was one of the great drinkers of literary history). He sends obscene postcards to his friend Sonia Trumpington (in *Labels* "Geoffrey," that is, Waugh, mails such postcards to an Englishwoman of his acquaintance). And it can hardly be a series of mere coincidences that makes Basil's age, from work to work, approximately the same as Waugh's.

Whereas the conservative in Waugh draws his sword on behalf of traditional art, the anarchist in him tosses bombs among the idols of popular taste. "I do not think," he says in *Labels*, "that I shall ever forget the sight of Etna at sunset . . . in a blur of pastel grey. . . . Nothing I have ever seen in Art or Nature was quite so revolting." When everyone else on the ship sees Gibralter, through Thackeray's eyes, as an enormous lion crouched between the Atlantic and the Mediterranean, Waugh sees it as a big slab of cheese and nothing else. As for the Sphinx, it is ill-proportioned and no more mysterious than Aleister Crowley.

At times Waugh's travels appear to be a succession of happy encounters with the grotesque and the eccentric. In Naples a charming small girl shows him two partially mummified bodies in a church crypt, puts her face to a slit in one corpse that reveals the lungs and digestive organs, inhales ecstatically, and invites him to do the same. In Haifa his driver tries to run over pedestrians and removes both hands from the wheel to light the Lucky Strikes that he smokes incessantly. The journalists in Abyssinia are a catalogue of oddballs including an Austrian in Alpine costume, a Soudanese traveling under a Brazilian passport and working for an Egyptian newspaper, and a German traveling under the name of Haroun-al-Raschid. In British Guiana and Brazil two characters on a grand scale turn up. Mr. Baine, a district commissioner, once had a horse that swam under water, and a guide with a parrot that flew ahead, flew back, and whispered in his ear what it had observed. Mr. Christie, a half-caste rancher, has dreams which indicate the nature of people who are about to visit him: he sees sometimes a pig or a jackal and often "a ravaging tiger." For thirty years he has preached five hours every Sunday without making one convert, for even his own family have the devil in them.

The meetings with fantastic characters are a matter of luck, but Waugh must decide which characters are appropriate to the travel books alone and which are the raw material of fiction. Mr. Baine is merely an amiable narrator of tall tales, and he makes no appearance in the novels, but Mr. Bergebedgian is a more complex discovery, and he becomes Mr. Youkoumian, Basil's assistant in the Azanian Ministry of Modernization. Mr. Christie develops into the terrible Mr. Todd, Tony Last's host and jailer in *A Handful of Dust*. It is worth noticing, however, that in his first novel, *Decline and Fall* (1928), Waugh invented on another basis or on none at all a marvelous religious maniac, the homicidal carpenter of Blackstone Gaol:

> "Well, one day I was just sweeping out the shop before shutting up when the Angel of the Lord came in. I didn't know who it was at first. 'Just in time,' I said. 'What can I do for you?' Then I noticed that all about him there was a red flame and a circle of flame over his head, same as I've been telling you. Then he told me how the Lord has numbered His elect and the day of tribulation was at hand. 'Kill and spare not,' he says."

The travel books record Waugh's interests in architecture, painting, etc., which began early and lasted all of his life. He was a student in a school of art (he did drawings for some of his books) and in a school of carpentry (did he meet a model for his homicide there?), and he was tutored in illumination and script. Therefore, he sees landscapes, cities, houses, churches, works of art with a trained eye. He devotes a long section of *Labels* to the architecture of Gaudi, who he says is to other practitioners of the Art Nouveau as the masters of Italian baroque are to the mediocrities who decorated the boudoir of Mme. de Pompadour. At the same time he notes in Gaudi's buildings a resemblance to the sets in the later U.F.A. films. He thinks of writing as a kind of architecture and cabinetmaking. In *Ninety-Two Days* he says that as a carpenter sees a piece of timber and wishes to square and plane it, he himself has certain haphazard experiences and wishes to turn them into the forms of fiction. In *A Little Learning* (1964), at the close of his life, he says that he makes and sells books as a man makes and sells chairs.

Waugh's travel books are accounts not only of his journeys but also of his temperament and his tastes, his pieties and his prejudices. Most of the accounts of the second kind square with those which he wrote later in life and with his novels — partly because of paradoxes which are common to all of them. There is also a kind of paradox which is peculiar to the travel books: encounters with the unfamiliar enable Waugh to understand the familiar. In foreign countries he learns about his own country what he could not have learned within it ("What should they know of England," Kipling asked, "who only England know?"). He learns about his religion likewise. It is only by witnessing the secretive Abyssinian Mass that he fully apprehends a triumphant fact of his own faith: that from the hidden and criminal sanctuaries of the early Church came "the great open altars of Catholic Europe, where Mass is said in a flood of light, high in the sight of all." Finally, in faraway places and in the company of strange men and women, Waugh learns about himself what he could not have learned in London, in Mayfair, in the midst of the Bright Young People.

Conclusion [On Waugh's Manuscript Revisions]
Robert Murray Davis*

Near the end of his career Waugh testified that the process of writing a novel took longer as he grew older: six weeks for the early ones, a year for *Men at Arms*, and, as we have seen [elsewhere], still longer for others. The problem, he continued, was that "one's memory gets so much worse. I used to be able to hold the whole of a book in my head. Now if I take a walk whilst I am writing, I have to hurry back and make a correction, before I forget it."[1] The various chronological accounts testify independently that the process became more difficult, but the objective evidence does little to bear out Mrs. Waugh's view that her husband "made increasingly more corrections and alterations as he grew older."[2] Although Waugh obviously had different intentions in writing *Unconditional Surrender* from those he had for writing *Decline and Fall*, the same kinds and degrees of meticulous revision are present in both manuscripts. And while details in the composition of the novels are more interesting than abstractions from more than thirty years of practice, the manuscripts do reveal fairly consistent, if artificially demarcated, kinds of concern, all the way from the phrase to form in the broadest and most obvious sense.

Waugh's view that "Writing [is] not . . . an investigation of character, but . . . an exercise in the use of language"[3] is, with some qualifications, obviously borne out by the manuscripts. Again and again — far more often than could be indicated in this book — they reveal him searching for just the right rhythm, tone, and shade of meaning and settling on a pattern that is unique and yet impervious to parody because all idiosyncrasy has disappeared. On the other hand, he confessed that "it is drama, speech and events that interest me";[4] this implies that his presentation of character, as opposed to "investigation" of it, is intimately connected with language. Many of his characters, from Mrs. Beste-Chetwynde and Mrs. Grimes in *Decline and Fall* all the way through Ludovic in the last two volumes of the trilogy, were discovered as he composed his novels, and most of the characters were enlarged, heightened, and made more individual not so much because of what they do as because of what they say. For Apthorpe, as for Grimes, the style is the man, and throughout his life as novelist Waugh's revisions helped the characters become more themselves and less like anyone else.

Frequently, as in *A Handful of Dust*, allowing characters to reveal themselves involved revision to give them the literal last word in a scene. In manuscript Waugh tended to skimp endings, whether of scenes, chapters, or whole books, and again and again, in looking over what he

*Reprinted from *Evelyn Waugh, Writer* (Norman, Okla.: Pilgrim Books, 1981), 333–36, by permission of the author. © 1981 by Robert Murray Davis.

had written, he took the opportunity to augment. Very rarely does he add action much beyond stage business; instead, he uses his own and the characters' rhythms of language to encapsulate theme and character. The manuscript of *Decline and Fall*, for example, ended, "So Peter went out, and Paul settled down again in his chair." In revising for the printed version, Waugh added: "So the ascetic Ebionites used to turn towards Jerusalem when they prayed. Paul made a note of it. Quite right to suppress them. Then he turned out the light and went into his bedroom to sleep." The added business emphasized, with help from the false parallelism of "So," the author's and character's lack of moral differentiation between the dynamic Peter and the static Paul and concludes the novel with an unmistakable finality of rhythm and action. In revising *Unconditional Surrender*, Waugh exhibited the same concern for rhythm in concluding the crucial scene. When Mme Kanyi describes men who thought "they could assert their manhood by killing or being killed," the manuscript continues:

> "Did none in England?"
> "God forgive me," said Guy, "I did."

This must have come to seem too curt, and the book reads:

> "Were there none in England?"
> "God forgive me," said Guy, "I was one of them."[5]

The revision subtly alters content as well as rhythm, for not only are the two halves of Guy's speech more equally balanced, but Guy places himself in a human context instead of insisting — as he had done at the beginning of the trilogy — on his isolation.

For a writer who said that in his youth he could "set a few characters in motion, write 3,000 words a day, and note with surprise what happened,"[6] the manuscripts reveal surprisingly few changes in basic conception. Waugh said that he had "very little control" over his major characters and that "I start them off with certain preconceived notions of what they will do and say in certain circumstances but I constantly find them moving another way." His example is Angela Lyne in *Put Out More Flags*: "I had no idea until halfway through the book that she drank secretly. I could not understand why she behaved so oddly. Then when she sat down suddenly on the steps of the cinema I understood all and I had to go back and introduce a series of empty bottles into her flat."[7] This account accords with the evidence of the manuscripts discussed in this book. For the most part, the sudden inspirations or revelations and subsequent changes in a character's fate occur with secondary characters like Mrs. Grimes, Sambo the parrot, and Major Hound. The major action, theme, and pattern seem to have been fairly clear in Waugh's mind — the theme of art in *The Loved One* is a notable exception — and in the novels after *Helena* all three elements seem to have been clearer in Waugh's mind before he began than they had in earlier novels. This does not mean that the process of composition was easier; it does mean that in all of his work, and especially in later work, Waugh devoted most of his attention to highlighting his themes by introducing or altering the actions of secondary characters.

The broadest if not the final concern in Waugh's revision for publication was structural. Day-to-day revisions and intermediate reconsiderations established the network of correspondences and allusions that hold the novels together from within, but like many writers more obviously committed to modernist experiment, Waugh took great care to guide his readers by means of external form. As the manuscripts of *Decline and Fall* and *Brideshead Revisited* show, he was sometimes torn between the claims of physical and thematic symmetry, and in the second novel he struggled through several principles of division before finding one that satisfied both. In other cases, as in *A Handful of Dust*, he completed the manuscript before settling on an external structure that would support and reveal this theme. In still others — notably *Scoop* and *The Loved One* — he went back and introduced new scenes (for Mrs. Stitch and Sir Ambrose Abercrombie) to balance earlier actions and to emphasize elements of the theme that had been neglected or underemphasized in first draft.

This aspect of Waugh's habits of composition reveals what textual study, by its concentration upon particulars, inevitably obscures: the novels are organic wholes, analyzable but indivisible. Waugh clearly stated this principle on at least two occasions. On the first, contrasting journalism with fiction, he asserted: "The value of a novel depends on the standards each book evolves for itself; incidents which have no value as news are given any degree of importance according to their place in the book's structure and their relation to other incidents in the composition, just as subdued colours attain great intensity in certain pictures."[8] Seven years later, admonishing Cyril Connolly, he denied that isolated passages could reveal much about style because "the style is the whole. . . . writing is an art which exists in a time sequence; each sentence and each page is dependent on its predecessors and successors; a sentence which he admires may owe its significance to another fifty pages distant."[9] When he was no longer "able to hold the whole of a book in my head" — if he did not exaggerate his youthful powers — he depended on increased diligence and a longer process of composition.

The major difference between Waugh and most of his modernist predecessors was that he regarded himself as a popular writer and grew increasingly impatient of technical innovations.[10] He knew a good deal about those innovations, however, and as he told Connolly in concluding the passage just quoted, ". . . even quite popular writers take great trouble sometimes in this matter." Waugh wanted to sell books; more than that, he wanted to have them read and understood, and, as this book has attempted to show, he always took great trouble in these matters.

Notes

1. Julian Jebb, "The Art of Fiction XXX: Evelyn Waugh," *Paris Review*, no. 30 (Summer-Fall, 1963):78.

2. Alfred Borrello, "A Visit to Combe Florey; Evelyn Waugh's Home," *Evelyn Waugh Newsletter* 2 (Winter, 1968):2.

3. Jebb, "The Art of Fiction XXX: Evelyn Waugh," p. 79.

4. Jebb, "The Art of Fiction XXX: Evelyn Waugh," p. 79.

5. Evelyn Waugh, *Unconditional Surrender* (London: Chapman and Hall, 1961), p. 300.

6. Evelyn Waugh, "Preface," *Vile Bodies* (London: Chapman and Hall, 1965), p. 7.

7. Evelyn Waugh, "Fan-Fare," *Life* 20 (April 8, 1946): 56, 58.

8. Evelyn Waugh, *Remote People* (London: Duckworth, 1931), p. 52.

9. Evelyn Waugh, "Present Discontents," *Tablet* 172 (December 3, 1938): 743.

10. See my "Evelyn Waugh on the Art of Fiction," *Papers on Language and Literature* 2 (1966): 243-52.

God and Taste   Jeffrey Heath*

Waugh was religious from his earliest years. His family tree "burgeoned on every twig" with Anglican churchmen, and his own youthful "ecclesiological interests" were Anglo-Catholic. When Waugh was nine his father gave him Mary MacGregor's *The Story of Rome*, having inscribed it: "All roads, they tell us, lead to Rome; / Yet, Evelyn, stay awhile at home![1] As a child Waugh attended Sunday services with Lucy, his nonconformist nanny. But in 1915 his parents began to take him to the Anglo-Catholic services of Basil Bourchier, a "highly flamboyant" and "totally preposterous parson" (pp. 91–92) who preached at St. Jude's Hampstead Garden Suburb. Anglo-Catholicism was not new to Arthur Waugh. At the time of his son's birth "he had a brief Anglo-Catholic phase and frequented St. Augustine's Kilburn . . . but he never took very seriously the doctrines taught there" (p. 68). Even though the elder Waugh took "the doctrines" lightly, they deeply affected his son, who later held his father responsible for leading him into a heretical belief.

Until 1915 Waugh's drawings had dealt with the usual exotica of childhood: slaves, Hindus, natives, war. After that time, they began to

*Reprinted from Jeffrey Heath, *The Picturesque Prison: Evelyn Waugh and His Writing* (Kingston and Montreal: McGill-Queen's University Press 1982), 30–36 by permission of the author and publisher. © 1982 McGill-Queen's University Press.

feature "saints and angels inspired by mediaeval illuminations" (p. 93).
One of these, remarkably well done, shows St. Augustine disembarking in
England.[2] Waugh now went about the countryside investigating "church
decorations and the degrees of Anglicanism — 'Prot, Mod, High, Spikey' —
which they represented" (p. 93). Waugh preferred the "Spikey." A representative diary entry from Waugh's eleventh year reads: "In the evening we
went to church. We struck a horrible low one. I was the only person who
crossed myself and bowed to the altar." Another reads: "It is a beautiful old
[church] and is very spikey. It has got some very Roman candles on sort of
rings standing on the ground but without the image in the centre. The
Blessed Sacrament is reserved in the Lady Chapel."[3] Waugh made a little
shrine bearing frontals and statues of saints, before which he burned
incense; chasubles and Erastianism were now considerations of major
importance. He expressed the desire to become a clergyman, but his
mother was not sympathetic. In emulation of Newman's "Dream of
Gerontius" he composed "The World to Come," a "poem about Purgatory
in the metre of *Hiawatha*."[4] Speaking in the first person, the young poet
describes his own death and introduction to the other world under the
tutelage of the angel Michael. He sees look-alike armies of warlike
Christians wielding crosses and Madonnas, and these are contrasted with a
Moslem "with a kind and gentle bearing."[5] The narrator's downward gaze
typifies the *sub specie aeternitatis* point of view which Waugh later
brought to bear on life and used in his novels.

Waugh's interest in Anglo-Catholicism persisted well into his years at
Lancing College where, in his second term, he "defied convention by
kneeling at the *incarnatus* in the creed at Holy Comunion." He suffered no
recriminations for his piety, for "if there was no great devotion at Lancing
there was a respect for religion" (p. 109). Church-going was of central
importance at Lancing, where the chapel was considered the most
"spectacular post-Reformation ecclesiastical building in the kingdom" (p.
98). Waugh did not find it excessive to attend chapel twice a day and three
times on Sundays. Indeed, he found "refuge from the surrounding loneliness", in the morning and evening services (p. 112), and he read *The Bible
in Art*, *The Divine Comedy*, and *The Child's Book of Saints*.

By the end of Waugh's stay at Lancing, his "phase of churchiness" (p.
94) was over. Chapel began to bore him, and he "lightheartedly" shed his
inherited faith under the influence of Pope, Leibnitz, and the Oxford
theologian, Rawlinson.[6] In his diary for 13 June 1921 Waugh notes, "In
the last few weeks I have ceased to be a Christian (sensation off!) . . . I am
sure it is only a phase." Tom Driberg remembers that when they were
sacristans at Lancing Waugh once prepared the communion table and
walked away, saying, "If it's good enough for me, it's good enough for
God." Yet he denies that Waugh ever completely lost his faith.[7] What
Waugh certainly *did* lose at this time, however, was his respect for the
authenticity of Anglicanism. As he later said to John Freeman, "Well, I

think I'd always — that is to say always from the age of 16 or so — realised that Catholicism was Christianity, that all the other forms of Christianity were only as good so far as they chipped little bits off the main block."[8] Moreover, Waugh characteristically exaggerated when he told Freeman that "from sixteen to twenty-eight I didn't go to church at all."

In later life Waugh rejected his "precocious religiosity" as an "absurd" hobby, based on merely aesthetic attractions. Yet he declined to "dismiss as pure fancy these intimations of truths which I was more soberly, but still most imperfectly to grasp in later years" (p. 94). Even through the "rollicking joke" of Basil Bourchier Waugh had "some glimpse of higher mysteries" (p. 92). The position he reached well before the time of his conversion was that Anglicanism and Anglo-Catholicism lacked validity as real forms of Christianity. Since they imitated Roman Catholicism and were derived from it, they were parodies and heresies. As Waugh wrote years later in letters to John Betjeman, "Many things have puzzled me from time to time about the Christian religion but one thing has always been self evident — the bogosity of the Church of England. . . . The nearer these people ape the ways of Catholics the nearer they approach flat blasphemy." "Catholics and Anglo-Catholics . . . may look alike to you," he wrote to Betjeman, adding that they were as different as "Trust House timbering and a genuine Tudor building."[9] Delusively beautiful as they were, however, Anglicanism and Anglo-Catholicism were not altogether worthless, for they could act as routes to the true faith, just as Charles Ryder's love of profane art foreshadows his love of God in *Brideshead Revisited*.

Waugh claims that he never attended chapel at Oxford. His life there seems to have been as pagan as the wood-cuts of Pan Dionysus which he liked to make. One of his Oxford short stories centres on a black mass.[10] And in his letters to Dudley Carew he is often sarcastic about religion. In an early letter he complains that the university has too much religion and too few brains in it; in another he recounts how he has steeled his heart like Pharaoh to escape conversion by an American revivalist.[11] But in a letter of slightly later date he confesses, "Chesterton beckons like a star."[12]

Despite the dissipation of his post-Oxford years, Waugh did not altogether forget religion. He still went to church;[13] furthermore, he was now talking about Roman Catholicism: "Claud and I took Audrey to supper," he notes on 22 December 1925, "and sat up until 7 in the morning arguing about the Roman Church." On 20 January 1926 he notes that Olivia's mother "has lent [him] von Hügel's letters to her to read." (These were letters of spiritual counsel from the Roman Catholic theologian, Baron von Hügel; the pious Gwen Plunket-Greene, later a Roman Catholic convert, exerted a strong influence on Waugh at this time. In *Decline and Fall* Paul Pennyfeather offers a copy of von Hügel to his friend Stubbs.) On 31 July 1926 he "got drunk in the evening and argued about foreigners and absolution." And on 20 February 1927 he records, "Next

Thursday I am to visit a Father Underhill about being a parson. Last night I was drunk. How odd those two sentences seem together." Father Underhill, alas, "spoke respectfully of the Duke of Westminster and disrespectfully of my vocation to the church." It would seem, then, that even during the riotous Twenties, and well before *Decline and Fall* and *Vile Bodies*, Waugh was still interested in religion. And this evidence comes from diaries which are especially reticent about spiritual matters.

From 23 November 1928 to 19 May 1930, Waugh's diaries are blank, probably destroyed in an attempt to expunge all trace of Evelyn Gardner. But profound changes were taking place, because only a month and a half after the diaries resume, Waugh notes, "To tea at Alexander Square with Olivia. I said would she please find a Jesuit to instruct me." Olivia Plunket-Greene succeeded, and six days later on 8 July Waugh noted that he had been to see Father Martin D'Arcy: "blue chin and fine, slippery mind." John Freeman Waugh later said, "I was under instruction—literally under instruction—for about three months, but of course I'd interested myself in it before, reading books independently and so on."[14] On 29 September 1930 Waugh entered the Roman Catholic Church. Characteristically, Waugh's decision was rational rather than sentimental: "and so on firm intellectual conviction but with little emotion I was admitted into the Church."[15]

Waugh was surprisingly open about this dramatic and highly personal development, and on several occasions attempted to explain what he had done. In a 1930 *Daily Express* article he drew a characteristic distinction, claiming that the present choice of Western civilization was not between Protestantism and Catholicism, but between (Catholic) Christianity and chaos; civilization "came into being through Christianity, and without it has no significance or power to command allegiance."[16] He argued that it was "no longer possible, as it was in the time of Gibbon, to accept the benefits of civilization, and at the same time deny the supernatural order upon which it rests." In "Come Inside" (1949) he argued, "England was Catholic for nine hundred years, then Protestant for three hundred, then agnostic for a century. The Catholic structure still lies lightly buried beneath every phase of English life; history, topography, law, archaeology everywhere reveal Catholic origins."[17] Logic showed him, he said, that "no heresy or schism could be right and the Church wrong": "It was possible that all were wrong, that the whole Christian revelation was an imposture or a misconception. But if the Christian revelation was true, then the Church was the society founded by Christ and all other bodies were only good so far as they had salvaged something from the wrecks of the Great Schism and the Reformation. This proposition seemed so plain to me that it admitted of no discussion." In 1953 he reverted to the same question when he said to Stephen Black, "I never in my life doubted that Roman Catholicism—never in my reasoning life—was the genuine form of Christianity. But for a long time I didn't believe in the truth of it."[18]

It is evident, then, that religion fascinated Waugh throughout his life, except perhaps in his Oxford years; thus his religious life by no means began with his conversion. From about his sixteenth year he believed that Roman Catholicism was the only true form of Christianity, that Protestantism was a heresy and Anglicanism only a pale copy. He never wholly repudiated them, however, because even through their mists of error they provided a glimpse of "higher mysteries." He believed that there has been a steady decline, through identifiable stages, away from the Catholic continuum in England so that at present Catholicism has returned, figuratively, to the catacombs. Finally, he was convinced that unless civilization is animated by correct religious values, it turns into a shadowy, insubstantial fraud. Since in the English Establishment only a "trickle of divine power survived the reformation & . . . petered out,"[19] Waugh depicts modern England as a fake society with less authenticity than the image on a film or the voice from a phonograph record. It is a society which recalls the echoing, distorted, and value-free world of Forster's Marabar Caves. The hollowness of civilization without grace is one of Waugh's major themes.

From the beginning of his career Waugh believed that the hollowness of modern British culture stemmed from a crucial failure of taste, although it was some time before he explicitly connected that failure with the absence of religious values. In Waugh's journalism right after *Decline and Fall* there is a preoccupation with what he liked to call the "bogus." Setting himself up as a spokesman for youth, he also became one of its harshest critics. He claimed that young people lacked "qualitative standards" and that they even preferred the second-rate: "People no longer speak of 'pearls' and 'artificial pearls' but of 'pearls' and 'real pearls.' . . . There is more or less of anything: a bottle of champagne or two bottles, but no idea that between one bottle and another differences of date and brand should suggest a preference."[20]

Waugh pointed to two main reasons for the rise of the "bogus" quantitative world: the "substitutes" of wartime and the failure of fathers to educate their offspring. No "imposition by rigid discipline . . . of the standards of civilization" ever took place, and so the younger generation became "the ineffectual and undiscriminating people we lament today."[21]

Waugh's early novels and travel books do not at first glance appear to be animated by a religious impulse; indeed, they seem to reflect the more dandified ideal of taste represented by Harold Acton. Acton and Waugh both scorned the fraudulent and the derivative, but Waugh's "disgusto," as one reviewer called it, sprang from deeper convictions than Acton's. We get fleeting glimpses of these when the dandy's mask slips from place. In

Rossetti, for example, Waugh implies that Rossetti's lack of "essential rectitude"[22] — Waugh's prerequisite for great art — stems from the fact that he had religiosity but not religion. Lacking valid taste, he could not produce valid art. Religion is important in *Decline and Fall*, too: Paul Pennyfeather studies Anglican theology and approves of the suppression of heretics; Prendergast, the lapsed Anglican rector who becomes a "Modern Churchman," is decapitated by a lunatic Calvinist. In *Labels* Waugh briefly remarks that Ruskin would have led a more valuable life if he had been a Catholic. And in *Vile Bodies* Waugh lampoons evangelism, theosophy, and Methodism while dealing out ambiguous treatment to the enigmatic Father Rothschild, S. J. Of course, these fleeting allusions to religion do not in themselves establish the Christian basis of Waugh's early novels, but taken together with "The Balance" they encourage us to admit it as a possibility. Waugh's early work manifestly concerns bad taste — the glass and aluminum King's Thursday, the barbarous Bright Young People. If it can be shown that this bad taste springs from bad faith, then these apparently superficial little books may take on fuller significance as Christian, perhaps even Roman Catholic satires.

What is, after all, the basis of good taste? Disregarding the maxim which says that the question cannot be solved, Waugh believed that good taste was the force which could vanquish the bogus ("the whole of thought and taste consists in distinguishing between similars")[23] and that it was rooted in a recognition of God's reasonable design for the universe. Good taste, he was convinced, was the special insight which came from the exercise of "right reason" — man's reason assisted by grace. Waugh believed that taste was a question of God, and dissented from the more fashionable view that God was a question of taste. In his view, art was not valid unless it was thematically concerned with God and formally incorporated decorum, clarity, and order. As a young man Waugh wisely avoided doctrinaire pronouncements on the subjects, and before *Brideshead Revisited* he treated it only obliquely.

As Waugh's career advanced, he became more explicit about his vision of history. He believed that the Reformation had crucially deflected British history from its proper course. Britain, in his view, was cut off from the vital springs of faith by that fatal sundering of the ways, and its culture was eviscerated as time compounded the initial folly. In *Edmund Campion* Waugh describes the long aftermath of schism:

> In these circumstances the Tudor dynasty came to an end, which in three generations had changed the aspect and temper of England. They left a new aristocracy, a new religion, a new system of government; the generation was already in its childhood that was to send King Charles to the scaffold; the new, rich families who were to introduce the House of Hanover, were already in the second stage of their metamorphosis from the freebooters of Edward VI's reign to the conspirators of 1688 and the sceptical, cultured oligarchs of the eighteenth century. The vast exuber-

ance of the Renaissance had been canalised. England was secure, independent, insular; the course of her history lay plain ahead; competitive nationalism, competitive industrialism, competitive imperialism, the looms and coal mines and counting houses, the joint-stock companies and the cantonments; the power and the weakness of great possessions.[24]

Waugh believed that England had been culturally maimed by the actions of Henry VIII, and needed a successful counter-Reformation to correct matters. As he wrote in 1955, "The determining events of our history are, two of them, conquests and one betrayal. It may seem to us now that for the fullest development of our national genius we required a third conquest, by Philip of Spain."[25] The zany events of Waugh's satires have much to do with the fact that no such conquest ever took place, and his "serious" novels all look forward to it. It is interesting to observe, finally, that Waugh talks about Catholicism in terms of freedom and amplitude. In *Edmund Campion* he observes that "the spacious, luminous world of Catholic humanism . . . ended with Henry's break with the Pope."[26] And in "Come Inside" he describes his own life within the Church as "an endless delighted tour of discovery in the huge territory of which I was made free."[27] Catholic life is ample, authentic, and free; existence apart from the Church is shrunken, false, and servile. This is why the hollow and culturally deprived England of *Decline and Fall* and *Vile Bodies* is so often depicted as tasteless, derivative, and confining: a spiritual prison. Although readers sometimes find it hard to believe that a moral vision animates Waugh's early books, it can be argued that they are images of a debased world ruled by bad faith, bad taste, and mere Fortune. Waugh does not endorse the chaos he so fascinatedly describes: instead, he uses irony and allusion to make disorder imply order and fraud imply truth. No moral judgment is expressed, but one is suggested everywhere.

Notes

1. Evelyn Waugh, *A Little Learning* (London: Chapman and Hall, 1964), p. 68.

2. See Alain Blayac, "Evelyn Waugh's Drawings," *Texas Library Chronicle* n.s. 7 (Spring 1974): 40–57.

3. *Diairies*, pp. 8, II.

4. Evelyn Waugh, "Come Inside," in *The Road to Damascus*, ed. John A. O'Brien (New York: Doubleday, 1949), p. 12.

5. *The World to Come: A Poem in Three Cantos* (London: privately printed, 1916).

6. "Come Inside," p. 14.

7. Interview with Tom Driberg, 25 February 1969.

8. "Face to Face," BBC TV, 26 June 1960.

9. *Letters*, pp. 268, 318, 243.

10. Evelyn Waugh, "Unacademic Exercise," *Cherwell*, 19 September 1923, pp. 152–53.

11. *Letters*, pp. 4, II.

12. At the Humanities Research Center Library, University of Texas at Austin.

13. *Diaries*, pp. 163, 178, 180, 202, 218, 224, 249, 292.

14. "Face to Face."

15. "Come Inside," p. 15.

16. Evelyn Waugh, "Converted to Rome: Why it has Happened to Me," *Daily Express*, 20 October 1930, p. 10.

17. "Come Inside," p. 15.

18. Stephen Black, interviewer, "Personal Call, No. 14," BBC radio, 29 September 1953.

19. *Letters*, p. 245.

20. Evelyn Waugh, "Matter-of-Fact Mothers of the New Age," *Evening Standard*, 8 April 1929, p. 7.

21. Evelyn Waugh, "The War and the Younger Generation," *Spectator*, 13 April 1929, pp. 571, 570.

22. Evelyn Waugh, *Rossetti* (London: Duckworth, 1928), p. 227.

23. Evelyn Waugh, "More Barren Leaves," *Night and Day* I (23 December 1937): 24.

24. Evelyn Waugh, *Edmund Campion: Jesuit and Martyr* (London: Longmans, 1935), pp. 3–4.

25. Evelyn Waugh, Foreword to William Weston, *The Autobiography of an Elizabethan*, trans. Philip Caraman (London: Longmans Green, 1955), p. vii.

26. *Edmund Campion*, p. 11.

27. "Come Inside," p. 16.

SELECTED
BIBLIOGRAPHY

PRIMARY SOURCES

Novels

Decline and Fall. London: Chapman and Hall, 1928. New York: Doubleday, Doran, 1929. Rev. ed. London: Chapman and Hall, 1962.

Vile Bodies. London: Chapman and Hall, 1930. New York: Jonathan Cape, Harrison Smith, 1930. Rev. ed. London: Chapman and Hall, 1965.

Black Mischief. London: Chapman and Hall, 1932. New York: Farrar and Rinehart, 1932. Rev. ed. London: Chapman and Hall, 1962.

A Handful of Dust. London: Chapman and Hall, 1934. New York: Farrar and Rinehart, 1934. Rev. ed. London: Chapman and Hall, 1964.

Scoop. London: Chapman and Hall, 1938. Boston: Little, Brown, 1938. Rev. ed. London: Chapman and Hall, 1964.

Put Out More Flags. London: Chapman and Hall, 1942. Boston: Little, Brown, 1942. Rev. ed. London: Chapman and Hall, 1967.

Work Suspended. London: Chapman and Hall, 1942.

Brideshead Revisited: The Sacred and Profane Memories of Captain Charles Ryder. London: Chapman and Hall, 1945. Boston: Little, Brown, 1945. Rev. ed. London: Chapman and Hall, 1960.

Scott-King's Modern Europe. London: Chapman and Hall, 1947. Boston: Little, Brown, 1949.

The Loved One. London: Chapman and Hall, 1948. Boston: Little, Brown, 1948. Rev. ed. London: Chapman and Hall, 1965.

Helena. London: Chapman and Hall, 1950. Boston: Little, Brown, 1950.

Men at Arms. London: Chapman and Hall, 1952. Boston: Little, Brown, 1952.

Love among the Ruins. London: Chapman and Hall, 1953.

Officers and Gentlemen. London: Chapman and Hall, 1955. Boston: Little, Brown, 1955.

The Ordeal of Gilbert Pinfold. London: Chapman and Hall, 1957. Boston: Little, Brown, 1957.

Unconditional Surrender. London: Chapman and Hall, 1961. As *The End of the Battle.* Boston: Little, Brown, 1961.

Sword of Honour. Redaction of *Men at Arms, Officers and Gentlemen,* and

Unconditional Surrender. London: Chapman and Hall, 1965. Boston: Little, Brown, 1966.

Collections of Shorter Works

Mr. Loveday's Little Outing and Other Sad Stories. London: Chapman and Hall, 1936. Boston: Little, Brown, 1936.

Work Suspended and Other Stories Written before the Second World War. London: Chapman and Hall, 1949.

Tactical Exercise. Boston: Little, Brown, 1954.

Charles Ryder's Schoolboys and Other Stories. Boston: Little, Brown, 1982.

Travel Books

Labels, A Mediterranean Journal. London: Duckworth, 1930. As *A Bachelor Abroad: a Mediterranean Journal.* New York: Jonathan Cape, Harrison Smith, 1930.

Remote People. London: Duckworth, 1931. As *They Were Still Dancing.* New York: Farrar and Rinehart, 1932.

Ninety-Two Days: The Account of a Tropical Journey through British Guiana and Part of Brazil. London: Duckworth, 1934. New York: Farrar and Rinehart, 1934.

Waugh in Abyssinia. London and New York: Longmans, Green, 1936.

Robbery under Law: The Mexican Object-Lesson. London: Chapman and Hall, 1939. As *Mexico: An Object Lesson.* Boston: Little, Brown, 1939.

When the Going Was Good. London: Duckworth, 1946. Boston: Little, Brown, 1946.

Tourist in Africa. London: Chapman and Hall, 1960. Boston: Little, Brown, 1960.

Biographies

Rossetti, His Life and Works. London: Duckworth, 1928. New York: Dodd, Mead, 1928.

Edmund Campion: Jesuit and Martyr. London: Longmans, 1935. New York: Sheed and Ward, 1935.

Ronald Knox. London: Chapman and Hall, 1959. As *Monsignor Ronald Knox.* Boston: Little Brown, 1959.

Autobiography, Diaries, Letters, Essays

A Little Learning: The First Volume of an Autobiography. London: Chapman and Hall, 1964. Boston: Little, Brown, 1964.

The Diaries of Evelyn Waugh. Edited by Michael Davie. London: Weidenfeld and Nicolson, 1976; Boston and Toronto: Little, Brown, 1976.

The Letters of Evelyn Waugh. Edited by Mark Amory. London: Weidenfeld and Nicolson, 1980. New Haven and New York: Ticknor and Fields, 1980.

The Essays, Articles and Reviews of Evelyn Waugh. Edited by Donat Gallagher. London: Methuen, 1983. Boston and Toronto: Little, Brown, 1983.

SECONDARY SOURCES

Recommended Critical, Biographical, and Bibliographical Works

Carens, James F. *The Satiric Art of Evelyn Waugh.* Seattle and London: University of Washington Press, 1966.

Davis, Robert Murray. *Evelyn Waugh, Writer.* Norman, Okla.: Pilgrim Books, 1981.

Davis, Robert Murray, Paul A. Doyle, Heinz Kosok, and Charles E. Linck, Jr. *Evelyn Waugh: A Checklist of Primary and Second Material.* Troy, N.Y.: Whitson Publishing Co., 1972. Revised and expanded as *Bibliography of Evelyn Waugh.* Troy, N.Y.: Whitson Publishing Co., 1986.

Doyle, Paul A., ed. *Evelyn Waugh Newsletter.* 1967–.

Heath, Jeffrey. *The Picturesque Prison: Evelyn Waugh and His Writing.* Kingston and Montreal: McGill-Queen's University Press, 1982.

Lane, Calvin. *Evelyn Waugh.* Twayne's English Authors Series 301. Boston: Twayne, 1981.

Littlewood, Ian. *The Writings of Evelyn Waugh.* Oxford: Basil Blackwell, 1983. Totowa, N.J.: Barnes and Noble, 1983.

Morris, Margaret, and D. J. Dooley. *Evelyn Waugh: A Reference Guide.* Boston: G. K. Hall, 1984.

Pryce-Jones, David, ed. *Evelyn Waugh and His World.* London: Weidenfeld and Nicolson, 1973. Boston: Little, Brown, 1973.

Stannard, Mark, ed. *Evelyn Waugh: The Critical Heritage.* London and Boston: Routledge and Kegan Paul, 1984.

Stopp, Frederick J. *Evelyn Waugh: Portrait of an Artist.* London: Chapman and Hall, 1958. Boston: Little, Brown, 1958.

Sykes, Christopher. *Evelyn Waugh: A Biography.* London and Glasgow: Collins, 1975. Boston and Toronto: Little, Brown, 1975.

INDEX